ALL
ABOUT
FUTURES

FROM
THE
INSIDE
OUT

& Thomas A. McCafferty
Russell R. Wasendorf

PROBUS PUBLISHING COMPANY

D1016085

ISBN 1-55738-296-4

Printed in the United States of America

IPC

2   3   4   5   6   7   8   9   0

Dedication

First, a "hearty thank you and well done!" to Gerry Martinson for the hours and hours of effort she expended on this book. And to our wives, Carol and Connie, who have no insight into the value of their assistance.

CONTENTS

THE NATURE OF THE FUTURES MARKET

Philosophers throughout the centuries have said that if God didn't exist, man would have invented Him. We don't wish to get into that argument, but it is our firm belief the creation of futures markets was just about as inevitable a concept.

Man has always had a love-hate relationship with the future. One day he can't wait for things to get better; the next he fears what will happen tomorrow. Individuals who can convince others that they know what is going to happen in the future can catapult themselves into positions of power. Much of the success of politicians, priests, and charlatans can be attributed to this skill.

On a more mundane level, businessmen have as much or more difficulty dealing with the unknown than the average person. How can they set firm prices for the products they sell or manufacture if they don't know what they'll have to pay for the raw materials they use? This question is at least 6,000 years old—that's when a futures market in rice was suspected to have first developed in China. By the Middle Ages, there was a sophisticated futures purchasing system for wheat and wool.

Our point is twofold. First, the concept of a futures market is as old as organized markets. The reason is that it solves a basic business problem—the need to control as much of the future as possible so one can get a good night's sleep.

For example, if you are an importer or processor of crude oil, could you have dealt with the uncontrollable pricing that took place following the invasion of Kuwait by Iraq—without the futures markets? If you are a seller of capital equipment to the Japanese and are to be paid in Yen 120 to 180 days from now, would you want to hedge the risk of the changing currency values of your payment? What's one of the most efficient methods for farmers to handle the price fluctuations they face each year while their crops are still in the ground?

The futures markets permit users of commodities—i.e., grains, meats, metals, financials, food, fiber, etc.—to set a price for their future requirements well in advance of when they are needed. Notice that today's definition of commodities stretches well beyond the physicals and includes security market futures, currencies, interest rates, and more. Producers can likewise lock in acceptable price levels (or profit levels) before their product is ready to be sold. This satisfies a very basic instinct within the human soul. That's why producers and users were destined to invent the futures market and why it continues to exist.

But Where Do the Speculators Fit In?

Speculators create liquidity in the market. They buy and sell thousands of contracts in hundreds of markets, allowing hedgers to easily transfer risk. If the futures markets were restricted to bonafide hedgers (producers or users of the commodities) only, the volume of many contracts and some entire markets would be so low that on some days they would not be able to trade. Volume is an essential key to discovering price; it is one of the most fundamental functions of all types of exchanges. The higher the volume is at any given time for a given commodity, the higher the reliability that its price reflects the current supply-demand situation.

Why? Simply because more people are putting their money where their opinion is. Confidence in understanding where the price of a commodity should be going—commonly referred to as the trend—inspires trading, thereby increasing volume.

Additionally, high volume markets are safer to trade. When you place an order for a trade, you have a better chance it will be filled when trading volume is high.

Therefore, the market function of the speculator is to create volume, so that anyone who wants to trade has a market. The speculator's objective, of course, is to make money from the ever changing ebb and flow of prices.

Who Should Be a Speculator?

This is a much more important question. It is also harder to answer. The term speculate means to engage in risky business transactions on the chance of generating great profits. There are three key terms: risky business, chance, and great profits.

The first key term, "risky business," distinguishes futures speculation from gambling, in our opinion. Gambling generally involves sport and pure chance. Futures speculation is more intellectual, involves research, strategies, and planning.

Detractors of futures trading have always tied their arguments to the second key term, "chance." There is always the element of chance when you attempt to forecast what is expected to happen at sometime in the future. This is true for commercial real estate investors, insurance companies, bank officers who set interest rates, and even individuals who buy homes. In other words, we all deal with the element of chance everyday. We have always suspected the speed at which the futures markets fluctuates is what makes its detractors wrongly classify it as a game of chance.

The last key term, "great profits," is what attracts aggressive investors to this form of investing. A goodly percentage of individual speculators wish to make a lot of money fast. They are greedy. This may be the single most important reason that most small traders lose. Success in the futures markets requires the patience to wait for high quality trades, to manage money judiciously, to study the markets and do the research required, to control emotional responses to fast moving opportunities when they are moving for or against your positions, and to have a clear head when everyone around you is losing their other end.

The debate surrounding the futures markets is similar to the one centering around firearm ownership. Are the guns intrinsically evil? Is the market evil? Does either become dangerous in the hands of someone who is irrational?

To carry this analogy a little further, we believe either can be handled by most anyone who is properly trained without getting hurt. Mishaps and accidents are always possible but can be greatly reduced by education. Does this mean anyone properly trained can make a fortune in the market? No, no more than anyone properly trained can fire expertly with any given firearm. The expert rifleman has extremely good eyes, a naturally steady hand and a feel for target shooting. That description does not fit everyone who can be trained to safely handle a weapon.

The same is true of the futures market or just about any other endeavor you name. There are rules to follow in the market that are designed to protect you against catastrophic losses, but you can't teach someone to trade successfully. "Natural traders" are as rare as "natural shooters."

The purpose of this book is to teach you enough about the futures markets and its rules so you can protect yourself. However, this knowledge is not a guarantee that you won't get wiped out. The market has a will of its own. Never forget that! If it moves violently against your position, you'll get burned.

But after careful study of this text, you should be able to decide:

- If futures trading will help you reach your financial goals

- How to go about entering the markets

- The various alternative approaches there are available to you

- Strategies to utilize initially to reduce or control risk, as opposed to all out exposure

Most importantly, you'll have an excellent overview of the futures and options-on-futures markets. This overview should give you enough background to decide intelligently how and if you want to pursue them.

The futures market is a zero-based market. At the end of each day, the books are balanced. For every buyer, there is a seller. For every seller, a buyer. That means one side wins and one side loses—every day. And every day, the losers must pay the winners in the form of margin money or reduced equity in their trading account.

Some days you'll win. More often you'll lose. Your objective is to be a net winner in terms of dollars invested. This is not an easy task, but it is achievable. The risk may be heavy, but the possibility of reaping very large profits over very short periods of time attracts the aggressive investor.

Carefully read the following text. Learn if this type of investment matches your financial goals. More importantly, try to determine if you are psychologically and financially suited for it.

CHAPTER 1

GETTING A REAL FEEL FOR
FUTURES TRADING

Key Concepts

⇒ What motivated the development of the futures market.

⇒ What fuels major price trends.

⇒ How to trade bull and bear moves.

⇒ Insights into analysis of price trends.

⇒ How to manage up, down and sideways moving markets.

Your first order of business is to obtain a firm understanding of the futures markets. Over the years, they have been grossly misunderstood by the general public and even the financial press.

When you "buy or sell a futures," what are you doing? The basic concept is extremely simple. First of all, you are buying or selling a futures contract, not just a "futures."

When you buy a futures contract, you agree to be contingently liable for delivery of a specific amount of a specific commodity at a specific time in the future at a specific price. Every futures contract is carefully defined as to size, quality, quantity, delivery location, and delivery date (see Figure 1.1 for an example and Appendix 5: Specifications of Futures Contracts). When you buy a contract, you are considered to be "long" the commodity—it "be-LONGS" to you. You "own" it at a given price.

On a cash commodity basis, when you are long, you have physical possession of the commodity. For example, a farmer with 5,000 bushels of # 2 corn in a bin on his farm or at a grain elevator is long cash corn.

When you sell a futures contract, you contingently agree to accept delivery of a specific amount of a specific commodity at a specific time in the future at a specific price and location. If you are a seller of a futures contract, you are short— you are currently "SHORT" of the commodity. On a cash basis, a farmer would be short corn if he currently does not have it in inventory. He has agreed to accept delivery of a specific number of bushels of corn of a specific grade (quality) at a specific location (grain elevator) at a specific time and price.

A little historical perspective may help in explaining this basic concept. The modern futures markets began to develop in the early 1800s. Chicago, because it was a strong financial center in the heart of the corn, cattle, and hog country, was one of the early centers—as it still is today.

Surplus to Shortage Problems

At harvest each year, farmers hauled to town the grain they could not use as livestock feed. Chicago became a natural basin for this excess grain because of transportation routes. During harvest, a time of surpluses, grain users (feed companies, stock yards, processors, etc.) pressed for low prices, often "forcing" farmers to accept ridiculously low offers.

Grain merchants stockpiled as much grain as they could afford at the low harvest prices, but storage facilities were limited. As the year progressed, the supply of stored grain shrank and users were forced to bid aggressively for the remaining supply still stored on farms. Thus began the annual cycle of surpluses to shortages. Violent price swings from harvest lows to late season highs drove the grain industry to search out an alternative marketing method—forward contracts.

Forward Contracts—A Useful Marketing Tool

To secure a steady grain supply, users sought out farmers who would agree to contract, grain for delivery at regular intervals throughout the year. Fearing the

Figure 1.1

Basic Futures Trading Strategy

Offset positions at a better price than you originally paid for them.

Long the Market

Objective:	Buy low, sell high
Example:	You decide to go long the Deutschemark because you believe it is going higher.
Initial Position:	Buy 1 June D-Mark at 55 cents on the IMM Exchange
Offsetting Position:	Sold 1 June D-Mark at 60 cents on the IMM Exchange
Results:	A 5-cent profit was realized. Since 1 cent equals $1,250 a total profit of $6,250 was earned. From this, a brokerage commission, National Futures Association (NFA), exchange and Futures Commission Merchant (FCM) fees would be deducted or approximately $100, more or less.

Short the Market

Objective:	Sell high, buy low
Example:	You decide to short gold because you believe it's going to decline in value.
Initial Position:	Sell 1 August gold contract at $500/oz. on COMEX
Offsetting Position:	Buy 1 August gold contract at $450/oz. on COMEX
Result:	A $50/oz. profit was realized. Since each COMEX contract contains 100 troy oz. of gold, a total profit of $5000.00 was earned. From this would be deducted the transaction costs (brokerage commission, NFA, FCM and exchange fees), which could be $100 more or less.

Note: See Appendix 5 for contract specifications. An offsetting futures position must be for the same commodity, delivery month, quantity and exchange, but on the opposite side of the market, as the initial position.

low prices of harvest sales, farmers willingly entered such agreements. The early contracts were tailored to a particular buyer and seller. They specifically stated the price, quality, quantity, delivery date, and location of each delivery. Through these contracts, farmers knew in advance the price of the grain they would receive at a future date. Contracting also gave the users the comfort of knowing they would have grain when needed.

Drawing up a contract for the future delivery became known as forward contracting. The term forward refers to a date forward in time. Forward contracts, sometimes called "to arrive contracts," were specified to fit the exact needs of the buyer and seller. Buyers and sellers of these contracts gave personal guarantees of performance. In fact, the buyer often paid the seller a portion in advance.

Once the farmer signed a forward contract, he locked in a price, thus eliminating the risk of a price decline. The price stated in the contract was exactly what he could expect for his grain on delivery day. One last risk remained for the farmer. A drought or crop spoilage (disease or insects) might prevent him from producing enough grain to fulfill the contract. In this case, he would be forced to buy grain on the open market to satisfy the commitment. At times, this could be a costly option, depending on the supply-demand situation.

The user was similarly bound by the contract, but in this case the danger was more likely price. If the grain price declined unexpectedly, the user would still have to pay the higher contract price. Despite these pitfalls, the advantages of the forward contracts definitely made them useful. Actually, they have stood time's test well. Even today, many farmers fix prices before delivery through forward contracts.

Inadequacies of Forward Contracts

Forward contracts suffer from an inherent problem. They lack flexibility. To understand the limitations of forward contacts, consider the following situation.

It is July 15. A farmer has 100 acres of land planted to corn. The crop seems healthy, and the farmer expects 100 bushels of corn per acre or 10,000 bushels. On the same date, July 15, a corn oil refiner checks his inventory and decides he needs 10,000 bushels at harvest time to meet his oil production schedule.

If, on July 15, the farmer feels confident that he will have 10,000 bushels of corn to deliver at harvest, he may want to find a buyer willing to set the price. If the corn oil refiner is sure that he will need 10,000 bushels at harvest time, then he may seek to lock in a price.

As the corn buyer and the seller bargain, they hammer out specifics of a forward contract. They agree upon price, let us say $2.50; quality, # 2 yellow corn; quantity, 10,000 bushels; delivery place, at the refiner's site; and time of delivery, Oct. 10. The seller of the grain signs the contract, obligating himself to deliver. If the price of corn declines during the contract period, the seller would be protected, but the buyer would have a loss of opportunity—the opportunity to buy at a cheaper price. If the price rose, the buyer would enjoy the lower "locked in" price, but the seller would lose the opportunity to sell at a higher price. Suppose that after signing the forward contract the corn farmer experiences a major crop failure that cuts his production in half. The forward contract obligates him to deliver 10,000 bushels, so the farmer would have to purchase corn in the cash (open) market, thus compounding his loss.

A similar problem could arise for the refiner if a decline in the value of corn oil were to dictate a reduction in oil output. The refiner is contractually bound to accept delivery of and pay for 10,000 bushels of corn. A portion of this corn might be sold in the open market at a lower price.

The forward contract was an improvement over producing and holding grain in the hopes of higher prices; however, it still proves to be an inefficient and inflexible way to market crops when supply or demand can change unexpectedly. Grain buyers and sellers need more flexibility.

Development of Contract Standards

As forward contracts became more common, speculators appeared on the scene. They hoped to make a profit by assuming temporary buy or sell positions in forward contracts. If a seller was interested in creating a forward contract to price the future delivery of grain but lacked a commercial buyer, a speculator might sign the buyer's side of the contract with the objective of finding a commercial buyer at a later date. The speculator hoped to profit by re-selling the forward contract at a higher price.

Let's assume a speculator takes the buy side of a wheat producer's forward contract. Shortly afterward, prices of forward contracts begin to rise. The speculator realizes that he can now sell his forward contract at a profit—say 10 cents per bushel higher. He may then sell the contract to a commercial grain buyer for a profit, if one could be found. In that case, the grain buyer must be willing to accept the specific details of the original contract. The 10-cent difference between the original contract price and the resale price is $1,000 on the 10,000-bushel contract.

As you can see, trading or speculating in grain by forward contracts can be cumbersome, inefficient, and restrictive. To encourage a smoother transfer of forward contracts, midwestern grain dealers established the Chicago Board of Trade in 1848. The existence of a centralized marketplace highlighted the need for streamlined trading procedures. Over time, these forward contracts acquired specific standards as to quantity, quality, commodity, delivery place and date. They, thus, became similar to modern futures contracts, one of the most flexible, innovative pricing mechanisms in the history of commerce.

Futures Contracts

Futures contracts have only one buyer and one seller at any moment in time. The creation of a contract simply depends on one buyer and one seller agreeing on a price. This is accomplished by "open outcry" in the pits on the floors of the exchanges. All other specifications, except for the number of contracts to be bought or sold, are standardized.

You, as a trader, transmit your trading order (to buy or to sell a futures contracts) to your broker. Your broker in turn communicates with the order desk on the floor of the exchange that trades the specific futures contract you want to trade. The floor order desk gives your trade to the floor trader in the pits. Once your order is filled, the process is reversed and your broker calls you with your fill (the price at which you bought or sold the contract(s)).

To offset your position in the futures market, you need only to find a substitute seller or buyer. You do this by giving your broker an equal but opposite order to your current futures position. Only about three percent of futures contracts are actually delivered. Therefore, initiating and offsetting futures positions are carried out in the same way.

Because futures contracts are standardized—ownership, transfer, and substitutions are accomplished without endangering the original purpose of the forward markets which is to set price, facilitate delivery, and transfer risk. Futures contracts can change hands many times before their delivery date (expiration). Historically, the increased use of futures by speculators makes the market more efficient and actually reduces price fluctuations.

Without active involvement of speculators, buyers' and sellers' price differences (the bid and offer price spread) would widen and prices would fluctuate more dramatically. Furthermore, without this speculative activity, the consumer would have to pay higher food prices to compensate grain dealers for the risk of violent price swings resulting from temporary gluts and shortages.

Role of Inventory Manager

To really get into the swing of what moves the markets, put yourself behind the desk of someone responsible for managing an inventory of a specific commodity, soybeans for example. We'll begin this scenario at harvest time when the bean supply is plentiful.

One of the first insights an inventory manager needs is how this commodity reacts to changes in supply and demand. This is called the "Principle of Elasticity." It can be defined as follows: a characteristic of commodities which describes the interaction of the supply, demand, and price of a commodity. A commodity is said to be elastic in demand when a price change creates an increase or decrease in consumption. The supply of a commodity is said to be elastic when a change in price creates a change in the production of the commodity. Inelasticity of supply or demand exists when either supply or demand is relatively unresponsive to changes in price.

Most food and feed commodities respond to changes in price. For example, if soybean prices shoot up, users look for a substitute or ration their usage of soybeans. Livestock feeders use other sources of protein; vegetable oil producers and users have a wide variety of substitutes available, e.g., sunflower seeds, corn, palm, and coconuts, etc.

The professional inventory manager knows soybean prices are elastic. The price stretches and contracts (rises and falls) in relationship to supply and demand. He knows at harvest the supplies are usually plentiful and prices are relatively low, from farmers who do not have or cannot afford storage.

Studying the seasonal price information indicates cash soybeans can be expected to bottom, approximately three out of four times, during the October-November period each year. Therefore, the inventory manager looks at harvest as a buying opportunity. But the question is still how much should he buy, or should he wait and buy as he can use (process) the beans? The next step he must take is to make an evaluation of the overall supply and demand (also known as fundamental) of the market. In late fall, the South American crop is planted. How many hectares? What yields are expected? How aggressively are the governments of Brazil and Argentina promoting production and exportation?

American farmers often carry soybeans for sale into the next tax year as a way of balancing their income, since most are on a cash basis accounting system. Traditionally, farm real estate debt comes due on March 1st. This generates another buying opportunity for the inventory manager. Within the same time frame, the South American crop is being harvested and supplies are again plentiful, if the South American crop is good.

In other words, the inventory manager must decide in November how much to buy between then and spring. Technical analysis can be a big help. (Discussed in Chapter 2). What do the charts tell him? Are prices near long or short term support areas? How much volatility is in the markets? This gives him an insight into how wide or narrow the trading range is expected to be. Keep in mind that beans are elastic. They will respond to changes—often wildly.

When you put yourself in the inventory manager's seat, all of the known and unknown variables come into sharper focus. This is true for virtually any commodity traded. For example, let's say you wish to trade the financials. You can evaluate interest rates from the standpoint of a bank officer inventorying money. What about the S & P 500? Put yourself in the shoes of a mutual fund manager. You have a $20,000,000 stock portfolio to manage—what do you do?

The object of this exercise is to gain an overview of the market you are interested in trading. Is the trend likely to be up, down or sideways? If your analysis indicates it is up, you would go long the futures or buy call options. If it is down, go short or buy puts. If it is sideways, stand aside or learn to trade within the price range.

Before trading, you must also gauge the strength of your conviction. Hold back when you get conflicting signals from the seasonals, fundamentals and other technicals. These will be discussed in detail later. Your confidence should increase when everything is synchronized.

One more caveat, timing can make all the difference—even when your analysis is absolutely correct. You can be dead right and still lose in the futures market, especially in the short term. On the long term, you must have the money and the patience to wait for the right time or to get in and out of the market with small, controlled losses until the timing is right for a big win.

Also, you can never assume your analysis is infallible. There are always unknown factors—dock strikes, floods, droughts, government intervention, etc.— that can stampede the market against your position. That's why you need to use special techniques, like protective stop orders, which will be discussed in Chapter 3, to cover your positions.

The beauty and value of the futures market is that every contract eventually reverts to the cash market. When a contract expires, it is either deliverable in the commodity or settled on a cash basis. The cash and the futures markets become one!

If you chart the cash price of a specific commodity at a given location and its futures price—particularly the nearby delivery month, you'll find these two prices usually move together. One does not mirror the other. But, the patterns are usually similar. Keep in mind that the cash price quote comes from a delivery point, such as a grain terminal. This geographical point has specific local influences that explains minor discrepancies that distinguish the cash and futures markets.

Also, the futures price is just that—a price for the commodity at some chronological point in the future. News, crop reports, cycles, seasonals, and all the other influencers of price usually impact the futures price first and with more impact than in the cash market. Then they trickle down into the cash market. It is common to see a 2 or 3 week differential in the trend changes between the futures and the cash markets. Eventually, they become one price at the expiration of the futures contract. This keeps the market honest and true to the supply-demand situation.

This is the reason users and producers closely follow the futures market, even if they don't trade it. They know that what happens in the pits will eventually be felt in the fields, or the mines, or the bank vaults.

Additionally, the inventory manager can be a hedger, shifting the risk of future usage from his shoulders to those of a speculator. This would be another reason for him to closely follow the futures markets.

Once you accept this close relationship, you gain insight into how to anticipate price activity by viewing the markets through the eyes of the inventory manager. Now, let's look at some specific price trend moves and decide what action an inventory manager would take.

Managing an Uptrend

Let's return to our soybean scenario. You work for a large soybean crusher. Your responsibility is to maintain a 30-day inventory of beans. Your annual bonus is based on the profitability of the operation, which means you must time your bean buying carefully.

Harvest is now over. The seasonal trend is up and the South American crop is in trouble. What do you do?

Each time you go into the market, the price is higher. Faced with this prospect, most inventory managers begin to build inventory. Each purchase becomes a little larger.

What does this do to the uptrend? It causes the trend to move sharply higher. As prices begin to "skyrocket," everyone panics. Herd psychology takes over. The buyers buy at any price. The sellers hold the product off the market because they think it will be more valuable tomorrow. The poor inventory manager fears he'll be completely shut out of the market and out of inventory.

At some point prices become ridiculous—$13 per bushel soybeans or silver at $50.00 an ounce. The manager of the soybean processing plant instructs the inventory manager to quit buying. Prices are too high to process the beans and generate a profit. It makes more sense to shut down the plant.

About the same time, the sellers realize they have a windfall and begin to send raw materials into the cash market. "Shorts" in the futures markets take delivery, thus squeezing the cash market even more. Then sellers begin to fear they are going to totally miss the boat. This causes them to sell as fast as they can, which drives prices down—just when the buyers have backed off. This behavior helps explain why markets tend to top with sharp peaks and fall twice as fast as they rise.

Managing the Downtrend

If the soybean market was trending downward, the inventory manager would not build inventory. He would buy from hand-to-mouth because each subsequent purchase would be made at a lower price. He may think, if he can just be patient enough, the producer will give him all he wants for "free."

This, of course, never happens, because abundant supply fosters increases in usage and, eventually, increases demand. A base is eventually built and prices level off.

Managing Congestion

What does the inventory manager do when prices are in a sideways or consolidating pattern? As prices move in a channel, the buyer perceives the top of the price channel as being too high or prohibitive. He backs off. Prices move lower and become a "bargain." He steps in and his buying generates support at the bottom of the channel.

Eventually something upsets this pattern. It could be some fundamental news, such as a drought or news of record yields. The supply-demand scale tips one way or the other and a new trend begins.

Your emotional or instinctual reaction to price changes are valid inputs. After all, the market is the sum total of all the players' reactions to what has happened, what is happening, and what everyone expects to happen. In short, it can be said a commodities futures price is the composite opinion of all market participants and influencers.

Get the Right Hat On!

When you put yourself in the position of an inventory manager, you must first give some thought to the specific situation you'll be facing. For example, an inventory manager can just as easily represent a *country* as a *company*.

Therefore, you want to match the commodity and the situation with the inventory manager's motives. If you are looking at the long term outlook for grains, you may want to look at the situation from a variety of viewpoints. Then you will be able to anticipate what each player will do and the cumulative impact on the price of grains.

For example, the motivation of the inventory manager of a South American country which is a net exporter differs substantially from that of an Eastern European country which is a net importer. At the same time, you must sort out the political situation of countries, like the United States, which has a history of using food as foreign policy.

In our current scenario, the grains appear to be making a technical bottom. What is going through the minds of inventory managers around the world?

The United States Department of Agriculture (USDA) has the Administration pressuring it to reduce its budget. Therefore, it wants to force the price of grain higher to cut down subsidy payments to farmers. At the same time, the State Department and the White House refuse to issue credits to the foreign country because of its human rights violation. Your analysis indicates that political pressure will be strong enough that the USDA will win. Credit will be given. This will have a positive effect on price.

The people in South America, who control the flow of grain, are also under a lot of political and financial pressure. They need the sales badly. Therefore, they will be aggressive sellers, but they are not in a financial position to offer credits. Which means, they'll probably discount prices.

As an inventory manager, you must analyze the net impact of this tug-of-war. You come to the conclusion that the need or the demand is so strong, it will push prices higher. But prices will move up slowly and in an orderly manner. The reason, you surmise, is that there are many willing sellers and, although the demand is extremely strong, the aggressive buyers are cash poor.

Historically, big net importers of grain, like the Commonwealth of Unified States, have been very active buyers of U.S. grains around harvest time. This is the cyclical low for the grain market. Inventory managers for these countries would naturally be buyers at this time of year. The scenario just described was for a bottoming market. What positions do inventory managers take when a market is topping?

First, you must distinguish whether you are thinking like an inventory manager for a seller or a buyer of the commodity. As a market tops, inventory managers for buyers try to hold back as much as they can—buying from hand to mouth. They are hoping the market will break before it breaks them.

Inventory managers for sellers might also hold back, expecting to sell their commodity at an even higher price tomorrow. This drives prices into a blow-off top, sometimes followed by a short-term rebound.

Open Interest is a Key to the Actions of Inventory Managers

Another key to understanding both topping and bottoming situations is open interest. It can be defined as the sum of all long or short futures contracts in one delivery month or one market that have been entered, but not yet liquidated, by an offsetting transaction or fulfilled by delivery. This information is reported by the futures exchanges and published daily in the major financial newspapers. Inventory managers, by virtue of their size, have a noticeable impact on open interest when they act.

If open interest increases when a market is near record lows and prices start to stabilize or move higher, you can bet your grain bin inventory managers for users are aggressively accumulating inventory. If, on the other hand, prices are topping and open interest is declining, the inventory managers for producers are selling.

Generally, speaking as the inventory managers go, so goes the markets they trade.

Please take this last statement as a warning. The strongest hands that ever hold a commodity are those belonging to a bona fide hedger. The bona fide hedger is a producer or has a business need for the commodity. He plans on selling it or using it. He can't conduct his business without it. He's not easily swayed by transient political or economic pressures.

But, and this is an important "but," he is not crazy or foolish. If prices get too far out of line, he'll relinquish his hold on the commodity in question. Therefore, you cannot blindly follow anyone into a position indefinitely.

Anatomy of a Bull Market

The scenarios just discussed touched on the concept of bull and bear markets. Understanding them is critical to success in the futures market, so it will pay to study them in a little more detail.

There are usually seven distinct stages in every major bull market. You must learn to recognize each stage before it is in full swing. By developing this skill, you'll be able to trade with the trend, which is often the difference between winning and losing in the markets.

Stage One—The Birth of the Bull

Surprisingly, the origins of a bull market are found in surplus situations. Surplus commodities widen the arteries, fill the pipelines, and foster new sources of demand. An industry whose raw materials are in surplus is likely to expand usage. Low-priced, surplus supplies build confidence in users—the confidence to expand, to develop new uses (corn sweetener, oils, gasohol, etc.), to solicit new customers, and to contract long-term commitments. All of these factors result in an increased appetite and a wider demand base.

From a technical analysis perspective (we'll discuss this in Chapter 3), a surplus market is observable as a rounded bottom, the early signs of which are progressively shallowing downtrends and narrower trading ranges. The absolute bottom of a rounded bottom often occurs when the fundamental information is the most bearish while the commodity price meanders sideways in a narrow range. You can be comfortable, for instance, with a major market bottom when all the news reports say that corn is going to the "price of gravel" while the corn price wanders aimlessly in a 2-cent range. Passive market activity in response to bearish news is your first bull sign.

Stage Two—Shallow Uptrend

The next benchmark is modestly increasing prices at the right side of the rounded bottom. It is a very shallow uptrend, usually accompanied by wider price ranges.

Fundamentally, there is little change in the supply of the commodity; although, commercial interest in the commodity changes slightly. A "what if" stage develops among the fundamentalists—e.g., what if there is a short wheat crop in Canada? What if Brazilian coffee has a freeze? What if housing starts increase by ten percent? What if war breaks out? Due to the intangible nature of the "what if" stage and the fruitless nature of most "what if" scenarios, stage two offers very little price improvement other than the gradual increase in price due to carrying charges. But this is the place to begin to build your position as the momentum builds.

Stage Three—The Breakout

The third stage of development is a very interesting one that often occurs with very little public supply and demand information. It is often described in business publications as a technical breakout, which is a way of saying: "The market has made a dramatic move but we don't know why."

Technically, the market is breaking out of the rounded bottom, and it usually shows a modest rally for a few days, sometimes weeks. This rally often subsides without fundamental follow-through and develops a platform or plateau. This is sideways market activity at the area of the rounded bottom breakout and a time of confusing information. Fundamental and technical data are often conflicting and often contradictory.

Stage Four—The Rally Begins

Stage four of the bull market develops as market information becomes more detailed. Often, seemingly minor fundamental (supply and demand) information comes into play, such as erratic weather patterns across the Midwest affecting the grain market. More "what if" scenarios also begin to develop. This is a nervous rally—it tends to be choppy with labored price increases and sharp, quick dips. The rallies and subsequent dips are usually able to hold a 45-degree trendline, and the traders feel confident in buying when prices dip back to the trendline.

Stage Five—The Explosive Newsmaker

On a technical basis, gaps are often left on the charts during this phase, while the bullish fundamental scenario gains wider acceptance. Users are often scrambling to purchase raw material, while sellers become reluctant to release supplies. Interestingly, advisory newsletters during this stage often become nervous and indicate a bias that the market may be topping.

Stage Six—The Steep Rally

The sixth stage of the bull market is typically a steep rally with few market retracements and wide trading ranges fueled by bullish fundamental information. Often, public attention turns toward the market rally and people who have never traded commodities suddenly think about trading the long side.

During this period, the news media reports users who are going bankrupt because they have left themselves exposed to price increases in raw materials.

Stage Seven—The Shearing

Stage seven occurs when investors decide to sell their blue chip stock at a loss and go long in the commodity market. This is when bullish information is being offered to the public, inspiring them to become involved. When you read about it in *The Wall Street Journal*, check to make sure you have your protective stop orders properly placed. Technically, the market will gap higher with limit up moves, even for two or more days; then, the sheep are shorn. It is after stage seven that the futures industry is plagued with outcries for greater regulation.

Bear Markets

Bear markets usually move down faster than bull markets move up. One of the reasons is volume is lower. The less volume, the more erratic and violent market moves become because there is less activity to absorb and cushion the fall. Low volume markets are very dangerous to trade for this reason. Avoid them, if possible, when you first start trading. By the way, the volume of each market is reported by exchanges and published daily in the major financial papers. Your broker should have it at his fingertips.

Like bull markets, there are several stages to these markets. The first stage occurs when bullish news enters the market, but it doesn't move higher. It appears that nobody believes the news or believes the market has already taken the information into consideration. Next, the market makes a severe retracement—usually 33 percent, 50 percent or 66 percent of the previous bull move. A lot of traders on the long side, often small individual traders, lose money and are forced out of the market. Since no new longs enter the market when this retracement starts, it is said to "fall by its own weight."

Once the market finds some support, completing the retracement stage, there may be a period where the market moves sideways or even up. This is a bear market rally. Traders are often very confused during this time period.

Sooner or later, the bullish news becomes scarce or non-existent. At this point, the market makes its final plunge lower, until it gets to the point inventory managers can't resist building inventories. This actually brings the bear market to an end.

The Price Discovery Process

Obtaining a firm grasp of how the market discovers price is so important to successful trading, we like to approach the concept using an analogy. What may appear to the novice trader as totally random price movement eventually conforms to recognizable and tradeable patterns.

Think about the futures market as a public poll. The futures brokers are the pollsters. They go out and survey the general trading public. "Where do you think the price of gold is headed? In your opinion, is the price of crude oil too high or too low?" The answers to all the questions are communicated to the trading pits, where they are processed. The results are published daily in various financial papers.

Keep in mind that the people who answer these surveys are very sincere about their answers—they have backed their opinions with margin money. Collectively, they represent all the thoughts, research, and emotions surrounding the entire financial community. The people polled may have been influenced by the media, their personal financial situation and what has and is happening in the world.

Can studying and evaluating all these surveys be meaningful? We think so, particularly when you're interested in finding long term trends. If you look at the trends—as someone like John Naisbitt, author of *Megatrends*, would do—you begin to think about them as being the collective response to stimuli. By reading, studying, and collecting a wide array of seemingly unrelated data, Mr. Naisbitt can deduct, with a good deal of accuracy, some various interesting trends, which planners and business people can use.

Mr. Naisbitt's work is very similar to fundamental analysis of the futures markets. You can often deduce the overall, long-term trend. But it doesn't necessarily tell you which specific opportunity or trade to take. More importantly it is not much help when it comes to timing. Most traders revert to technical or chart analysis at this point.

Left and Right Brain Trading

While we're discussing how pricing is made, let's talk for a minute of how trades are selected. As we've learned from scientific research, the brain has a left and a right hemisphere. The left side deals primarily with the logical side of our nature, the right with the creative or artistic.

Therefore, you use your left side to do fundamental and technical research. Once all your homework is done, either by yourself or in consultation with your broker, you need to digest the facts. At this point, the hard data moves to the right side of the brain for interpretation. The artist in the trader uncovers the patterns in the charts. Intuition takes over in many successful traders. They may trade what appears to be hunches, but it is, in reality, a synergistic blend of the left and right brain functions.

With several of our best customers and brokers, we often see a behavioral pattern where they study the facts, sleep on the information, and trade successfully the next day. We don't think this is an accident.

Also, if you have every followed a good CTA (commodity trading advisor) for an extended period of time, you often find that he or she substantiates their analysis at different times with different analytical tools. One time you think the CTA is a fundamentalist; the next, a strict technician. The cynical observer accuses the analyst of using whatever technique fits the preconceived conclusion.

The truth of the situation is usually just the opposite. The experienced analyst selects the correct analytic technique based on the current market conditions. For example, some techniques work well when the markets are trending up or down, but are useless—or worse, dangerous—in choppy, trendless markets. Some chart formations are more reliable than others. Sometimes, the fundamentals are clear and meaningful. At other times, they are conflicting.

One of the keys is that nowadays there is so much access by traders and advisors to both technical and fundamental information, that the well-known signals become self-fulfilling prophecies. Everyone sees corn break a trendline or drop through a support level. This causes a rush to the short side of the market. The lower prices foretold by the broken trendline are realized.

This often prompts the question: Wouldn't a totally automated system be best?—perhaps a freestanding computerized trading system that eliminates the need for subjective judgment on the part of the analyst. You wouldn't want this anymore than you would want to ride in a plane that didn't have human pilots who have the capacity to override the autopilot, when conditions warrant it.

Futures trading is a blend of cold, calculating statistics and a warm, human touch. Traders who rely too heavily on either—to the neglect of the other—have not, in our opinion, been very successful. This brings us to the "Law of Probability." You must accept this concept to be able to handle the stress of futures trading. It simply means that futures trading can be a hit and miss type of investment. Some trades work, others don't. For a fact, most traders lose money. You must keep trying one trade after the other until you pick the profitable trades. Thus the origin of an important adage: "Cut losing trades short and let winners run."

You diversify your portfolio by trading several different markets in order to increase the probability of being in the right trade at the right time. Discipline and money management, which will be discussed later in great detail, are essential for you to survive the markets and utilize the law of probability to your best advantage.

CHAPTER 2

IS FUTURES TRADING FOR YOU?

Key Concepts

⇒ Whether you are financially and psychologically suited to the risk involved.

⇒ The five secrets and four major obstacles to success.

So far, we tried to give you some general insights into how the futures markets work. As mentioned several times, futures prices and price trends reflect the composite response to the current supply-demand equation of everyone who is in the market. If the overall attitude is bullish, the market moves higher. If traders are bearish, it plunges. If nobody is sure or opinions are conflicting, it slides sideways. This all sounds very simplistic, but gauging traders' attitudes or forecasting price is an extremely complex activity, as we'll see in the next chapter.

Now, we need to become introspective for a moment. Are you suitable to trade futures? This is a question your broker must also determine, as per the federal regulators who govern the industry. Your broker is charged by NFA (National Futures Association) and the CFTC (Commodity Futures Trading Commission) to find out if you are indeed suitable. That's why they ask you a series of personal questions. What is your net worth? Profession? Age? Investment experience?

With this information, your overall suitability is reviewed on several levels. First, your broker makes the first screening. He then passes your account forms (see Chapter 9) or account papers to his supervisor, who is usually on the IB (Introducing Broker) level. From here, it goes up the ladder to the FCM (Futures Commission Merchant). The FCM is the entity that actually does the trading in the pits. It is the clearing—as in clearing trades through the system—member of the exchanges. An IB is the link between you (the general public) and the FCM. It introduces you to the market.

Who's Suitable?

There are a variety of ways of determining suitability for futures and options trading. One of the measures is the person's net worth, annual income, and liquid assets.

Before we get into specific evaluation methods, we need to distinguish between futures and options trading. The reason is simply the amount of risk.

With futures, the risk is unlimited. If you're in a futures position and the market makes a limit move against your positions, you must immediately meet the margin call, if your account does not include excess equity. And, there could be more than one day in a row of limit moves. Once the live hogs contract limited down six days in a row. The limit move was $600 per day or $3,600 for those six days. If you had ten positions, it would have been over $36,000 when you include commissions and fees. This doesn't account for days when the limit might have been extended. Margin calls can be in the millions of dollars.

Buying exchange traded futures options involves a more defined risk. It equals the amount of the premium for the option and the transaction costs. These latter costs are defined as the broker's commission and fees. There are NFA, exchange, and FCM fees to be paid on both futures and options trades. Let's keep it clear: we are talking about buying options (calls or puts) when we discuss options trading. If you write options, you'll have the same risk as a futures trader since you are contracting to deliver a futures position, if the options you write are exercised. We'll get into this in more detail later.

Therefore, the futures trader faces more risk. The options trader can lose 100 percent of the amount invested, but the amount is known in advance.

This analysis of the risk facing both types of traders explains why the net worth and liquid asset requirements differ for each type of account. The FCM (Futures Commission Merchant), which is the entity that holds the investor's capital and executes (or arranges to execute) the trades, sets the standards.

When approving an account for trading, the FCM compares the prospective customer's resources with their anticipated trading activity. Are they financially suitable? For example, many FCMs will not approve an account that plans to trade more than 10 percent of his or her liquid assets. When and if a margin call is made on the account, the customer has 24 hours or less to meet it. Therefore, only liquid assets can be considered in the evaluation.

If the customer has a high annual income, let's say in excess of $100,000 per year, they may be approved even if their net worth is unremarkable. Or if they are not very wealthy, they may be approved to trade (buy) options since the risk is defined and the entire investment is usually made in advance.

Other Suitability Questions

A customer's financial position is not the only consideration. Brokers are required by federal regulations to "know their customers." (Not, of course, in the biblical sense.) But, at least, they must learn the following, in addition to the financial information:

- The customer's true name, address, and principal occupation or business;

- Approximate age; and

- An indication of the customer's previous investment and futures trading experience.

The FCM and the federal regulators (NFA and CFTC) want to get an insight into the experience and sophistication of the investor. For example, very young or very old people may require additional investigation by the FCM before they are accepted. Investors who have traded futures in the past or traded stocks on margin would be considered reasonably experienced.

Risk Tolerance

Besides learning about an investor's financial background and previous investing experiences, good futures brokers delve into the risk tolerance of their customers. This is a critical consideration when developing a trading plan designed to reach specific objectives—yet one the customer is comfortable trading.

When doing this, a good broker attempts to classify his or her customers' attitudes toward risk. Each customer is an individual and each one reacts differently to risk. If a broker doesn't deal with this, a lasting bond of trust will not be created.

When classifying attitudes to risk, economists use the term "utility," which is a measure of personal satisfaction. If something provides a feeling of greater satisfaction than whatever it is compared to, it is said to have greater utility.

As experienced brokers discuss trading strategies and risk-to-reward ratios of specific trades with their clients, they learn to classify customers as adverse, neutral or aggressive risk takers. For example, a risk adverse person may not be interested in a trade that would be projected to return a dollar for every dollar at risk. These traders want to take little or no risk and are satisfied with low, but dependable, returns. If you fit the risk adverse description, you probably should not be trading futures.

The risk neutral traders may consider trading options and/or what appears to be the most conservative of futures trades. The aggressive risk takers are the ones most commonly thought of futures traders. These people are willing to take the risks required to get high utility (satisfaction) from making successful trades.

When you consider your suitability to trading futures, look closely at all three of these areas—financial situation, investing experience and risk tolerance—before you fill out the account papers and send in your check.

We Have Met the Enemy

Just because you are suitable, doesn't mean you'll be successful. Studies of futures traders indicate most lose money. That brings up two questions:

(1)   Who will be successful in the futures markets?

(2)   What is the most important element of a successful trading system?

When active traders get together at a conference or seminar, there is often a heated discussion centering around trading systems. Which one works best? Can the fundamental trader know and evaluate all the possible facts that influence the supply-demand equation? How reliable are technical signals and how should they be interpreted? When using both technical and fundamental analysis, or when you selectively override your system, when are you relying on skill and when on luck?

What are some of the characteristics of successful people? Think about someone you admire who has reached the pinnacle of his or her field. It could be an executive, professional, athlete, or futures trader. My point is simply that most successful people possess some similar characteristics.

Self-Knowledge

Key among these characteristics is an innate understanding of themselves and their mission in life. They seem to have a little secret that they won't share—no matter how much you probe them. That secret guides their lives and spawns several other very important traits, namely patience, persistence, discipline, and independence.

Their secret is simply the fact that they have clearly defined goals. And they work hard each day to achieve these goals. These objectives are usually reached in stages, with each step of the journey clearly defined.

How does this apply to the futures traders? Why do, as conventional wisdom tells us, 95 percent of futures traders end up net losers?

The obvious answer is that they do not set realistic goals. Perhaps they get in the market on a whim. Someone gives them a tip that corn is going to $4 or silver to $10 in the next 3 weeks. They call a broker and put on a futures position or buy an option. Or a broker might have called them with the "trade of the century." Their odds of winning are the same as someone who purchases a lottery ticket—very few win, many lose.

The Serious Player

The serious futures trader is no different than the serious athlete. To be a professional football player, you start in grade school. This is usually followed by eight or nine successful years on the high-school and college levels. After ten to twelve years of hard work, you're a rookie! With a few more years of sweat and bruises, you may be taken seriously in the NFL, with a visit to the Pro-Bowl or Super Bowl.

Most commodity traders do not spend ten years preparing for their first serious season in the markets. To them it's more like a carnival. They walk up to the barker, give him a dollar, pick up the big hammer with both hands, swing as hard as they can and hope they ring the bell on the first try. If they can afford it, they try until they are out of money. Then they lick their wounds and go home. Six months or a year later, they may try it again when the "carnie" comes back to town.

The Secret of Successful Trading

It really doesn't matter what type of trading system you employ. We've seen extremely successful systems of all sorts.

Success in the markets goes deeper—into your psyche. You must know yourself! Know what you believe in. Back your beliefs with commitment.

Here's a few over-simplified examples. If you look at a head and shoulders topping chart formation that projects a 22-point move lower and feel in your heart it is all hocus-pocus, you should not be a technical trader. Or, if you feel totally overwhelmed by all the information you need to be aware of to be a fundamental trader, that's probably not your calling. We've also seen traders develop sophisticated systems requiring one or two hours of daily updating, only to learn they didn't have the time or inclination to service the systems.

Your system must suit you, your psychological make-up, and the time you have available to administer it. Additionally, you need to believe in it, trust it, work with it, and refine it until it makes money for you. Without the patience, persistence, and discipline mentioned earlier, you'll never succeed as a futures trader.

This brings us full circle to the "secret of success." It's not the "magic system" that reaps success in the markets. You need achievable objectives, a plan to reach those objectives, and a system in which you have faith that matches your personality. Then you need to be able to withstand the bruises and bumps you'll experience on the way to a winning season. Last of all, you must learn to conquer serious opponents—pride, hope, fear and greed.

What Can Oedipus Rex Teach You?

The ancient Greeks would easily relate to how an intelligent, aggressive trader—with a strong market position—ends up taking a massive loss on that position. The Greeks coined a word for what often happens to otherwise skillful traders. It was "hubris." Its common definition is simply "overbearing pride." How many times have you talked to a trader about his or her position only to get the response, "Don't worry about me. I KNOW where the market is going!"

You'll often find three witches accompanying hubris. They are hope, fear and greed. We personally believe this foursome has brought more people, who could have been successful in the market, to their financial knees than just about anything else.

How Do You Control Hope, Fear and Greed?

The answer may also be hidden in the past. Just as the ancients offered an ox or a goat to the gods, you must make sacrifices. We often refer to it as "swallowing one's pride." One way of doing this is being brutally honest with yourself in your trading diary. In Chapter 6, you'll learn how to create a trading journal.

Let's say your system flashes a sell signal while you are holding a long position. You override it, only to watch your profits evaporate as prices head lower. In your diary, if it is to be of any real value to you, you must state how you violated the system. Your journal must force discipline upon your trading. If it does only this, it will be well worth all the time and trouble it takes to maintain.

Sacrifices must be made to the witches as well. Let's take greed as an example. You must prove to the market that you have "conquered" or at least can manage greed.

How can you do that? One way is to take "surprise" or windfall profits. Let's say you're short silver. Your analysis indicates it should go down a quarter over the next 30-90 days. Shortly after you get your order filled, silver drops a half dollar—25 cents more than you expected. What do you do?

(a)   Take your unexpected profit?

(b)   Wait for it to go down further?

(c)   Place a close stop to protect profits?

If you selected "b," you're testing the gods. And, the gods and the markets punish mere mortals who challenge their authority. If you chose "a," you pocket $2,500 (minus transaction costs) and the gods are pleased you accepted their gift.

Those of you who selected "c" are still fighting greed. But you have shown at least some management. You're still in the market. You still have a profit, at least on paper. If the gods smile on you, you'll eventually be stopped out with a profit. If not, the market will limit through your stop and skyrocket higher until you see the evil of your ways.

If you trade multiple positions, you can demonstrate your mastery of greed to the gods by closing out part of your position when it becomes profitable—for example, let's say to trade in three lots. You're long corn. It moves up to within a range from one-half to two-thirds of your objective. You close out one position at this point. Then you close your second when your objective is hit, and you speculate with the third using a stop. This approach should please you and the deities that watch over these matters.

Hope Springs Disaster!

Eternal hope can put you in the poor house. You may survive on hope in your personal life, but it can be extremely damaging in the markets. The usual scenario evolves around a position that is moving against all your best judgments. Just about everything indicates you are wrong—but you keep hoping the market will turn in your favor.

Hope is addictive, numbing your discipline. Open your diary and write down why you are staying in this market. If you're frank with yourself and write "because I hope it will go my way tomorrow," you're in trouble. Cut your losses short. If you still think the market will turn, place a stop reversal order in the market. But, do it only after re-evaluating the situation and entering it as a complete new trade that meets all your criteria for a new trade.

The last witch is fear. It's one we face daily in the markets. Fear of losing money. Fear of making a stupid error. Fear of looking foolish in the eyes of our peers. Fear, fear, fear.

Probably the most effective way of controlling fear is by sacrificing a portion of our profit. The old adage—bears win, bulls win, hogs lose—evolves from those that have learned to deal with fear. For example, you can limit some market fear by not trying to pick tops or bottoms. If you are riding a bull market to seventh heaven, get off at the sixth cloud. Take your profits and bank them.

Or, you can hedge your position. If you are into a large position on the long side, consider buying some puts that are near in-the-money as protection. This is not a sign of weakness. It is a sound business decision.

Another suggestion is to continually take excess profits out of your account. Then, when you do have a drawdown, it is not as crushing. You still have profits to show. You don't feel as threatened and fear doesn't overwhelm you. Futures trading is a very personal challenge—are you prepared? To check your preparedness, complete the Financial-Psychological Worksheet (Figure 2.2).

Figure 2.2

Financial Psychological Worksheet

1. Never invest any more than I can afford to lose in highly speculative investments. Futures and options trading fall into this category. I will invest no more than 10% of my net liquid assets (those that are cash or can be converted to cash within 24 hours) in the futures market and no more than 10% of this amount on any one position.

Net Liquid Assets (NLA)

Cash-savings/checking accounts	$ _____
CDs and money market funds	$ _____
Bonds-treasury, etc.	$ _____
Publicly traded stocks	$ _____
Other	$ _____
Total	$ _____
Risk Capital - 10% of NLA	$ _____

If this is less than $5,000, I will consider trading options rather than futures.

2. Before opening a futures or options trading account, I will make sure I have the following:

   _____ Adequate life insurance
   _____ A sufficient net worth, so that if all or part of my NLA are lost, it will not affect my life style.

3.   I rate myself, regarding my attitude toward risk as

       _____   Risk adverse—avoid futures trading programs
       _____   Risk neutral—consider options or managed programs
       _____   Aggressive risk taker—consider futures and managed
                     programs

4.   I am looking for an annual percentage rate of return from the funds I commit
to the futures market of

_____	25%	_____	100%
_____	50%	_____	150%
_____	75%	_____	200% or higher

I understand that, the higher the expected return, the higher the risk will
normally be.

5.   I rate my investment experience as

  _____ Minimal   _____ Adequate   _____ Experienced

6.   I understand the futures market

  _____ Very Well   _____ Medium Well   _____ Not at all

7.   I understand myself and my motivation for trading futures

  _____ Very Well   _____ Medium Well   _____ Not sure
  _____ I'm after profit, not excitement.

8.   I withstand pressure in the following way:

  _____ My heart speeds up when I write checks for $10,000 or more
            for an investment.
  _____ Losing money keeps me awake at night.
  _____ I take the good and bad in stride.
  _____ I constantly gamble and take changes.
  _____ The following describes my behavior under financial pressure:

     _____

(figure continues)

9. I can deal with the following negative news:

_____ I realize I will probably have numerically more losing trades than winning ones.

_____ I understand that my trading account will regularly experience drawdowns of equity.

_____ I am ready to face an occasional margin call.

10. I am ready to do whatever it takes to trade successfully—that is,

_____ Cut losing trades short, let winners run.

_____ Control my pride, greed, hope and fear.

_____ Write a plan which includes goals.

_____ Keep a trading journal.

_____ Develop a trading system.

_____ Select a broker that compliments my character and limitations.

_____ Fund my account adequately.

There are no right or wrong answers to these questions. After answering them honestly, review them with someone you trust. Then carefully and thoughtfully make your decision as to whether you are ready to become a futures trader.

CHAPTER 3

HOW TO ANTICIPATE THE DIRECTION OF FUTURES PRICE MOVEMENT— BEFORE THEY BEGIN

Key Concepts

▐▶ Fundamental analysis-the study of all underlying factors influencing the supply-demand equation, which determines the price of commodities.

▐▶ Technical analysis—the study of commodity price charts and other statistical data to determine commodity price trends.

▐▶ You must master the use of the following basic technical analysis signals and chart formations: trend lines, volume, open interest, ten technical trading rules, rounded bottoms, consolidations, tops, bottoms, support, resistance, retracements, reversals, head and shoulders, continuing formations, triangles, coils, boxes, flags, pennants, diamonds, moving averages, momentum oscillators, seasonals, cycles, Elliott Wave and Gann Numbers.

O nce you get a general feel for the futures markets and decide you are financially and psychologically suited, you need to consider the area of price trend
forecasting. Futures trading requires you to make a simple decision—should you
go long or short? Do you think the price of whatever commodity you want to
trade is headed higher or lower? If you can't do this, there's no point in considering
an individual trading account. You should think of some type of alternative strategy, such as those described in Chapter 5.

There are basically three methods of forecasting price trends. You can use
fundamental or technical analysis. Or you can use a combination of the two.

What Is Fundamental Analysis?

To quote the National Futures Association's *Glossary of Futures Terms*:

Fundamental Analysis: The study of basic, underlying factors which will
affect the supply and demand and hence the price of a futures contract.

In theory, it is quite simple. When the supply of a commodity becomes scarce,
the price goes up. When it is plentiful, the price goes down.

Unfortunately, it doesn't always work this way. For example, some of the
toughest factors to accurately quantify are those of supply and demand. How much
of a given commodity is enough? Where is it, and is it in a usable form?

Agricultural commodities are a good group to use to illustrate this point;
most people are familiar with them, and they are very responsive to supply and
demand factors.

To make an accurate price projection for corn, for example, here's what you'd
need to know for a given crop year:

- Existing stocks (On-farm and Commercial Inventory)

- Production (Projected Acres/Yields)

- Usage (Food, Feed & Seed)

Now this seems reasonable—until you try to gather all the facts needed to
make these three estimates.

First off, keep in mind you're doing this on a global basis, and many of the
countries from which you need vital information will be uncooperative. The developed countries may share only the information that suits their side of the
supply-demand equation. If they expect to be corn buyers, they might provide
inflated figures on supply they have on hand or expect to produce. Their objective
is to drive prices down—to get more kernels of corn per ruble.

Undeveloped countries may do the same thing. Additionally, they may not have an established infrastructure to gather, process, and evaluate what information they have on their crop.

As you attempt to piece together all the facts on production and usage, you quickly come to the conclusion that much of the information is unreliable for a variety of reasons. With agricultural products, the weather is always a major uncertainty. Too much or too little rain, even over a short period of time, can drastically impact prices.

Other groups of commodities are equally influenced by seemingly uncontrollable factors that are virtually impossible to predict. Consider what wide swings in political unrest or interest rates can do to the price of precious metals.

Our point is simply this: the accuracy of fundamental analysis often hinges on fast changing information—much of which is not easily obtained, nor can it always be accurately interpreted.

How Do You Do Fundamental Analysis?

For years, number crunchers have attempted to quantify supply and demand statistics. It's been like the search for the Holy Grail or the goose that lays golden eggs. Who wouldn't want a mathematical formula that can accurately forecast prices three, six or nine months into the future? We would be tickled pink with one that would be good for tomorrow's prices.

Statisticians have tried linear and nonlinear regressions analysis, double exponential smoothing, probability and trigonometric curves, multi-variable analysis, and just about every other technique they could think of. Hopes were raised with the advent of computers. Wharton School of Business and Chase Manhattan Bank were two well-known leaders in the field of econometric modeling. These were sophisticated computer programs that attempted to account for just about every variable affecting price.

We've used several conditional words—tried, attempted, etc.—in this description. The reason is that fundamental analysis has not been particularly successful in day-to-day trading of the futures markets. The reasons are threefold:

- Projections have been marred by unexpected events. The invasion of Kuwait by Iraq is a typical example.

- Another perennial problem is attempting to take all variables into consideration. One or more critical ones always seem to be missing (or misinterpreted) after the projections are made.

- This type of analysis is long-term in nature, while most futures trading tends to be short- to medium-term.

If you combine all this with the fact that fundamental analysis is not self-cor-recting, as we'll see in the next part on technical analysis systems, you can begin to get a feel for the problem. By this we mean if a fundamental analyst determines that $2 is a cheap price for corn, and goes long, what does he think when the price drops to $1.50? Does he absorb the loss and continue to buy? How can he square his analysis with what the market is doing?

Is Fundamental Analysis Useless?

No, definitely not. There are some CTAs that have found it very effective. They often use a particular aspect, weather for example, to make projections. They are position traders who take long-term approaches to the market.

More often than not, the CTAs who use it do so by combining it with technical analysis. Fundamental analysis can provide the overview, the Big Picture, the long-term trend. Technical analysis is used to signal the short-term entry and exit points.

Since fundamental analysis deduces its conclusion from external or underly-ing factors influencing supply or demand, it is very unique to each commodity. Therefore, we covered the specific factors for each commodity in the individual "overview sections" at the end of this chapter and Appendix 1.

What Is Technical Analysis?

Technical analysts confine their prognostication of future price trends solely on the analysis of price activity. The price of a futures contract, they contend, reflects

Figure 3.1

Supply-Demand Equation

- Existing Stocks

- Plus Production

- Less Usage

- Equals Supply

Fundamental analysis is based on an analysis of the comparative strength of the opposing forces of supply and demand. If supply exceeds demand, prices usually decline. If demand outstrips supply, prices usually rise.

---

the impact of every single bit of fundamental information known by anyone who can even remotely affect the price of the commodity. This is a big statement. Think it over for a moment. Every fact that is known about supply, demand, and, most importantly, the psychology of the public—ends up on the price charts.

Price action is the composite opinion of everyone that is willing to put their money where their mouth is!

That is why learning to analyze price action is so important to anyone trading stocks, futures or options. The function of technical analysis is to determine through the analysis of price change the probable strength of demand compared to the pressure of supply on a futures contract at various price levels—and then to predict the direction, length, and velocity of the next move.

History Repeats Itself

In the commodity markets, history does repeat itself. Past price action can provide clues as to future price action. On commodity price charts and indexes, price movements tend to repeat themselves with remarkable consistency.

You'll learn that some patterns or formations indicate that demand is greater than supply. Others suggest the reverse is true. And, some imply that supply and demand will remain indefinitely in balance.

This occurs for two reasons. First, technical analysis can be a self-fulfilling prophecy. It is self-fulfilling because so many professionals use it. They all see the same patterns and often expect the same results. Therefore, if enough of them act the same way to the same chart signal, the signal fulfills its promise. This occurs regularly with the most common and widely known signals.

Secondly, the market is anticipatory, and you can see price movement first in the charts. For example, major buyers, like the Chinese, have been known to go long the futures market before they announced a big grain deal. They entered the futures market to cover their cash sale. Therefore, the first alert something is about to happen often occurs on the futures price charts.

Entering the market causes a price movement before the fundamental facts are known. Technical analysts are alerted in advance, before the fundamental information is public. Supply and demand factors are still the prime movers, yet technical analysis is the earliest indicator of movement.

If you use technical analysis, you don't have to understand or acquire all the fundamental information in the world in order to trade. The impact of all the activity affecting price comes to you in the form of price movement. If you don't understand what is causing the price movement, you can exit the market until you do.

Is It Fool Proof?

There is no infallible system—technical or fundamental—for trading the futures markets. Chart signals, just like fundamental news, can be misleading. You don't always have to be right to enjoy trading futures and options, but you need to have structure in your approach to the markets. Technical analysis can give you that structure.

Since technical analysis is probably the only forecasting technique an individual investor can utilize, we're going to discuss the most common tools and signals. Fundamental analysis, because of the enormous amount of information necessary and enormous amount of time required to absorb all the fundamental factors, is usually too costly and time consuming for individual investors.

The Trend Line

The most common technical analysis tool is the trend line. Prices tend to follow straight lines. They almost cling to them. If they bounce off a line, they are drawn back to it. There are sound psychological reasons why prices trend.

Figure 3.2   Uptrend Formation

The Uptrend Formation is probably the most common and most followed of chart formations. Traders using this trend believe prices will continue to increase.

Chart courtesy of "Pocket Charts."

First, let's describe what a trend line is. It is a line drawn between at least two points on a price chart. Uptrend lines should be drawn so they connect lows and are drawn below prices. Downtrends connect highs and are drawn above prices. Sideways trend lines are drawn below prices and connect lows.

Why Do Prices Cling to Straight Lines?

It is simply human nature. A trader will resist paying more for a commodity than what others are willing to pay, unless he thinks it will continue to increase in price. The converse is equally true.

Therefore, if a price is going up, traders will watch the trend. As long as it moves higher, buyers will continue to buy. If it increases a little too fast, buyers hold back and the price returns to the trend line. The more buying (volume) taking place, the more confidence traders have that prices will continue to rise.

We're all more comfortable when others are behaving the same as we are behaving. This is referred to as herd psychology.

We can sometimes quantify the herd's psychology through the measurement of volume and open interest. Volume is the total number of contracts traded in a day. Open interest is the number of contracts outstanding at the end of a trading day.

Other human psychological tendencies also come into play. The inventory manager, who is responsible for buying a commodity for his company, increases his purchases as he sees prices go up, fearing that prices will be even higher in the future. This increases consumption.

The person who owns the commodity holds out for higher prices when he sees prices increasing. This reduces the supply. And the uptrend continues.

The Law of Price Trend Inertia

Human resistance to change has a strong impact on trends. Nobody wants to be the first one to go against the crowd.

This brings us to Rule number 1. When a commodity is found to be following a trend, it is likely to continue along on that trend.

Spotting trends is simply a matter of drawing trend lines on price charts. The key to technical analysis is recognizing which trends are significant and reliable. Technical analysis is more of an art than a science.

Rule number 2. The longer the term of the chart, the more reliable the trend line. A trend line on a monthly price chart is more reliable and significant than one on a weekly chart. One on a weekly is better than one on a daily. A daily means more than an hourly, etc. The reason is that the longer something lasts, the more comfortable we are with it, and the less likely we are to want to change it.

Figure 3.3

Ten Technical Analysis Trading Rules

1. When a trend is established, it is likely to continue.

2. The longer term the chart (15-minute, hourly, daily, weekly, monthly), the more reliable the trend line.

3. The greater the volume of trading when a trend is established, the greater its significance.

4. In uptrending markets, when prices move too far too fast, trading volume decreases and prices decline.

5. In downtrending markets, volume is higher when prices are declining than when they rally.

6. Markets tend to give warnings before major trend changes occur. Be alert for these signals.

7. If a market is in an uptrend, volume usually drops just prior to it reversing its direction.

8. Volume usually increases in downtrending markets, just before a reversal of trend.

9. Markets tend to test their trend lines, by making shallow penetrations, before they plunge through them. These dips are warnings of impending trend reversals.

10. The steeper the trend, the more unstable it is and the more likely a reversal of trend is imminent.

Figure 3.4   Downtrend Formation

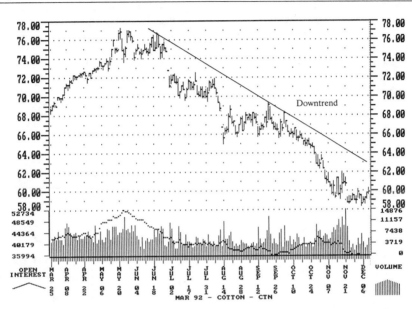

Up, down and sideways trends are usually drawn by connecting
highs or lows. Trends tend to continue until something upsets the
supply-demand equation.

Chart courtesy of "Pocket Charts."

How Do You Confirm a Trend is a Trend?

One of the answers is volume. The more trades behind a price move, the stronger
the conviction there is in the marketplace of the trend. Rule number 3: The greater
the volume, the greater the significance of a price trend.

Volume also tells you when traders think prices are moving too far or too
fast. In these two situations, volume decreases and prices reverse. For example, in
the normal uptrending market, when prices move too far above the trend line,
volume will decrease until prices return to the trend line. Conversely, in a downtrend, the volume is usually greater when prices are falling than when they are
rallying. These are Rules number 4 and 5.

Markets are like rattlesnakes—they make a noise before they bite. Each time
an established trend line is penetrated, it's a warning that the market may reverse
(Rule number 6).

Substantial changes in volume are another rattle from a market that it is about to reverse. If the market is in an uptrend, volume usually decreases before a reversal. If it is a downtrending market, volume usually increases before it reverses (Rules number 7 and number 8). The reason is that prices can fall from their own weight; but, they need constantly increasing buying activity to trend higher.

The first sign to look for when a market is changing direction is a violation of the trend line. A small dip below an uptrend doesn't necessarily mean the trend has changed. But it is a warning (Rule number 9).

Variations on a Theme

There are several different types of trendlines besides the basic up, down, and sideways. There is the Fan Formation, for example. It is a series of trend lines extending from the same point, but drawn at different angles.

Figure 3.5   Sideways Trend

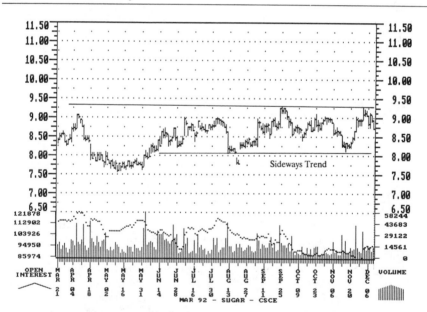

Traders commonly say: "The trend is your friend." This simply means prices will continue in the established direction until there is a reason for change of direction.

Chart courtesy of "Pocket Charts."

The Fan Trend Line Formation develops when an established trend line is broken; but, the price continues to move in the same direction forming a new trend line. This can happen two or three times, rarely four or more times (Rule number 10). After the third, be very alert.

It also occurs when prices heat up. Each successive trend line becomes steeper and steeper as a market heads for a blow off top.

The Internal Trend Line is an interesting formation. It develops out of a broken uptrend line. After the uptrend is broken, the market retraces and eventually the highs are attracted to the bottom of the old trend line. This is also an example of the "pull back" effect.

What Does All This Mean to a Trader?

Trend lines are your basic signals as to whether you should be on the long or the short side of the markets. Additionally, they tell you how much conviction traders

Figure 3.6   Fan Formation

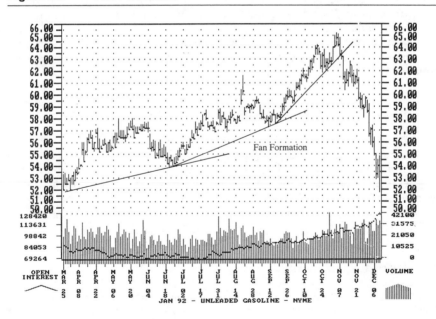

As prices reach a peak (high or low), the trend line becomes increasingly steeper. This is a warning to experienced traders that a trend change is imminent.

Chart courtesy of "Pocket Charts."

have in their positions. They warn you when investors are losing faith in their positions. They tell the contrary trader what the herd thinks about where prices are headed.

The trend can be your friend—if you learn how to read it. And, always analyze it in light of volume and open interest.

A Chartist's Dream Formation

The chart formation known as the rounded bottom is a chartist's dream because is it easy to recognize, it is reliable, and it alerts you to an upcoming long-term price move. Most important of all, this formation gives you time to make your decision. If you miss taking advantage of a rounded bottom, it's your own fault.

The formation starts with prices gradually moving down. They bottom. Then gradually increase.

Like any meaningful chart formation, there are some good psychological reasons behind it. A rounded bottom develops out of an increasing over–supply situation. As supplies of a commodity become plentiful, inventory managers (buyers) purchase from hand to mouth, believing the commodity will become less expensive tomorrow.

Volume on the exchanges for the commodity drops off, as traders wait to see if the movement is a major bear market or just a retracement. The supply-demand equation becomes balanced, and a long, flat bottom develops.

Great Bull Markets are Children of Over Supply!

Once the price stabilizes at a low price, the users of the commodity begin to take advantage and increase their usage. Demand builds. Inventory managers sense future price increases and add to the demand by laying away inventory.

Traders anticipate increased activity and begin bidding prices up at the exchanges. The volume of trades mirrors the price activity. A bull market often erupts from the rounded bottom formation. Refer to the *Anatomy of a Bull Market* in Chapter 1.

Periods of Consolidation

A variation of the rounded formations are horizontal channels or flat formations. These occur when a commodity or index has developed a base for a major move in the future.

They appear on the price charts as long sideways patterns. Prices trade in a very narrow range. Volume is low because traders feel that the market has little potential. Speculators are bored by these markets. They become flat or stagnant.

Figure 3.7   Rounded Bottom

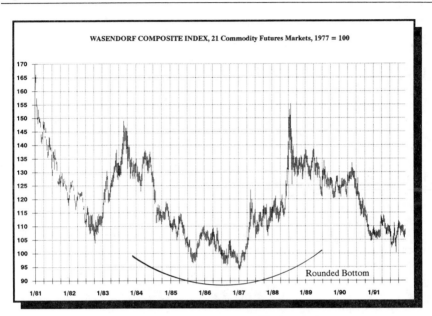

WASENDORF COMPOSITE INDEX, 21 Commodity Futures Markets, 1977 = 100

The Rounded Bottom Formation is a harbinger of a major uptrend in prices. They often take a long time in developing.

Chart courtesy of "Pocket Charts."

This formation can develop at major tops, major bottoms, or intermediate formations, occurring somewhere between major highs and lows.

This formation is often a harbinger of a major move, which could just as easily be up as down. Some people describe them as trading plateaus. The longs and the shorts are neutral, until something positive or negative heats the market up. At that point, a major move often occurs.

Spiked Tops and Bottoms

This formation is as unpredictable as the rounded bottom is predictable. It strikes without warning. Almost as if all the traders in a given market got together and decided to sell or buy at one time.

First we'll describe the spiked bottom. The price of a commodity drops sharply. Hits a point substantially below where the fall began. It stops and begins moving up sharply. The turn around usually is done in a single day of trading, although the decline can occur over a few days. After the bottom, the climb from the bottom continues for some time.

You must draw a steep trend line along the downtrend portion of the formation. You cannot be sure the bottom is in place until this trend line is broken.

Take care that you don't get whipsawed. This occurs when you prematurely reverse your position—move from long to short, or short to long—before you are sure the trend has changed. This can happen with spiked moves. Then the market moves sharply down, then pauses, only to plunge even deeper.

The psychology behind spike formations is the same herd psychology that causes cattle to stampede. To begin with, the market is nervous—very uncertain about what to expect. Often it has recently experienced some totally unexpected news. Everyone's confidence in their analysis is at a low. No one really believes anyone knows what will happen next.

Then, out of nowhere, more very grim unexpected news occurs. Traders sell the news. Then panic and rush to get out of their longs. The market makes a spiked move downward.

Just as suddenly as the market learns the facts, which are nowhere near as devastating as the "news" seemed to be, traders begin buying the facts and the market recovers.

Multiple Tops and Bottoms

Double and triple tops and bottoms are among the most common, yet most deceptive of chart formations.

The double top resembles the letter "M." Prices rise sharply to a point, fall back about half as far, rise again to the previous point. Then they decline beyond the point where the formation began. The double bottom looks like the letter "W" and is the reverse of the double top.

We characterized these formations as deceptive for a few reasons. It's very common for commodities to trend up and down. Inexperienced chartists begin seeing "M" and "W" formation on every chart. So many of these are false signals.

Secondly, it is nearly impossible to definitely call a double top or bottom until the reversal in trend has become pronounced and prices have moved below the initial starting point. To confirm an "M" or "W" formation, prices must fall or rise, respectively, beyond the vertex that's between the double top or bottom. By this time, the formation is complete, and a good deal of the move and opportunity has been missed.

Lastly, the move could be a triple top or bottom. If you act when it is only a double, you could be whipsawed.

The normal pattern for volume shows increases around the peaks. But again, this is not reliable. Studies have shown a lot of variation in volume.

Figure 3.8   Spiked Bottom Formations

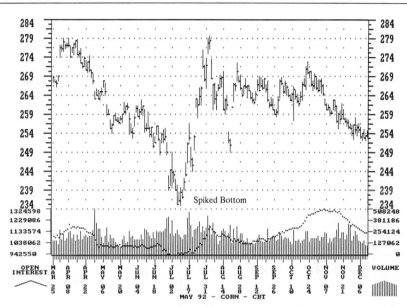

Spiked Tops and Bottoms can strike fear into the most experienced traders.
They occur without warning and result in a major trend change.

Chart courtesy of "Pocket Charts."

Support and Resistance Areas

Have you ever watched a commodity move up or down in what can be described
as a stair step movement? The commodity, for example, moves up ten or fifteen
points, consolidates for a few days, and then moves up again.

Or have you ever followed a bull market move up to a certain point and then
stop? Or watched a commodity retrace, after a bull move, to a level it had been
previously trading?

These are often examples of support and resistance levels. A support level is
a price or price range at which you can expect increased demand for the commodity. For example, a commodity drops in price until it hits a point where traders or
inventory managers (buyers for the users of that commodity) can't resist buying.

Figure 3.9   Double Top Formation

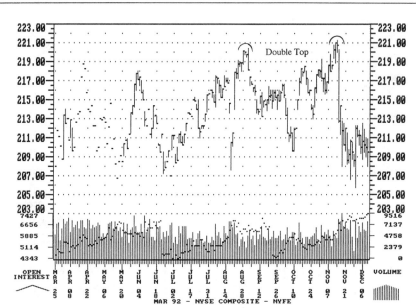

Double Top Formations are sometimes referred to as "M"
formations. They signal a change in trend. Warning: They can
become triple tops, which can whipsaw traders.

Chart courtesy of "Pocket Charts."

One way to detect this activity is by watching volume. As the price of a
commodity decreases, it is common to see the volume decrease. There simply isn't
any buying activity to bolster prices higher, so they fall by their own weight.

When the commodity reaches a level that is attractive to buyers, volume
increases as they take advantage of the "bargains." Prices trade sideways or rebound slightly on the charts. This becomes a support level.

Resistance levels are just the opposite. They are price levels where you can
expect a lot of selling. Prices reach a range where traders no longer see the potential
for further increases. Prices consolidate or retrace to lower levels.

Changes in volume and open interest alert you to resistance levels. Therefore,
if volume, open interest, and prices are all down, you know traders are closing out
their long positions. For whatever reason, a resistance level is created on the price
charts.

Figure 3.10   Support and Resistance Levels

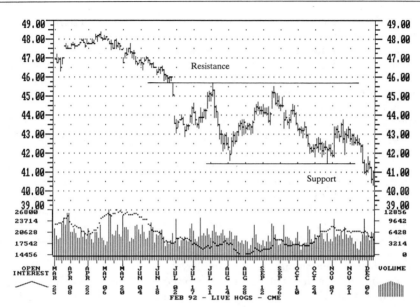

Chart courtesy of *"Pocket Charts."*

These are pricing levels where the majority of traders actively trading think prices have become too high (resistance) or too low (support). Therefore, price moves stall.

Serious technical traders study the long range charts looking for these areas of support and resistance. They know that when it comes to technical analysis, history repeats itself.

By knowing where prices are likely to stall during a bull move or likely to find support in a decline, technicians time their trading. The information gives them clues as to when to enter or exit markets, where to place protective stop orders, and insights as to the size and length of anticipated moves.

Another interesting technical phenomenon you'll notice as you study charts is that previous resistance levels often become support levels, and vice-versa. For example, a commodity breaks through a resistance level based on some bullish news. Once the move is exhausted, it retraces to find support at the level that previously had been the resistance level to the initial bull move.

Retracements

A retracement is a market reaction to the main trend. If the main trend is up, the market may often decrease or retrace the ground it just covered.

Always keep in mind that there are good psychological reasons for every chart movement. When traders think a market has moved too far or too fast, many will take their profits and exit the markets. Others short the market because they feel it is unstable. This causes a retracement.

But how much of a retracement will occur? How far down or up will the market go? Retracements often pull back or rally to areas of support or resistance respectively. It is also common for retracements to occur in calculable mathematical proportions.

The first step is to calculate the distance from important highs to important lows. Next, you analyze how the particular market previously performed under similar circumstances.

What you learn is that most markets often have repetitive retracement patterns. Market analysts accept retracements of 33 percent, 50 percent and 66 percent as most common. This means that a market that begins to retrace will probably retrace 33 percent, 50 percent or 66 percent of an amount equal to the distance between the previous significant high and low.

Again, you use this information as a timing device, or to help you select a point where you will take your profits, or re-enter the market, or buy/sell an option.

Key Reversals

Key reversals can occur either at market tops or bottoms. They are very reliable indicators that the current market trend is likely to reverse for an undetermined period of time.

Here's a description of how one takes shape on the charts. Look for key reversals when a market is in a steep up or downtrend. Next, see if the trading range widens. A new high or low is often made. The market closes near the high in the case of a top or near the low in the case of a bottom.

On the following day's trading or the key reversal day, prices move higher than the previous day's high and lower than the previous day's low, closing near the low of the day for a key reversal top. This reversal is more definitive if accompanied by high volume—sometimes record high volume—and new contract or all-time highs. An opposite pattern occurs for key reversal bottoms, again on high volume.

Figure 3.11   Retracements

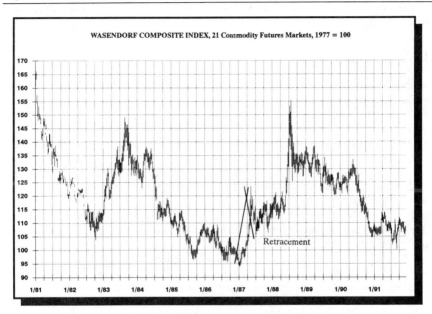

WASENDORF COMPOSITE INDEX, 21 Commodity Futures Markets, 1977 = 100

Prices move in uneven, stair stepping patterns. It's common for them to move higher, then retrace before moving higher again.

Chart courtesy of "Pocket Charts."

Island Reversal

An island reversal is similar to a key reversal, but usually involves a few more trading days and requires a gap at either side of the island formation. Typically, the gaps are at approximately the same price level.

Continent Reversal

The continent reversal is identical to the island reversal except that it may take weeks or even months to form.

These chart signals alert you to the possibility of a trend change. You must analyze them in light of the entire situation for the commodity you are studying. Do not use them as your sole decision making guide.

The Very Reliable Head and Shoulders Formation

For several reasons, many technical analysts get excited when they see a head and shoulders chart formation developing. First, it is probably the best known chart formation. And, since technical analysis can be a self-fulfilling discipline, the more traders who recognize it, the more likely its promise will be fulfilled. Even dyed-in-the-wool fundamental traders cringe at the thought of trading against a head and shoulders formation. They'll stand aside first.

Head and shoulders formations are among the best known because they stand out on the charts. Everyone sees them and tries to trade them. For these reasons, they have become to be known as one of the most reliable of formations, in our opinion. Novice technicians, as well as experts, are eager to take advantage of them. Head and shoulder formations are not only reliable as reversal indicators but they also project a price objective.

A head and shoulders formation is a harbinger of a major reversal in the trend of the commodity or index being charted. This formation can be either a head and shoulders or an inverted (reverse) head and shoulders.

The head and shoulders formation signals the end of an uptrend. The inverted head and shoulders formation alerts traders to the end of a downtrend.

The head and shoulders formation simply portrays three successive rallies and reactions. The second or middle rally reaches a point higher than the other two rallies. The formation looks like the silhouette of a person. The left shoulder is the first rally, the head is the second (middle), and the right shoulder the third.

Volume Is the Key

As previously mentioned, the volume of trading must be watched closely. It is the key that tells you what the market is really thinking.

For example, during the first rally and reaction represented by the left shoulder of the formation, volume expands materially on the rally and contracts noticeably on the reaction. The overall volume is considered heavy during the development of this shoulder.

During the second rally and reaction, which forms the head, volume is high on the rally phase. But, the overall volume may be lower than the overall volume that occurred during the formation of the first shoulder.

When the right shoulder forms, the overall volume drops even lower. This third rally fails to reach the high established by the second (the head) rally and is a distinct sign of weakness.

As soon as the third rally fails, the technician draws a line connecting the lows created by the failure, or reaction, that occurred when the right shoulder and

Figure 3.12   Key Reversal Formations

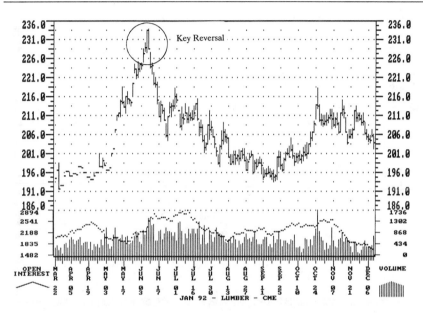

**Key Reversals can occur at the top or bottom of a market move.
They signal a major change in the direction of the trend.**

Chart courtesy of "Pocket Charts."

head were formed. A line drawn using these lows forms the neckline of the formation.

Special Note: No head and shoulders formation is considered complete or reliable until subsequent price action breaks the neckline.

Another unusual phenomenon often occurs at this point. It is called the "pull back" or "return" move. Once the neckline is broken, prices drop below the neckline (or above it in the case of an inverted head and shoulders) and then are drawn back up to the trendline (or down to it in the case of an inverted formation).

This characteristic of trend lines was discussed earlier. A broken uptrend line, after it has been penetrated by the bear move, often becomes a resistance area for future bull moves. Prices seem to be attracted to and cling to straight lines.

Technical traders, who are convinced a valid head and shoulders formation has been formed, use the "pull back" move as their signal to enter the market or add on to their position. If volume increases after prices bounce off the neckline, it confirms the fact that a major trend reversal has occurred.

Figure 3.13   Inverted Head and Shoulders

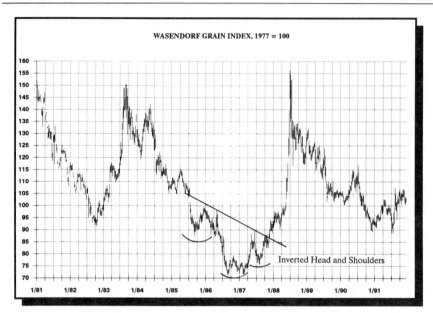

WASENDORF GRAIN INDEX, 1977 = 100

Inverted Head and Shoulders

The Head and Shoulders Formations are considered by many
chartists as one of the most reliable. Besides heralding a trend
change, they often indicate the size of the next move.

Chart courtesy of "Pocket Charts."

How Do You Calculate Objectives?

The first price objective of a head and shoulders formation is calculated by mea-
suring the distance between the neckline and the high (or low) made by the top
(or bottom) of the head. Multiple objectives can be calculated by doubling or
tripling this measurement.

Once the move begins, you must double-check and confirm the action by
referring to other price trend indicators. For example, in order for a trend reversal
to continue to make a substantial move, other technical formations are likely to
come into play and be fulfilled. Confirmation chart formations are also useful.
These are discussed later.

Volume and open interest provide additional clues. Once the trend reversal
starts, volume should increase and open interest must be building in the direction
the market is now trending. You also look to see what the large traders with

reportable positions and the commercial hedgers are doing. This information should be available from your broker and is reported by the Commodity Futures Trading Commission (CFTC).

You should highlight on your charts the areas where the move is most likely to encounter resistance. Then study the price action as these points are reached. Does the volume increase and the price bust right through the resistance? Or does the price movement and volume slow down? This tells you if you should stay in the market and look for a second, third, or fourth objective, or take your profits and look for a new trading opportunity.

The Look of Abstract Art

Head and shoulders formations can more closely resemble a Picasso than a Renoir. It's common for them to have two or three shoulders or even multiple heads. Sometimes the formations are angular, reminiscent of Picasso's cubist period. Seldom are they simple and perfectly formed.

One last caveat. Head and shoulders formations can be misleading, especially when the right shoulder is formed. If it doesn't break the neckline, prices can continue sideways for a long time or even move in the unanticipated direction. Even when the neckline is broken and the formation is complete, they may be highly reliable; but, it could be a very expensive lesson if you bet the farm on the first objective always being reached.

Continuation Chart Formations

As we discussed earlier, the most common charting formation that indicates a price trend will continue is the trend line. But what do we do when a trend line is broken? Do we immediately reverse our position, close it out and stand aside or wait out the reversal until the market decides where it is headed?

Much of the decision depends on how the trend line is broken and the changes that take place in volume and open interest at that time. Also, you must consider how close the price is to major support and resistance levels.

Always remember that even the strongest trends do not roll on indefinitely without an interruption. It sometimes helps to think of them as long distance runners, who must occasionally back off to get their wind.

There is a very interesting financial reason for this. It's called profit-taking. Following a sharp move—up or down—some of the traders on the correct side of the move will want to cash in their position and pocket their profit.

There are other reasons as well. The move may enter a support or resistance level causing traders to evaluate their positions. Or, some fundamental news or a well circulated rumor can cause a trend to stall or temporarily congest.

At these junctures, traders become uncertain. Not sure whether they are looking at a trend reversal or just a place where the move is pausing to catch its breath.

Figure 3.14   Coil Formation

The Coil Formation indicates prices are going to make a major
move. Unfortunately, it is not always clear whether the break out
will be up or down.

Chart courtesy of "Pocket Charts."

Triangle or Coil Formations

The triangle formation develops when a trend hits a price level where the buying
dries up. The move stalls. Profit-taking develops. The "bulls" second guess themselves. The market moves sideways and each successive high is lower and each
successive low is higher. A triangle is formed where the uptrend line and the
downtrend line meet.

Prices move into the apex of the triangle which forces them to make a move
up or down. In the majority of times, about 60 percent, prices continue in the
direction they were going when they entered the triangle, thus continuing the
trend.

Sophisticated technical analysts categorize triangles into four groups: symmetrical, ascending, descending, and inverted triangles. This approach increases
the reliability of the signals. The symmetrical triangle is the one just described.

With the ascending triangle, the top line is horizontal, while the bottom line slants to meet the top line. This formation suggests that a supply of the commodity is available at the price level of the top line, but there are no sellers below it. Prices are drawn up and finally break out to the upside. The descending triangle is just the opposite and is a harbinger of lower prices. The horizontal line, like the base of a right triangle, is on the bottom. The hypotenuse descends to meet the base and prices break out to the downside.

The inverted triangle looks somewhat like a funnel and represents a very nervous market. Prices can go either way out of this formation.

Boxes, Flags, Pennants, Diamonds

These chart formations are more reliable than the triangles. Their graphic names help you to spot them easily.

Figure 3.15   Flag Formation

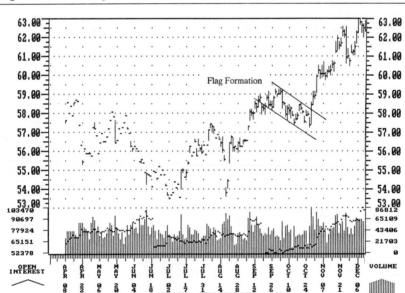

Flag Formations can be bullish or bearish depending on the direction it is "flying." The flag pole gives clues to the length of the next price move.

Chart courtesy of "Pocket Charts."

The box formation takes weeks or months to develop. Prices move sideways with the highs and lows staying at the same levels or in a channel. A vertical line drawn at both ends of the trading channel forms the box.

The box occurs when there is a tug-of-war going on between equally matched teams of bulls and bears. The breakout of the box is usually valid and usually goes in the direction prevalent at the time prices entered the box.

The flag formation is similar to the box, but the channel is on an angle. If the angle is down, it is an up flag because that is the way prices will be headed when they break out of the formation. A down flag has the channel angles headed up and prices will be going down. The flag formation looks like a parallelogram with the top and bottom on a 45-degree angle.

Some analysts claim the tighter and neater the flag formation is, the more reliable it will be. Flags formed quickly are more dependable than slowly, sloppily formed ones. The length of the flag pole supporting the formation can also be an indication as to how far the price trend will continue after it breaks out.

Pennants fly from "poles," like flags, but they look like symmetrical triangles. The up pennant forms out of bull moves and signals a continuation of the uptrend. Again, the tighter the pennant, the higher its level of reliability.

The diamond formation develops during a period of wide swings in price. It is an exciting time with traders wildly bullish one minute and bearish the next. Prices seesaw back and forth with greater and greater swings on high volume. Then the excitement ends and the prices taper off. Thus the diamond is formed. Diamond formations are hard to predict. They can just as easily alert you to a reversal of the price trend as a continuation of the trend.

Volume Tells the Story

As always, pay close attention to volume when analyzing formations just described. It usually dips as the formation develops and then increases as the breakout occurs. These formations are not as reliable as the head and shoulder formations discussed earlier. Use them as guides only. Find confirmation from other sources.

Price Smoothing and Filtering Techniques

Grandad used to say, "When the joint gets raided, they haul in all the girls—and the piano player!" He wasn't talking about the commodity market, but the axiom applies.

When a major trend takes hold of the market, all the commodities are usually affected. It's rare that an individual commodity can move in the opposite direction of a major trend.

That's why it is so important to have the trend at your back—moving your position in the desired direction. But commodity prices often make very jerky and erratic moves. Trends are not always clear cut.

Changes in trends can be equally difficult to spot early. If you act too soon when you're anticipating a trend change or planning to take profits out of a position, you may miss a good deal of the move because you mistake minor corrections for major trend changes.

Technical traders who face choppy, sawtooth price charts have developed some techniques to overcome this roadblock. One of the methods they use is moving averages.

Simple Moving Averages

Moving averages combine the price activity of a commodity over a period of time and smooths it out. For example, to calculate a four-day moving average, you would:

1.   Select the first four days' prices

2.   Total them.

3.   Divide by four.

4.   Subtract the first day and add the fifth day.

5.   Divide the new total by four.

6.   Subtract the second day and add the sixth day.

7.   Divide the new total by four.

8.   Continue doing this with each day's price.

Refer to Table 3.1 for an example of a 4-Day Moving Average using the closing prices for twelve trading days of a corn contract. You can use the high, low, open price, as well as the close. You must be consistent in your choice to keep the data meaningful.

Once the moving averages are calculated, you simply chart them on a graph. Some analysts like to chart them right on their daily commodity price charts so they can compare them with the actual price activity. In a downtrending market, the moving average usually remains above the current price. In an uptrend, it tends to stay below the current market price. The point at which the moving average crosses the actual price is a critical point.

Some technical analysts use moving averages to simply indicate the trend. The 4-day moving average described above would provide the short-term trend. An analyst looking for a bigger picture might use a 200-day moving average to represent the long-term trend.

Table 3.1   **Moving Averages**

Day	Price	Total	4-Day Moving Average
1	282.25		
2	283.75		
3	280.25		
4	279.25	1125.50	281.38
5	277.75	1121.00	280.25
6	271.75	1108.75	277.19
7	273.75	1102.25	275.56
8	273.25	1096.25	274.06
9	265.00	1083.50	270.88
10	268.50	1080.50	270.13
11	259.00	1065.75	266.44
12	262.00	1054.50	263.63

Other analysts use moving averages to generate specific buy/sell signals. It becomes a mini-trading system within itself. To do this, you need to chart two different moving averages. Common ones are the 4-day and the 9-day moving average.

The slower one, the 9-day, requires more days in its calculation and determines the long-term trend. The faster one, the 4-day, signals the short-term trend.

If you want to buy a market, both moving averages should be moving higher. Place buy orders in the price range between the averages. Place stops below the slower moving average. Wait for prices to dip into the zone below the slower moving average to buy.

If you want to sell a market, both moving averages should be moving down. Sell orders are placed in the price range between the averages. Stops are placed above the slower moving average.

Wait for the market price to rally into this zone. Sell short only when this occurs.

When you're placing a long-term trade or trading options, you want to make sure both moving averages are headed in the same direction. You'll also want to use a long-term moving average, perhaps a 50- or 100-day moving average.

A Weighted Moving Average

Some analysts like to give more emphasis to the current price. They believe it helps them anticipate trend changes sooner.

To calculate a weighted average, arrange the numbers to be averaged in chronological order, the most recent number last. Multiply the oldest number by one, the next by two, the next by three, and so on, until you reach the most recent which will be multiplied by a factor that is the total number of entries. If you are averaging five numbers, the most recent number will be multiplied by five.

Now, add all the results and divide by the sum of the multipliers. This will give you the weighted average. See Table 3.2 for an example.

Notice that the weighted average is greater than a simple average because greater emphasis is placed on the most recent values in this rising market.

No matter how you do it, moving averages are an excellent tool to use to confirm trends. But like all our trading techniques, they need to be tempered with experience and good, common sense.

Table 3.2

Weighted Moving Average Table

Day	Price		Weighing Factor	Result
1	$2.52	×	1	$2.52
2	$2.57	×	2	$5.14
3	$2.56	×	3	$7.68
4	$2.60	×	4	$10.40
5	$2.61	×	5	$13.05
Totals	$12.86		15	$38.79

Weighted Moving Average $= \dfrac{\$38.79}{15} = \$2.59$

Simple Moving Average $= \dfrac{\$12.86}{5} = \$2.57$

CHAPTER 4

UNDERSTANDING THE FOUR BASIC APPROACHES TO TECHNICAL ANALYSIS

Key Concepts

➠ Trading contrary opinion.

➠ Developing your own trading system—money management, analysis, a entry-exit mechanism, and discipline.

➠ Overview of soybean, live hog, pork belly, silver, and stock index markets.

Now that you have a feel for what technical analysis is, let's categorize it into basic types. There are basically four general approaches to technically analyzing commodity markets. They are price charts, trend-following, structural, and character-of-market. So far, we have dealt with the first two because they are the most widely used and recognized.

Price chart analysis involves finding chart formations or patterns that often repeat themselves. We studied reversals, support-resistance areas, head and shoulders, continuing formations, and others. We also studied some trend-following types of analysis, namely, trend lines and moving averages. Structural analysis presumes the market moves in established, recognizable patterns—like seasonal, cyclical or wave patterns. Once the analyst can exactly locate the current position of the market, he can predict the next move or price objective. We will discuss this type of analysis shortly.

Character-of-Market Analysis

We consider character-of-market analysis to be very sophisticated because it attempts to measure the quality of a price movement, and then, take a position that may be opposite of the current trend. The other types of analysis try to spot existing trends or certain formations that are reliable harbingers of future price activity. The prudent trader uses them as a guide and waits for confirmation before acting.

With character-of-market analysis, the technician seeks what are known as "overbought" or "oversold" conditions. If the market is found to be overbought, it is sold. If it is found to be oversold, it is bought. This approach is a 180-degree turn from what we talked about with the trend-following approaches.

The psychology behind character-of-market analysis is simply that when a market becomes too top heavy, it falls. Or, when everyone gives up on prices ever rising again, they will. It is a contrarian approach to technical analysis.

The trick is determining when a market is overbought or oversold. Some of the better known systems are oscillators, Williams' %R, and Wilder's Relative Strength Index.

Oscillators

Oscillators are concerned with price changes over a period of time. Simple oscillators utilize the difference between two moving averages. The departure between them indicates overbought and oversold conditions.

More complicated ones use the difference between daily prices. It can be the settlement, high-low or opening price. Take a simple five-day settlement price oscillator as an example. It is computed by subtracting the settlement price of the fourth-previous trading day from the current settlement price. If the settlement price has risen, you get a positive remainder. A negative remainder occurs if the price has fallen. If the remainder is exceptionally high or low, the analysts will consider the market overbought or oversold and take the opposite position.

Analysts using oscillators usually use more complicated ones than this simple example. But the basic concept is the same.

Williams' %R

An example of a more complex approach is the Williams' %R (Copyrighted 1979 by Larry R. Williams). For example, A five-day %R is computed as follows:

Subtract the settlement price of the latest trading day from the high price of the five-day period. Then divide that difference (i.e., the "change") by the difference (i.e., the "range") in the high price and the low price of the five-day period. Finally, multiply that result by 100. The range of %R is 0% to 100%.

According to Williams, when the value of %R enters the 90-100% range, the market is considered to be oversold. When the value enters the 0-10% range, the market is considered to be overbought.

Wilder's RSI

Another example of this intricate approach to the markets is the Relative Strength Index (Copyrighted 1978 by J. Welles Wilder, Jr.). It can best be described using the following formula:

RSI	=	$100 - (100/(1 + RS))$
Where RS	=	Up Avg/Dn Avg
Up Avg	=	Up Sum/1
Dn Avg	=	Dn Avg/1, and
L	=	number of days in RSI

Again, this is a system that measures the change in price over a period of time to determine overbought-oversold situations.

Let's look at a fifteen-day RSI. To calculate RSI, the Up Sum is first computed by tabulating the positive changes in the settlement prices of successive trading days over the fifteen-day period and adding those changes. The Dn Sum is computed by tabulating the negative changes in settlement prices over the period and adding those changes. Then, Up Avg is computed by dividing Up Sum by fourteen, similarly for Dn Avg. Next, Up Avg is divided by Dn Avg to get RS. And, finally, RSI is computed by adding one to RS, dividing this sum into 100, and subtracting that result from 100.

According to Wilder, when RSI exceeds seventy, the market is considered to be overbought. When RSI is less than thirty, the market is considered to be oversold.

Clearly these are not calculations you can do on your fingers. The computer has come to our rescue. These very complex mathematical calculations are available on computer software allowing the average trader to exploit them. Many of today's electronic quotation systems include them as special features.

When Do You Use Character-of-Market Analysis?

This approach works best in choppy, zigzagging markets. If you use them in a long trending market, you may get burned badly. You need many tools on your technical analysis workbench. These are excellent ones to have when the market appears to be confused or erratic—but never rely on just one approach to analyzing the market.

Structural Analysis

You can set your watch by the tides. Animals always know when to migrate or hibernate. Winter follows summer, night follows day.

From earliest times, man has been fascinated by the workings of nature. The ancient Greek philosophers developed the concept of Natural Law. All the religions of the world reaffirm that some known or unknown force has implanted an order on the physical world.

The great advances of science have been predicated on the concept that the laws of physics, chemistry, biology, geology, etc., can be understood. Man's mind seeks out structure in his every activity.

Why Not in the Commodities Market?

Several very successful technical traders have developed theories about the market that begin with the assumption that the universe, in general, and the markets, in particular, work in very precise patterns. More importantly, these theorists believe that these patterns can be discovered and exploited for profit. We'll now review four of the most prominent theories.

Seasonals

Seasonal patterns are the easiest to understand, especially if you consider the agricultural commodities. The seasonal price trends these commodities undergo reflect the regular annual changes that take place in their supply-demand equation.

Think about a typical crop year. First of all, we anticipate planting intentions. Then we worry and fret through the weather markets of the growing season. Finally, we usually have an abundant supply at harvest.

Studies have shown, for example, that 70 percent of all seasonal tops occur between April and July for soybeans. While 80 percent of the time, soybean prices bottom between August and November.

How can you use this information? If you know the seasonal patterns for the futures contracts you trade, you can use these patterns to confirm signals you get from other methods of analysis. Some traders will not trade against reliable seasonal patterns without having a very strong reason for doing so.

Seasonal patterns have been uncovered for virtually all futures markets. Learning the ones for the markets you trade is as basic as learning which chart formations are most reliable for those markets.

Cycles

Cycles are similar to seasonal patterns, but they can be longer than twelve months or extremely short in duration. Cycles are built on the observed phenomenon that events have a tendency to repeat themselves at more or less regular intervals.

As mentioned earlier, much of man's life is governed by repeatable patterns or cycles. Since man made and controls the markets, it seems fair to assume that the market would also possess definable cycles, at least that's what a cyclist will tell you. Understanding these cycles within the price trends of the market is another key to successfully trading the markets.

Cycles measure the time between each high or low (peak and trough). By knowing the time span between each high and low and the previous high and low, you are in a better position to anticipate the next high or low. Time is often measured in calendar days, as opposed to trading days used by some systems. Calendar days are used for the simple reason that people and nature do not take weekends off—money continues to change hands and events affecting cycles continue.

A long-term cycle generally last a year or more, an intermediate cycle less than a year, and short-term cycles last a few weeks or days. As a general rule, allow approximately ten percent leeway in the length of a cycle when establishing your expectation for the next top or bottom.

Elliott Wave

The Wave Principle states that social and market behavior trends and reverses in recognizable patterns. These patterns or waves reoccur. Prices unfold in "five waves" of crowd psychology when moving in the direction (up or down) of the primary trend. Then they move against the trend in "three waves." The wave pattern reflects life's starts, stops, false starts, and reversals. Progress is made in a jerky, sawtooth pattern, rather than a smooth up or down trend.

By isolating the exact position of the current price activity within the wave patterns, the trader can profit by anticipating the market's next move. Once your trading becomes synchronized with the wave pattern, you can successfully ride the economic waves of the market, or so the theory goes.

Gann Numbers

The best known structural analyst is probably W. D. Gann. His book, *How to Make Profits Trading Commodities* published is 1942, was the first important treatise on this subject. He believed that precise mathematical patterns govern everything, particularly the commodity market. More importantly, he believed these patterns could be uncovered and exploited. Since his price predictions became legends in his own time and he claims to have made millions in the market, we can only assume he discovered many of them.

Integral to his trading system are Fibonacci Numbers—again a throwback to natural law—and angles of price trend movement. His numbering system uncannily alerts traders to highs, lows, support-resistance areas and reversal points. His work must be studied by every serious trader.

Other Types of Technical Trading Systems

There are many technical trading systems besides those already described. Here's a brief description of the "rate of price change," "counter trend," and "counter cyclical systems."

The theory behind rate-of-change systems is simple. Mathematical formulas are devised which indicate to the trader when a market is about to change directions. Think of it as the momentum in a football game. As one team moves the ball down the field, it has the momentum. Yardage gained on each successful play is longer, and successful plays become more frequent.

Then something happens, and the defense tightens. Gains per play become smaller and less frequent. Eventually, the defense holds, and the offense is forced to give up the ball. This activity is often accompanied by a switch in momentum.

Rate-of-price-change systems evaluate price changes on a periodic basis, usually on the day's closes. As the rate of change diminishes, the trader prepares to close out the current positions and open new ones on the opposite side of the market. In other words, you would close out long positions, for example, and enter shorts. Or, offset calls and open puts in the options market.

In certain very orderly markets, these systems perform wonderfully. But like all systems, they are not loss-proof. For example, when the markets are highly volatile and choppy, these systems have problems. To return to our sport's analogy, it's like when one team fumbles and the other team recovers. Only to have the team that fumbled immediately intercept a pass to get the ball back. The momentum gained by the fumble recovery is lost by the interception.

Counter Trend Systems

The rate-of-price-change calculations just discussed can be used to develop a counter-trend system. This is a system that attempts to buy at the low and sell at the high. Traders try to anticipate the next market move—catching all major moves early or before they begin.

Keep in mind when using this type of system, you must use protective stop loss orders. It's not like a trend-following system that eventually corrects itself by establishing an offsetting position. With a counter–trending system, you are net long or net short until you close out your position. That's why we recommend stops.

There are several types of counter-trend systems, but we only have room to discuss a few of the most common. The fading-minimum-move system is a typical example. A sell signal is triggered when the market rallies by a pre-determined amount above the low point, after the last counter-trend buy was signaled. The reverse is true for buys. The size of the price change required to generate a signal can be either a percentage or a nominal figure arrived at through testing or analysis of past moves. The size also determines how sensitive the system is.

Like any other system, you can require confirming signals before a buy or sell signal is taken. It's common, for example, with counter-trend systems to wait a day before placing a trade—just to make sure the trend has changed.

The use of oscillators are also common with counter-trend systems. Oscillators, mentioned earlier, are technical indicators that measure market momentum.

A popular oscillator is the RSI, also discussed earlier. This stands for relative strength index and was developed by J. Welles Wilder, Jr. His oscillator attempted to solve one of the big drawbacks of these tools. How much is too much? When is an oscillator indicating a change in trend—60 percent or 90 percent? Wilder's RSI pegs tops when its values are above 70 percent and lows when they penetrate 30 percent.

Counter Cyclical Counting

You could also use cycle analysis to develop a counter-trending system. By plotting the anticipated highs or lows, you would generate entry and exit signals. You position yourself on the short side of the market when your cycle analysis indicated a top was due—or long in anticipation of a low. Again, we strongly recommend the use of stops for this sort of trading system.

Buying into Fear

Another approach to forecasting price trends is known as Contrarian Investment Strategy, or Buying into Fear!

Basically, this is the concept of going against the crowd. Trading the opposite side of the market from the popular thinking of all traders as a group.

Your first question might be, "Where can I get this kind of information?"

A good place to start is *The Wall Street Journal*. Three important pieces of data are published daily on the *Commodity Page*: estimated volume for the current trading day, actual volume for the previous day, and open interest. You'll also find the high, low, settlement, change, and the lifetime high/low. It is very critical in estimating market sentiment to grasp what these numbers mean.

Understanding Volume and Open Interest

Volume and open interest figures benchmark the degree of activity and the amount of trader participation in the individual futures markets. Volume is the velocity of trading and open interest measures the number of contracts held at the conclusion of a trading session.

Volume reported daily by the commodity exchanges is published in *The Wall Street Journal* and indicates the number of contracts traded during that day. Remember, this is the number of contracts traded during the day, not the sum of the buyers and sellers. For every contract traded, there is one buyer and one seller. To determine the volume of trading, simply count either all of the buyers or all of the sellers. The number of contracts traded includes the creation of new contracts, the transfer of either the buy or the sell side of a contract, or the liquidation of a contract.

Open interest is a measure of the number of contracts outstanding at the completion of the trading day. Consider it a description of participation—traders show their conviction to market participation by taking their positions "home" with them, at least overnight. Many transactions may occur in a given day without initiating any new contracts or eliminating existing contracts—existing futures contracts may merely change hands.

To understand open interest and volume, follow the example below:

Day 1:   Trader A buys one contract.
            Trader B sells one contract.
            Trader C buys one contract.
            Trader D sells one contract.

If these were the only transactions on the first day, the open interest would be two contracts. Volume is two contracts, also.

Day 2:   Trader E buys one contract.
            Trader A sells to offset one contract.

If these were the only transactions taking place on the second day, the open interest would still be two contracts. Volume would be one contract. Trader A simply transferred his position to Trader E.

Day 3:   Trader F buys one contract.
            Trader G sells one contract.
            Trader B buys to offset one contract.
            Trader C sells to offset one contract.
            Trader E sells to offset one contract.
            Trader D buys to offset one contract.

At the end of the third day, only one contract survives; the open interest is one, but volume is three contracts.

After the dust clears, open interest indicates the number of contracts that are held by participants in the market. Notice that for every buyer, there was a seller. The next step is to analyze the interrelationship of these statistics. See below.

Open Interest	Volume	Prices	Interpretation
UP	UP	UP	Very Bullish (strong participation and volume with higher prices
DOWN	DOWN	DOWN	Slightly Bullish (weak participation and volume with lower prices)
UP	DOWN	UP	Mildly Bullish (strong participation but weak volume with higher prices
UP	DOWN	DOWN	Mildly Bearish (strong participation but weak volume with lower prices)
UP	UP	DOWN	Very Bearish (strong participation and volume with lower prices)
DOWN	DOWN	UP	Slightly Bearish (weak participation and volume with higher prices)

Once you know how all the other traders are calling the market by their actual trading activity, you can determine what position you wish to take.

The phrase at the top of this section, "Buying into Fear!," was coined by Bernard Baruch. He strongly believed that once you determined what most of the market place was going to do—you should do the exact opposite. This philosophy worked well for him.

Options are an excellent tool for the contrary trader. You can take a position opposite to what everyone else is doing and limit your risk of the cost of the premium plus the transaction costs (sales commission, exchange and NFA fees).

Also, never forget as you trade futures, "You must be more than right. You must be right at the right time!" Buying options that do not expire for sixty to ninety days provides some time to "become" right.

What does this mean? Let's say you analyze the futures market. Everything is up, up, up—open interest, volume and prices. If you go with the crowd and purchase a call, your premium is high if the option is "in or near in-the-money." By the time the underlying future increases enough to bring your option to break-even or a modest profit, the market has began to retrace.

Would you have had more success if you had purchased a put? You can buy them economically when everyone else is wildly bullish. Then you sit in ambush waiting for a retracement.

Buying Options Into a Bull Market

By nature, most people come to commodity trading as bulls. We all just feel more comfortable making money when prices are rising, rather than taking advantage of a declining market.

An additional reason is that bull markets last usually longer than bear markets, which gives us more time to trade them. There are seven distinct stages to the classical bull market which were described in Chapter 1.

Options are an excellent investment tool to take advantage of an upcoming bull market. You can plan your trades enough in advance to be in the right market at the right time.

For example, once the options trader spots a commodity that has a good fundamental reason for becoming a runaway bull market, the trader begins to study the price charts. You're looking to spot Stages 2 or 3. First the long term downtrend is broken, followed by a modest rally.

These are your signals to get into a call that is in or near in-the-money. You'll want one with as much time left on it as possible. At this point, you are acting contrary to what most traders are doing. They are still on the sidelines totally unaware of the developing situation.

You ride the bull market through Stage 6. Again you want to be a contrarian, which means take your profits before the blow off top. Don't forget the old trading axiom: Bears win, bulls win, but hogs get slaughtered!

Many traders, after successfully marking profits in Stages 3, 4, and 5, hold out to pick the top. This is a very dangerous strategy. As mentioned earlier, the market usually declines substantially faster than it rises. Those who wait are often disappointed. Options trading is risky business. You can easily lose your entire investment. The surest way to do that is to overstay a position or to try to pick tops or bottoms.

When the blow off top begins, you again do the opposite of what most traders are trying to do. Instead of getting in the market long, you're looking for a put. One that is reasonably priced with enough time to take advantage of the impending bear market.

Success in the commodity market often means thinking and doing the opposite of what most traders would do in the same situation. You buy your call before other traders have spotted the opportunity and sell the day you see a story about the price run up of your commodity on the nightly news.

Are You Vulnerable to Mass Hysteria?

As we all know hindsight is 20/20. Looking back, we really wonder how people can get caught up in the silly things they do. We often think of ourselves as being too logical or level-headed to be turned around by some bizarre social reality. Did you ever buy a hoola hoop? Is Elvis alive?

We all are vulnerable to some extent, and we all have our Achilles' heels. If you understand how these phenomena of herd psychology work, you'll be better prepared to deal with them. And, as a contrary trader, you must be able to see reality for what it is in order to profitably trade reality. Let me first give you a few examples to illustrate this point.

In London, in 1524, the city awaited its doom. Numerous astrologers and fortune tellers had foretold a massive flood. The great Thames, one of the world's best behaved rivers, was to jump its banks and engulf the entire city on February 1. Doom and gloom was the general prediction. Over 20,000 citizens, nearly the entire population, moved to higher ground.

On February 1st, nothing happened. But the charlatans had an answer. A minor miscalculation had occurred. The flood was coming in 1624. Londoners were safe at least for a while. Sound like any economic forecasters you know?

If you think these things only happened in the Middle ages and that only the "poor unwashed masses" are caught up, think again. The "red bating" frenzy of McCarthyism even engulfed the ACLU (American Civil Liberties Union). It is a group which considers itself above mass hysteria. The fact is it, too, was swept along in the 1950's and refused to defend suspected communists.

This type of behavior occurs in commodity trading regularly. Traders get caught in a powerful mass delusion—"Prices are going through the ceiling! There's no end to this bull move!"—that causes them to lose control of their trading.

The contrary trader must be prepared to recognize these situations and take advantage of them. Let's take a quick look at how these fantasies develop.

Two Types of Beliefs

Our personal and collective body of beliefs can be roughly divided into two distinctly different types. The first is deeply rooted in physical fact. If we touch something very hot with our bare hand, we get burned. It is extremely difficult for anyone to get us to change our minds regarding these beliefs.

The second type of beliefs are just as important, but they are not based in physical fact. Some of these may be our religious, political or financial beliefs.

When we get into very complicated areas in which we have strong feelings, yet our understanding is somewhat vague, we tend to rely on others whom we consider authorities. In the case of religion, they are ministers or priests. In politics, they are politicians. In finance, they are bankers and advisors.

Commodity trading is no different. It is certainly complex and vague. We look to CTAs, journalists, brokers, and newsletter writers. When they get caught up in the image of what "everyone" thinks is happening, they can whip traders into a wild frenzy. This pulls the average investor in off the street. Everyone thinks the market will never stop.

You, as the contrary trader, recognize it as a blow-off top of a classical bull market. But how do you resist? How do you call your broker, when he's foaming at the mouth, and get him to buy you a put when the rest of the world wants calls?

You need the discipline—that comes with an understanding of the mass psychology—to overcome this trap. Add to this the courage to stand up to your broker when he says: "You want to buy a what? The market isn't even half way to my first objective?"

How Do You Measure Market Psychology?

First, we need to refer back to the concept of open interest and how it differs from volume. Open interest measures market participation by telling us the number of contracts outstanding at the completion of the trading day. Volume is the velocity of trading.

Contrarian traders study these figures. Volume interest them because they want to know how active or how "hot" the markets are. The hotter they are, the more emotional they become, which gives strength to major moves.

Open interest is even more important, especially if you can determine who is holding the positions. One way to learn who's doing what is to study the daily reports supplied to the Commodity Futures Trading Commission (CFTC). The CFTC requires clearing members of the exchanges, futures commission merchants (FCMs), and brokers to report each trader's position on their books that, in any future month of a commodity, exceed certain levels. These are the large traders usually with "strong hands" and good information sources.

Here are a few examples of the reporting levels by commodity:

Commodity Reportable Level

Corn	500,000 Bushels
Silver	150 Contracts
Treasury Notes	200 Contracts

Besides supplying the CFTC with the number of contracts, the reporting entities must also give the classification—non-commercial or commercial. A commercial trader are hedgers as defined by the Commissions' regulation. These are usually companies, even countries, who are willing to take physical delivery of the commodity and use it in their business. An example would be a grain merchant who hedges an upcoming cash sale on the futures markets. Non-commercials include individual traders. Non-reportable positions are ones that are below the reporting limit.

This information is often published in commodity newsletters and other periodicals on a weekly or monthly basis. It is put into index or graph formats known within the industry as the bullish or bearish market opinion or consensus.

Picking Overbought/Oversold Markets

Traders may study the data to determine if a market is overbought or oversold. They use it as a guide to determine when to switch from the long to the short side, or vice versa.

The problem the contrary investor faces is avoiding getting caught up in the illusions and mass hysteria fast moving and rapidly rising markets create. You need rules to follow to avoid this pitfall. For example, when they see the open interest numbers rapidly increasing in non-reportable positions (the small traders) and decreasing in reportable positions (the large traders), a good contrarian may conclude that the "public" has a hold of the market. This means it may be time to begin picking an exit or reversal point.

Another important indicator of the general thinking of traders is the number of puts or calls for each option. If there are substantially more calls, most options traders are bullish. More puts indicate a bearish outlook. These numbers are found each trading day on the *Commodity Page* of *The Wall Street Journal*.

Since most people, including traders, are followers as opposed to leaders, by the time the majority get on board, it is time to switch sides of the market. An excellent example occurred when the stock market crashed on October 19, 1987.

On Friday, October 16th, there were 32,045 calls and 30,087 puts. On the day of the crash, there were 34,971 calls and 25,685 puts. The next day saw 35,183 calls and 24,327 puts. A week later we still had more calls than puts—38,346 versus 25,432.

Our point is simply this: The majority doesn't rule the commodity market. Your best opportunities materialize when you resist following the crowd.

Developing Your Own Trading System

Perhaps the biggest single mistake investors make when they begin to analyze the market is that they fail to put together a trading system. Clearly an analysis procedure is not a trading system. Most traders are attracted to technical analysis because they use or are exposed to a technique, like moving averages or chart formation analysis, that works. They then want to apply this specific technique to every situation.

All technical tools described have been used to successfully trade the futures markets at one time or another. But neither a single technical analysis tool, nor combination of analysis tools, makes up a trading system. Analysis is only a part of a trading system—often a small part!

Also, there are many, many technical approaches we do not have time or space to describe. Here's a partial list:

Astrological
Complementary Angles
Harahus Pentagon
Japanese Candle Sticks
Parabolic
Point and Figure
Price Bar Congestion
Speed Resistance Lines
Stochastics
Swing Charts

The list goes on and on and on.

True trading systems are composed of three major components. The first—and most important—is a money management technique. The second is the analysis of the market, and the third, a market input-output mechanism.

CHAPTER 5

DEVELOPING YOUR OWN
TRADING SYSTEM

Key Concepts

➠ Realistic goals must be set.

➠ Commodity portfolios selected.

➠ Strategies evaluated.

➠ Overview of soybean, live hog, pork bellies, silver and stock index markets.

Let's begin our discussion with the analysis procedure. All too often, would-be futures traders use analysis procedures to support their preconceived notion of the direction of market prices. Your preconceptions invariably will get you into trouble—financial trouble.

Remember the old adage: "The market is always right." This simply means that the market—no matter how hard we study or analyze it—functions independently of our analysis. The harder you work at figuring out the market, the more you want it to go your way. You become enamored with your analysis. A technical analysis procedure should be designed to reduce subjectivity to a minimum. Market opinions based on emotional subjectivity are seldom successful.

Consider the following guidelines for selecting an analysis system.

1. Choose an analysis procedure, or better yet, a series of analysis procedures, in which you have a high level of confidence.

2. The system(s) should be qualifiable and quantifiable. It must be specific: it must not only tell you to go long or short, but at what price.

3. Your procedures need to be able to withstand serious, historical testing. You must be able to use historical market data and to run simulations—which can be done quite easily on today's personal computer systems.

4. Choose optimizable analysis procedures. This will help you avoid using yesterday's factors for tomorrow's markets. Optimizing is a fine–tuning procedure. It does not mean abandonment of analysis principals. Optimizing adjusts your analysis procedures based on a change in market conditions, such as a major change in market volatility—not a change in your opinion.

5. The analysis procedure should tell you when to get into a trade and when to get out. You'll want a procedure that can "admit when it is wrong," and "tell you to take a small loss and try again."

Using the above checklist, we have found computer based systems "fit the bill" better than systems that are difficult to computerize. Computers take much of the opinion out of decision making and allow more accuracy in determining historical track records and hypothetical performance.

An Options Trading System

If you're planning to trade options rather than futures, the trading system you develop may need some extra refinements. Also, you'll want to refer to Appendix 4 for additional background information on exchange traded options.

The value, and therefore the price movement, of an option is related to the price movement of the underlying futures contract. If the price of the underlying futures trends upward, so will the price of the option in most circumstances. The same is true in bear markets.

However, options-on-futures are distinctly different from the underlying futures market. They have characteristics that sometimes cause their price movement to react differently than the futures on which they are based. You must keep these differences in mind when you attempt to relate the signals from a futures trading system to the anticipated price action of an option. And, you cannot evaluate an options trading system exactly the same way you do a futures trading system.

Similarities and Differences

The special attributes of options bring their own set of problems to investing. The premium values for options are determined by a bid/offer open–outcry auction, just as futures prices are determined. Buyers and sellers of options get their lead from the futures markets.

But there are other important considerations that make options trading less responsive to those trading systems that are used successfully in futures trading. First consider the delta factor. It is the value change of the premium price relative to the price change of the underlying futures market. Under optimum conditions the delta factor for an option will be .5, meaning that the value of the premium will move 50 percent of the value of the price change for the futures market.

If you are considering a trading system that has performed well for futures markets, then you would have to make an adjustment to compensate for the delta factor. In other words, if your futures trading system anticipates a 50-percent increase in the price of the underlying futures contract and the delta was .5, you would look for a 25-percent increase in the price of the option.

It is typical for lower cost premiums (i.e., out of the money) to have low delta factors, thus reducing the positive affects of the high level of financial leverage provided by options. Actually, in the money options will provide the closest relationship between options and futures. They can have a delta approaching one.

Dangers of Liquidity

As you test trading systems, the accuracy of your hypothetical results will depend a great deal on how closely your projected entry and exit prices resemble reality. When testing futures market trading systems, it is common to add an extra cost factor of $100 per trade to cover slippage and brokerage commissions. The degree of slippage depends on liquidity and the spread difference between bid and ask prices.

For grains such as soybeans, where high liquidity typically exists, slippage for an individual trade may only be a quarter of a cent per bushel or $12.50 per 5,000 bushel contract. But in less actively traded markets, such as orange juice, slippage may be as much as $200.

The problem of slippage is compounded in the case of options. The reason is that for each individual commodity option there are a large number of strike prices. For each strike price there are bids and offers for puts and bids and offers for calls. Also, actively traded options have less liquidity than actively traded futures. Therefore, you must plan for a wider disparity between the bid and offer prices.

To be assured of a fill, the premium of an option must trade at a price significantly less than the price offered. In other words, if we expect to be filled with an option at a premium of ten, it may be appropriate to only consider a fill if the premium drops to eight, when calculating hypothetical results.

In the case of nearly every option on futures markets, the expiration or declaration date precedes by a number of days the last trading day for the underlying futures markets. Since the option expires first, it may lose the benefit of the trading period within which the futures market most resembles the "real world" cash market.

Matching Money Management with Analysis

Let's talk a little about money management. You can't trade successfully if your system constantly drains your trading account of equity. Successful traders talk about the necessity of "surviving" the rough, choppy markets so that they are in a position to profit when the market smoothly trends up or down. To succeed, you must first survive.

Surviving simply means preservation of risk capital. You must be able both financially and psychologically to withstand some losing trades. You should cut your losses quickly and let your winners run. The trading system you select or develop should have a definite procedure for protecting positions with stops or "bail out" points.

It is our opinion that money management is often more critical than the analysis facet of trading system. Even the best analysis procedure is seldom more than fifty percent right. Good money management preserves your "chips" during the times that the analysis is wrong. It should provide readouts of risk-to-reward ratios.

How Much Can You Afford to Trade?

Greed often raises its ugly head when traders decide to get into the markets. Greed is an extremely strong emotion. If not kept in check, it can distort the trader's perceptions. Greed, like most everything else, is not intrinsically evil. There are a lot of positive aspects to it. Without a certain amount of greed, we wouldn't accumulate what we need to survive and prosper. Businesses—that provide a means of support for most of us—would not exist without a healthy amount of greed on the part of entrepreneurs.

Like chocolate mousse, bourbon 'n' branch water, even jogging—too much of anything is too much. We have always held the philosophy that a person's strength is also his or her weakness. For example, we have a friend who is extremely well organized. It is a pleasure to work with her—most of the time. Everything needed for a project is at hand before we begin to work. But her organization skills can become a stumbling block when something unexpected occurs. She just can't adjust quickly or easily. Once a task gets out-of-hand, she usually has to go all the way back to square one and start over.

Another associate of ours is very creative—generating idea after idea. That's wonderful, except he can never get around to completing anything he dreams up.

Greed can work for or against you. It's positive when it prompts you to take a chance—to take a controlled risk with the expectation of a substantial reward. However, it becomes detrimental when out of control, as is the case with compulsive gamblers.

Trading Limits

If you can select the correct amount of money to trade that suits your emotional make up, you can reduce the negative influence of greed. At the same time, you need to invest enough to make the risk taking involved in the futures markets worth your while.

It's common for beginning traders to over trade. They often select markets that are cosmetically exciting and require large margins—for example, gold and silver.

Equally common are the "nervous Nellies" who invest too little. They have not fully accepted the concept of futures trading. If traders only stick one toe in the water, investing one percent or two percent of their risk capital, a doubling of their money makes little impact.

There are a number of formulas for selecting the proper risk capital that should be devoted to high risk investment opportunities. The following formula has proven to be effective.

First, determine your net liquid assets (NLA). NLA includes assets that are cash or can be converted to cash within twenty-four hours. This would be savings accounts, CDs, common stocks, etc. It would not include real estate, life insurance policies, IRAs, etc.

Once the NLA has been determined, no more than 10 percent of this capital should be earmarked for high risk situations. For example, if an individual has net liquid assets of $50,000, the amount of investment capital will be ten percent, of $5,000. This is the smallest investment we would justifiably recommend to a beginning commodity trader.

Some informal studies have indicated that the larger the amount of investment capital placed in commodity trading, the greater the chance for success. The rough percentages are as follows:

With $5,000 in a commodity trading account, the probability for success after one year is approximately one out of ten.

With $10,000, it is two out of ten.

With $20,000, it is three out of ten.
With $50,000, it is 50-50.
With $100,000, it is six of ten.

Notice that the odds are stacked against the trader with less than $50,000 in an individual commodity trading account. (This certainly heightens the importance of good money management techniques.)

The success ratio improves for two reasons as the investment capital available increases. The first is diversification. The more money in an account, the more markets you can test. The more markets you are in, the more likely you'll be in the market(s) that make the big moves.

The second reason is staying power. If you have a very small amount to invest, you may only have enough equity for one or two trades. The odds get better of hitting a "winner" when you have enough money to make fifteen, twenty-five, or sixty trades.

W. D. Gann Money Management Advice

W. D. Gann is one of history's most noted Wall Street successes. During his commodity and stock trading years in the early part of this century, he supposedly amassed tens of millions of dollars while documenting his trading techniques in a market newsletter and numerous books.

He summarized his money management techniques for stock trading into twenty-four rules. In the following pages, we have revised these twenty-four rules to be applicable to commodity trading.

1.   Determine the Proper Amount of Capital to Use—Divide the amount of risk capital that you are devoting to the commodities markets into ten equal parts and never risk more than one-tenth of this risk capital on any one trade.

2.   Use Stop Loss Orders—Always protect a trade with a protective stop.

3.   Never Overtrade—One often makes this mistake after reaping a considerable profit from a recent trade. Confidence will have built up and the trader will make the mistake of entering the market with a larger than usual position. Overtrading also occurs when a trader tries to recoup losses.

4.   Never Let Profit Run Into a Loss—Once you have a profit, raise your stop/loss order so that you will not lose capital on the trade.

5.   Never Buck the Trend—It is particularly important to know the trend of the market before you buy or sell.

6. If You Don't Know Why You Are in a Trade or Are Not Confident of the Market's Direction, It Is Best to Abandon Your Position—Never enter a trade when you are in doubt.

7. Trade Only Liquid Markets—Those are the active commodities traded. There are plenty of good, viable commodity markets offering profit without going into "left field" and trying to trade the markets that are thinly traded and dominated by commercial or local interests.

8. Diversify Your Risk—Trade commodities from various grouping (grains, meats, metals, financials, food/fiber) to balance your account. Try to avoid tying up all your trading capital in one commodity or commodity grouping.

9. Trade Only with Market Orders—Fixing a buying or selling price can be dangerous and should only be used when you have a specific purpose in entering a limited price on your order. We'll discuss orders in more detail in the next chapter.

10. Don't Close Out Your Trades Unless You Have Good Reason—Following the trade with a stop/loss order will protect your profits but will not allow you to exit the market on a whim. Let the market tell you what should be done. If you are wrong, let the market kick you out by hitting your stop.

11. As You Produce Profits, Place These Profits into a Surplus Account to be Used Only in an Emergency—This will help you to avoid becoming egotistical about your commodity trading and will discipline you to stay on the original track that you have set out for yourself.

12. Never Enter Commodity Trading for Tax Purposes Alone.

13. Never Average a Loss—If you have a loss in the market, do not increase the size of your position to lower your average loss. This is one of the worst mistakes a trader can make.

14. Do Not Lose Patience in Your Positions—Don't exit the market simply because you have lost patience or because you are anxious from waiting. This is particularly true for options traders.

15. Avoid Taking Small Profits and Large Losses.

16. Never Cancel a Stop/Loss Order After You Have Placed It.

17. Avoid Churning Your Account—Avoid getting in and out of the market too often. Position your trades and stick with them.

18. Don't Be a One-Way Trader—Be willing to sell short just as often as you are willing to buy. Let your object be to keep with the trend and make a profit.

19. Don't Buy Because You Think the Commodity is Oversold or Too Low. Don't Sell Just Because the Price Seems Too High.

20. It is Dangerous to Pyramid at the Wrong Time—The best time to pyramid is when the commodity has broken resistance levels and has become active. Treat a pyramided position as a totally new position. If you would not buy if you didn't already have a position, then you shouldn't be pyramiding the position. Remember that at the bottom of all the great pyramids, there's a dead pharaoh.

21. It is Best to Pyramid on the Buy Side if the Open Interest Has Dipped. It is Best to Pyramid on the Sell Side After the Open Interest Has Risen.

22. Never Spread Off a Loss—If you are in a loss position, get out. Do not spread the position and compound your error.

23. Never Change Your Position in the Market Without Good Reason.

24. Avoid Increasing Your Trading after a Long Period of Success or a Period of Profitable Trades.

Besides money, there is another type of asset that is just as vital. Unfortunately, nobody can check for its presence but you. It's a shame you can't ask your broker or a friend: "Am I psychologically set to trade?" "What's my stress level?" "Is it above the red line?"

Like money management, there are some rules to follow to help you conserve or manage stress. Here's our list:

1. Rule numero uno is to follow all the money management rules. Money at risk is, of course, a very serious source of stress. If those rules are violated, following the other ones described below will not do you much good.

2. Experiencing losses in the futures market is not failure. It's the normal course of business. You can equate it to trying to hit a baseball. A hitter who has a .300 batting average gets a hit about every third time at bat. Two-thirds of the time he loses. Worse yet, of the three in ten hits, only

a small percentage of them are home runs. An even smaller percentage of the home runs are grand slammers. A lot of the hits are singles.

In commodity terms, singles break even and may pay, or partially pay, the transaction costs (commissions and fees).

The batter who hits .300 or has a lifetime average that high will be a success. So will the futures trader whose every third trade is profitable. The law of probability will see to it that he gets a few homers and an occasional grand slam.

3. Don't run your mind through the wringer on every trade. Once you make up your mind on a position stay with it, unless you uncover some overwhelming reasons to abort the trade. Avoid listening to the advice of others once your mind is made up.

4. Closely related to number three is the ability to live with your trading decisions. You must accept full responsibility for them and that's that!

5. At the same time you're accepting responsibility for your actions, you cannot marry positions. Stay impersonal. Be prepared to cut losing positions early through the use of stops.

6. When you feel the market is dragging you down, walk away for awhile. Take a trading vacation.

7. Take pride in yourself and your trading skills. It is only thing that keeps us going sometimes, but the market can be a "great humbler." Therefore, you need to control your reaction to success and stay humble. Pride often induces over trading which can result in serious financial damage.

8. Trade as "James Bond" would—with cold, calculated precision, once you have decided what to do.

9. Maintain the maximum amount of self-discipline. Set concrete rules for yourself—for example, stop trading for a day or a week after taking two consecutive losses—and stick to them.

10. Master yourself. As part of your diary, include remarks about your behavior. Then work at correcting any flaws. You must work against natural instincts to be stubborn, emotional and inflexible. Find your character flaws and overcome them. We go into detail in the next chapter about how to set up a trading journal and what should be in it.

11. Always be open and responsive to changes in the market place, particularly changes to the basic facts on which your decisions have been made. When necessary, change your mind and reverse your position.

12. Before each trading or decision making session do a "gut check." Are you ready to trade? Is your left and right brain in sync? Do you feel comfortable making decisions at this time? If the answer to any of these questions is no, take a cold shower and trade some other time.

13. Eliminate all distractions.

14. Never trade when you are physically or mentally ill or under stress from non-trade related pressures.

15. Resist pressure from all outside sources.

Serious traders almost make futures trading a religious experience. They become monks of the market. Just as Franciscan monks submit to the will of God, practice humility and obedience, so must the monk-trader become submissive to the will of the markets, obey the laws of probability and respect the market's whims. Thus the adage: "The market is always right!" (Hopefully, the monks and the traders will differ in regards to the vow of poverty.)

These rules, and the money management ones detailed previously, were constructed to help serious traders conserve their two most critical assets—their financial and psychological strength. If you neglect or ignore them, you do so at your own risk.

This brings up the concept of trading discipline. Discipline for the futures traders centers around three critical areas:

• Trading System Discipline

• Money Management Discipline

• Personal Discipline

Let's look at each of these in turn and then discuss some strategies to improve our discipline.

But first, let's define the term. Discipline is training intended to produce a specific character or pattern of behavior or, more simply, controlled behavior. We want to train ourselves to do something as nearly perfectly as possible.

We're talking about a major commitment.

Success requires that we become specific and record our progress. Success requires clearly stated goals. We must regularly record our results and honestly evaluate how we're doing.

Most traders lose what they gain through lack of commitment. Written goals, written plans, follow–up procedures—they're all fine, but without the whole hearted commitment they mean little.

You, as a futures trader, must train your behavior. The first area of concern is your trading system. Studies seem to indicate there are a wide variety of systems that can make money in the markets.

All trading systems have a few functions in common. They give specific trade entry and exit signals, along with some type of a timing mechanism. Your function is to take the appropriate action.

If this is carried to the limit, the ideal trading system would be totally automatic. You'd hook it up to a computerized order placing system and have the profits wired to your bank.

We don't think this would work—even the most automatic of systems needs the human touch to adjust to the idiosyncrasies of the market.

On the other hand, the human touch must be gentle and timely or we face the dreaded "operator error" syndrome. It's discipline that keeps us on the straight and narrow. Discipline also makes sure we do our homework—updating the system regularly, reviewing it, and following the signals.

Money management is the second critical area. We discussed its potential when we spoke about W. D. Gann's 24 Money Management Rules. You need to be sure that you adopt rules applicable to your trading style. You need to put them in writing and keep them in front of you.

The last area refers to personal performance. You must discipline your emotions—particularly your pride, greed, hope and fear. These are the emotions that lead you back to your old losing ways.

How Do We Stay on Track?

We begin with honesty. If you want to win in the futures markets, you must say: "I'm going to enter some losing trades—there's no avoiding some loss. But I'm not going to let that bother me because I'm going to follow my trading system's rules, my money management rules and my personal emotional rules. I'm totally committed to making money in the futures market."

From here, you must develop specific strategies to accomplish our mission. For example, following rules can be made easier if you set a firm schedule. Update and review charts daily by 7:00 p.m. every trading day. Discuss markets with broker at 8:00 p.m. each night. Think about possible trading opportunities overnight and call broker in the morning to place orders. Update data and journal before leaving for work. Check the market at noon.

You must back up your schedule with checklists, so nothing gets overlooked. It helps to match your homework with your personality. If you are not the type to do a lot of detailed number crunching each night, you need a simple system that doesn't require it.

If you simply don't have any time, you shouldn't be trading. Successful futures trading requires a lot of work. If you aren't up to it, consider an alternative approach to the markets, like a discretionary, guided, or managed account.

Your trading plan, which includes your objectives and trading system, is your road map to success in the futures market. Discipline is your navigator that keeps you on course. Be sure to listen to your navigator—so you'll end up where you want to be.

"Garbage In, Garbage Out!"

Now, let's move on to another important area. All trading systems demand information. You must feed them their daily ration of prices, open interest, volume, or whatever they utilize. It is critical that this information is accurate, timely, readily available, and reasonably priced. If not, your system cannot function over the long term.

The computer axiom "Garbage In, Garbage Out" applies to trading systems as well. If you don't input clean, accurate data, you can't expect reliable output. Not to belabor the subject, state-of-the-art personal computers and modems makes data retrieval accessible to nearly everyone.

Classes of Data: On-Line

Futures (or stocks for that matter) price information is usually defined into three classes based on how and when you receive it. You can be "on-line" and receive "real–time" prices. These are prices that are transmitted directly from the exchanges. They are sometimes called tick-by-tick prices.

To receive the on-line pricing, you have to pay a fee to the exchanges, as well as the monthly charge to your vendor. This type of service, depending on the bells and whistles included in the system, can run several hundred dollars per month. This price doesn't always include the equipment, usually a personal computer.

Additionally, you'll need a communications link. This could be a satellite dish, dedicated telephone line, FM radio antenna, cable TV, or similar arrangement. Keep in mind that as long as the markets you are following are trading, your equipment is tied up.

A less expensive variation of on-line services are the fifteen-minute delayed price quotation services. These cost less because you no longer have to pay the exchange fees, which can run from less than $10 to over $100 per month per exchange. If you supply your own equipment, usually a TV set, these types of services can run less than $50 per month for individual investors.

With on-line services, you also need to consider if and for how long you are going to capture the data coming across the screen. Retaining the prices requires computer memory. Some systems are set up to capture and store data for the life of thirty, fifty, or 100 contracts. They send the price to memory every five minutes or every fifteen minutes. Often you have a choice. Naturally, the more frequently you save date, the faster the computer's memory is filled up.

The data saved can then be used to perform technical analysis. Most current price quotation systems include very sophisticated studies as part of their packages. When shopping for a system, find one that includes software with the appropriate analytic tools needed for the type of trading system you plan on trading.

Call-Up Information

Let's say you can't plant yourself in front of a monitor during trading hours, but your system requires you to review each day's trading tick-by-tick. You could utilize a call-up or dial-up service.

These are computer service bureaus that sell you access to their database to retrieve whatever pricing data you want. Some will allow you to select market by market, while others offer packages of ten, twenty, thirty-five, or fifty markets.

All you do, usually after 5:00 p.m. EST, is connect your computer through a modem and telephone line to their computer. You punch in your identification code and down–load the information you've agreed to purchase. You're then billed on a monthly basis.

Once you have the day's data, you can study it at your leisure. You can combine it with previously collected data to get the longer-term view or run your favorite technical analysis studies.

Historical Data

The least expensive pricing information is historical data. You can acquire this data on diskettes or you can down–load it to your system. With historical data, you can go back to when a contract or a market first began trading. System developers use this type of data for evaluation purposes. They can use it to hypothesize how well a trading program performs over a wide variety of market conditions.

Where Is this Data Available?

Keep in mind that not all the services are reliable. Further, the chances for errors—human and mechanical—are compounded when the data is inputted from the pit to a computer, is repeatedly up and down linked via satellites, is up and down loaded to computers, and finally is delivered to the users in a variety of formats.

You have two basic sources: the full service vendor or the specialists. Your choice probably evolves around your use of data.

If you're just interested in keeping track of what's going on, you might select a very general service, such as Compu-Serve or the Dow Jones News/Retrieval

Service. In addition to futures prices, these services provide stock quotes, news, weather, and even entertainment. More serious users have about 25 service bureau choices. You can locate them via magazines, like *Futures*, which has an annual reference volume. See Appendix 3 for details.

A System Must Be a System!

The three components of a trading system described above must complement each other—they must work to a single goal. Your analysis, for example, cannot violate good money management principles. And the data input must suit the analysis component. They must work like the Three Musketeers: "All for one and one for all!"

We'll now quickly review five popular futures and options-on-futures markets. This will give you a feel for both the fundamental and technical factors you need to be concerned with as you develop or select a trading system. Appendix 1 includes fifteen additional markets. You will notice, as you peruse these market overviews, there is a lot of fundamental and technical information needed in order to successfully trade any market. You must decide in which markets you want to become an "expert" in.

Overview of Soybean Market

Soybeans have been commercially cultivated for at least the last 5,000 years, primarily in the Orient and specifically in China. It's cultivation relatively new to the United States (circa 1930), yet we are now the world's largest producer. Beans are grown in this country from the southern delta to the Canadian border. Iowa and Illinois are the largest producing states.

From a fundamental analyst's point of view, you must determine what will influence supply and demand. Think of it as a balance scale. When supplies are heavier than demand, the price declines. When demand out weighs supplies, prices increase.

Supply Side

One of the keys to the soybean price equation is production. How many acres will be planted? What will the yield be?

The key to production is weather, but it is a very difficult factor to predict, especially over the entire growing seasons throughout entire world. Is there enough moisture to germinate the crop? Will there be rains through the entire growing season? Will harvest be dry and free of snow?

In the Northern Hemisphere, August is a particularly sensitive month—the crop can be made or lost. Pod filling occurs primarily during the first two weeks of August. You should be particularly attuned to rainfall markets during this month. The slightest shower, particularly in Chicago, can send prices plummeting. Any prolonged dryness and prices will take off like the space shuttle.

Several South American countries, particularly Brazil and Argentina, have complicated the production side of the supply/demand equation over the last decade. Their soybean production usually exceeds one billion bushels. The crop year for these countries is essentially the opposite of ours: they plant in November and harvest in March and April.

Soybeans also have a lot of competitors. When the bean is crushed, it produces oil and meal. A few of the oil competitors are sunflower, palm, and coconut oil. With regard to meal (or protein) competitors, the most common replacement feed is wheat.

Demand Side

The meal is used as feed for livestock, so you also need to keep an eye on hog and cattle prices and numbers. The acreage, yield, weather, etc., for the other oil producing crops mentioned earlier must be tracked closely.

Demand or usage depends on the beans being in the right place at the right time at the right price. Therefore, you need to be aware of any export (i.e., embargoes, dock workers strikes, etc.) or transportation (i.e., frozen rivers in inland waterway systems, barge rate, etc.) problems.

Since about fifty percent of the U.S. crop is exported, the strength of the dollar is critical. The lower the dollar, the greater quantity foreign countries can purchase. One of the largest importers is Japan. Being aware of their needs for food and feed and their economic condition can make the difference between picking a winning trade or not.

Technical Factors

As you can see, following the fundamental side of the market is a staggering task. That's why so many professionals rely on technical analysis.

One of the most reliable tools is a seasonal analysis. At harvest, you can expect a lot of beans on the market. Therefore, prices are likely to be lower. Prior to harvest, processors use up last year's production and prices tend to increase.

This analysis has been finely tuned. Studies indicate that seventy percent of all seasonal tops occur between April and July. Eighty percent of all seasonal highs are made by the end of July. Price bottoms—up to eighty percent—occur between August and November.

The theory of cycle analysis states that price action will repeat itself in a predictable fashion. For soybeans, two dominant long term cycles have been identified—a 24- and a 39-month cycle—by the Foundation for the Study of Cycles. Weekly and even daily cycles have also been isolated.

Chart analysis of soybean price activity has been known to be quite reliable. It is often a trending market that can be interpreted fairly accurately. But certain chart formations, like triangles, are very unreliable. Other chart formations, like head and shoulder formations, are very reliable, but are seldom formed.

Overview of the Live Hog and Pork Belly Markets

On a worldwide base, the United States ranks third in pork production, behind China and Russia. But since there is a negligible import-export business, we'll be discussing only the United States markets.

Iowa has the largest production in the United States. Nine other states (Georgia, Illinois, Indiana, Kansas, Minnesota, Missouri, Nebraska, North Carolina, and Ohio) are major producers. Together these ten states account for approximately 75 percent of total U.S. production.

Pork producers have a special vocabulary of their own:

Farrowing: The act of giving birth.

Gilts: Female swine that have not given birth to a litter.

Boars: Male hogs used for breeding.

Stags: Boars castrated after sexual maturity.

Barrows: Male hogs castrated before maturity.

The reason for castration is simple. It increases the rate of weight gain and reduces aggressive behavior (fighting).

The production cycle for hogs is relatively short.

- The gestation period is approximately four months.

- Sows are bred twice a year.

- Litters range from five to fifteen with an average of approximately nine, of which seven reach maturity.

- Gilts reach sexual maturity and slaughter weight at six months. At this point, they can be held back for breeding or sent to the packing house.

- Barrows reach slaughter weight (220 pounds) at six months.

- It takes about one and one–half years from the time a pig is born to the time a pork chop from its offspring reaches the dining room table.

Supply Side

Hog farmers often integrate their production. It is common for producers to grow much of their own feed (corn/soybeans), farrow their own feeder pigs, and finish them out to slaughter weight. It is not unusual for a pig to spend its entire existence, until slaughter, in the same building or adjacent buildings—moving only from the nursery to the feeding floor. Pig farms, such as the one described, are known as a "farrow-to-finish" operations.

In the past when hogs farrowed in pastures and were fed in open lots, all females were bred at the same time—spring and fall. This gave a seasonality to production. Now, with more sophisticated facilities, production has leveled off somewhat.

A 220-pound market hog yields an average 153 pounds of pork, trimmings and lard. Fresh hams account for about 18.5 percent; pork bellies (bacon), 17.5 percent; loins, 15 percent; trimmings, 18 percent; picnics, 8.5 percent; other, 22.5 percent. The six commercial cuts are hams, loins, picnics, Boston butts, bellies and spareribs. These represent 40 percent of the live weight and 90 percent of the value of a hog.

Demand Side

Pork has always been an important part of the American diet. Over the last 20 years, pork has faced some stiff competition from beef, chicken and fish. It has been fighting back for a market share in the media.

Unlike beef, in which most is consumed fresh, much of pork is processed or stored—smoked, canned or frozen. Pork bellies, for example, can be stored (frozen) up to one year before processing. The storability of pork products means that the forecasters of futures prices must take supplies, as well as production, into consideration.

What Are Pork Bellies?

The pork belly is the layer of meat and fat from the underside of the hog. Each hog has two bellies, one on each side, which extend from the front to the rear legs. They weight between ten and twenty pounds. Most bellies weigh fourteen to sixteen pounds. Almost all bellies are cured, smoked and sliced into bacon. A well developed cash market exists in bellies, which impacts the futures markets.

Fundamental Analysis

Fundamental analysts usually take the pipeline approach. What are the number of farrowings? How many feeder pigs are available? How many gilts will be held back for breeding? How many market hogs are in the system and at what weights? What are storage levels? You must rely for numbers on USDA quarterly reports ("Hogs and Pigs" report) released on or about the 22nd of March, June, September, and December. It covers the top ten producing states.

Hog Cycles

The hog cycle is considered to be a four-year cycle. It may range from as low as three years to as high as six. During the last fifty years, there have been twelve cycles averaging 4.1 years. The expansion phases lasted 2.4 years on average and the contraction phase 1.7 years.

Seasonality

As mentioned earlier, the seasonality of the production cycle has become somewhat less meaningful over the years as production techniques have changed. Still, hog prices tend to have a definite seasonal pattern. Hog prices tend to bottom in late spring and the fourth quarter. Most highs are made in August. With pork bellies, the inventory level on hand tends to impact any seasonal pattern. There is also the BLT factor—demand in late summer for bacon, lettuce and tomato sandwiches.

Price Determinants

Naturally, the supply–demand equation is the most important price determinant. You must be on top of the size of pig crop, hog slaughter, slaughter weights, direction of two-way gilts, etc. Other determinants are:

Hog-Corn Ratio: This is the price of corn (major feed component) compared to the price of hogs. If the ratio is low, feeding is profitable. If high, it isn't. With the increase investment in buildings and the cost of feed supplements, this ratio has become less reliable in recent years.

Weather: Unusually hot or cold weather can impact weight gain. This is somewhat mitigated by the confined feeding systems currently being used, but not entirely.

As mentioned in past sections of this series, such things as fashion, health considerations and promotions can impact prices by influencing demand.

Trading and Technical Analysis

Pork belly contracts are a favorite of day traders and aggressive position traders because of the wide price ranges in which they trade. But the volatility factor should be taken as a warning to neophyte traders.

Both the bellies and the hogs lend themselves well to spread trading strategies. Nearby contracts usually gain enough on the distant in bull markets—and lose enough in bear markets—to make the spreads attractive, especially when you take the lower margins and somewhat more manageable risk (compared to a straight futures position) into consideration.

Always trade these markets with stops. They respond violently to unexpected news, weather, or reports.

Overview of the Silver Market

Silver was first used by man sometime around 4000 B.C., which is slightly after man learned to use gold and copper. The earliest known mines of "native" silver (pure silver found in nugget form) were in Asia Minor.

The first use of silver was decorative, primarily jewelry and armor. Inscriptions found in the Royal Tombs of Chaldaea indicate that by the fourth millennium B.C., silver had become a medium of exchange. It was the ancient Greeks who popularized the use of minted silver coinage. Europe remained silver poor until the discovery, by Spanish and Portuguese explorers, of vast deposits in the Americas during the sixteenth century.

Supply Side

Total world production ranges between 300 and 500 million troy ounces per year. The main producing countries are Australia, Canada, Mexico, Peru, USA and Commonwealth of Unified States.

Most native silver mines have played out. It is now primarily produced as a by-product of the mining of base metals, such as copper, zinc, and lead. Additionally, silver is often found in association with gold ore. The fact that most silver is produced as a by-product makes production somewhat insensitive to demand. Increased demand for the base metals, on the other hand, can create over supply situations for silver.

People have a habit of hoarding precious metals. This can distort the supply side of the supply/demand equation. When silver became very precious, hoarders will dump their silver—thus driving prices sharply lower. The magnitude of this problem can best be seen by looking at India. It is estimated that Indians hold 5,000 million ounces of silver—approximately a twelve and one half year supply!

The French are also known as world-class silver hoarders. There are no accurate figures as to how much silver is hidden away.

Recently, new and efficient technologies have been developed to recover silver from photographic solutions; thus, adding recycled silver to the supply side of the balance sheet.

Demand Side

The demand for silver as a medium of monetary exchange has all but dried up, only about seven percent of silver supplies are still manufactured into coins each year. It's traditional use, i.e., as jewelry, silver place settings, and art objects, still represents a major portion of annual consumption.

The really big users are the electrical and photographic industries. Silver has several very desirable physical characteristics. It's a better conductor of heat and electricity than copper, for example. And some of its salts are light and radiation sensitive and form the active ingredient in almost all film emulsions. In photography, about half of the silver consumed is for X-ray plates.

Marketing of Silver

In London, which is the silver marketing capital of the world, there are two very distinct silver markets. The first is the bullion market. Three brokerage firms—Mocatta Metals and Goldsmith, Samuel Montager and Sharps Pixley—hold a daily "fixing" meeting each morning. At this meeting, they set the price they are willing to pay for silver. This "fixes" the cash or spot price and gives brokers around the world a price to bid around.

The other market, of course, is the futures market. The two major futures exchanges trading silver are the New York Commodities Exchange (COMEX) and the Chicago Board of Trade (CBT). The Far Eastern silver markets, particularly Hong Kong, Singapore and Tokyo, have been steadily gaining in importance.

Fundamental Analysis

There are five key areas the investor in silver must analyze from a fundamental point of view. First is industrial usage. Is the use of photographic film and emulsions expected to increase or decrease? Some electronic discoveries in the use of digitalized images threatens this market. How serious is this challenge? Other industrial uses of silver, such as an electrical conductor and as a catalyst, must be gauged as well.

The second area of concern is currency fluctuation. Silver prices reflect the values of stronger currencies; although, they are not a perfect hedge against inflation.

Third, you need to evaluate the impact of the political situation. Unstable world conditions encourage the hoarding of silver and other precious metals. Governments have often tried to "control" or legislate the price of silver. Other governments, like India, have attempted to restrict the export of this precious metal. Can you predict what political action is going to occur? How effective it will be? And, it's impact on silver prices?

Next, you must estimate production and recovery. Normally, more silver is consumed each year than is mined. Yet, we haven't run out, nor do we appear to be about to.

Lastly, you must take the unpredictable into account. For example, a major producers have been known to disrupt the market to gain a political advantage.

Technical Analysis

There are two technical formations that work well for silver. Major lows in the silver market are usually made in rounded bottoms. Rounded bottoms may take years to develop, as was the case from 1974 to 1978, or from 1968 to 1973.

After creating a rounded bottom, silver often makes a spectacular rally—often doubling or tripling from its previous high. Highs, on the other hand, occur in a matter of seconds. A reversal from a top is often a spectacular spike top with "island reversals" and other kinds of violent formations.

Seasonally, you should expect silver to create its lows during summer, and its highs are often made in January.

Overview of the Sugar Market

Basically, two types of sugar exist: cane and beet. Cane accounts for approximately 60 percent of the world's production. It's a perennial crop with an 18-month growing season. After harvesting, the stubble left in the fields produces another crop. With each successive crop, the yield diminishes. Eventually, it has to be replanted.

Production of cane sugar is widely distributed around the world; it is one of the few crops harvested year-round. The four major producing countries are Brazil, Cuba, India and Australia. They account for approximately 45 percent of the world production of cane sugar.

Beet sugar accounts for the other 40 percent of total production. Europe accounts for 85 percent of this sugar, which amounts to one-third of the total world production.

Sugar beets are an annual crop. Therefore, plantings can be estimated in the spring and followed throughout the year. Since the European crop accounts for so much of the world's production and the cane crop is harvested all year long, the beet crop critically influences the supply-demand equation.

Supply

The statistical sugar season begins September 1st and ends August 31st. Like all food commodities, year-end stocks play a big role in price analysis. To this is added estimated production. The first official indication as to the size of the new crop each year is made by the F.O. Licht's estimates of European sugar beet plantings. The first estimate of total world crop is not released until October of each year.

The supply side of the supply-demand equation is further distorted by the impact of competitive products. High-fructose corn syrup (HFCS) is a popular sweetener as a result of depressed corn prices. To a lesser degree, Nutrasweet has become a substitute. But Nutrasweet has only found a modest degree of acceptance in highly developed countries.

Demand

Sugar consumption has grown steadily over the years at a rate averaging a little over three percent per year. HFCS put a damper on this growth for awhile, but it appears to have recovered. Since sugar has a well defined usage pattern, it is relatively easy to project consumption from year to year.

Hear are some reasons for the steady pattern:

1. In many countries, sugar prices are strictly controlled by the government. Only fifteen percent of the world's annual usage requirements are traded on the free market. Domestic usage by producing countries is high.

2. For many uses, there is no substitute.

3. Even when HFCS can be substituted, this is done reluctantly because of the fickle nature of consumer tastes. This has been particularly evident in the soft drink industry, where changing formulas is a high–risk decision.

4. In non-industrial usage, demand tends to be inelastic since the cost of sugar used is not a significant amount of the user's budget.

Therefore, projecting consumption can be a relatively simple matter. If there has not been an extremely active bull market in recent seasons that would substantially increase plantings (especially of perennial cane sugar), the previous usage gains for the last two to four crop years can be used. If there has been a bull market recently, then you can anticipate a modest consumption decline.

Price Forecasting

Sugar pricing has an unusual pricing history. Many analysts liken it to the "tulip-omania" that occurred in seventeenth-century Holland. It was a period of speculative frenzy that drove tulip bulb prices to incredible heights—only to crash with equal momentum.

Take the 1974 bull market in sugar as an example. At the market height in November 1974, sugar prices had increased eightfold over 1973 levels. In the final months of this wild bull rally, futures prices shot up 36 cents/lb. in two months. Thirty-six cents is three times higher than the prior post World War II high!

It started with some very bullish fundamentals. The year-end (1973-74) stock/consumption ratio was a low 20 percent. The sugar beet crop in Europe was faced with some adverse growing conditions. Fundamentals might account for 20- or 30-cent sugar, but it more than doubled that price to over 65 cents. There was talk of dollar per pound sugar. Then it came down faster than it went up, leveling in the 15- to 20-cent range. A similar market "panic" occurred in 1980. It was not as severe, but sugar rallied to 45 cents that time.

The point is simply this: sugar has a propensity to move way beyond what could be expected based on fundamentals. It can be a very emotionally driven market. Keep this in mind.

Technical Analysis

Because of its emotional nature and unusual pricing history, sugar can be traded using technical chart formations. They will catch the big moves.

The seasonal pattern projects the annual low around September with the high in January or February. The cycles for sugar have been described as "bizarre." They are characterized by extremely sharp but relatively short-lived upside bursts, followed by extended periods of dormancy at depressed levels. This may be the result of some fundamental factors, such as the year-long harvesting of the crop.

Overview of the Stock Index Futures Markets

These indexes are relatively new to the futures and options–on–futures markets. The first index, the Value Line Composite Index (Value Line) futures contract, commenced trading on February 24, 1982 on the Kansas City Board of Trade. The others followed shortly thereafter.

Besides the Value Line, there are the Standard & Poor's 500 Stock Index (S & P 500), New York Stock Exchange Composite Index (Composite) and the Major Market Index (MMI) futures contracts. There are options on futures for the S & P 500 and the Composite indexes.

Each of these indexes reflects a different type of stock portfolio. For example, the S & P 500 and the Composite represent a broadly based portfolio. The S & P 500 includes 500 stocks, while the Composite is composed of over 1,500 stocks. Both of these indexes are weighted by capitalization. The MMI mimics the Dow Jones Industrial Average and the Value Line mirrors stocks with low capitalization. The MMI is priced weighted, and the Value Line gives equal weighting to all stocks.

Stock Market Risk

The index contracts and their options were developed to either manage or capitalize on the risks inherent in the stock market. We need to discuss this risk in order to properly understand the uses of the indexes.

There are basically two types of risk associated with the stock market. The first type relates to the changes in the price level of the overall stock market. Is the stock market bullish (going up) or bearish (going down) overall? Which direction are the Dow and other indexes going?

The second type of risk relates to price changes of individual stock issues relative to the level of the overall stock market. The first type of risk is commonly called market risk, and the second, stock-specific risk.

You, as an investor, must look at individual stock prices as they compare to the overall market. This is called volatility. If a stock is highly volatile, it's price level will swing up or down in a wider range than the overall market.

Volatility is measured by use of "beta" coefficients. For example, if the price level of a given stock increases by 1.5 percent when the overall market goes up only 1 percent, this stock has a beta coefficient of 1.5 and is considered highly volatile. The opposite is also true. With stocks with low betas or low volatility, their price levels do not change as much as the overall market.

Stock portfolio managers want to be in stocks with high beta coefficients when a bull market is in progress. The price level of these stocks should outperform the averages or indexes. In bear markets, the portfolio managers want to be in low beta stocks or out of the stock market completely.

Index Trading Strategies

The investor or portfolio manager can combine actually trading the stock market with the use of stock indexes and options trading. Let's say you expected the overall stock market to go up, but you are not sure what to expect from a specific stock or group of stocks you are holding. Remember, a specific stock does not necessarily move in the same direction as the overall market nor with the same volatility. Therefore, you could hold onto the stock and purchase a stock index futures contract or option to take advantage of the expected upward move. If you're bearish, you could short the futures market or purchase a stock index put option.

What we are talking about is hedging a stock or a portfolio. You can select the futures contract that most closely resembles your stock portfolio. For broad-based portfolios, use the S & P 500 or Composite, the Value Line for small stocks, and the MMI for portfolios similar to the Dow Jones Industrial Averages.

Price Determinants

Naturally, you can speculate about the direction of the stock market through the use of stock index futures and options without owning any specific stocks. But like all other futures markets, you need to have an opinion as to whether the market is going up or down and when.

There are at least two technical approaches to analyzing the stock market index futures contracts. The first utilizes the analysis of charts and chart formations, including several types of moving averages, algorithms, oscillators, and relative strength indicators. The second technical approach uses several stock market indicators, such as short interest, specialist short interest, advance/decline ratio and odd lot buying and selling.

Other stock market analysts use fundamentals, such as,

Corporate Profits—higher corporate profits usually equates to high stock prices and an increase in the indexes.

Interest Rates—higher interest rates usually means lower corporate profits and lower index levels.

Economic Conditions—here's a "Catch-22." Better economic conditions lead to higher corporate profits and eventually higher interest rates. The indexes go up for awhile and then down.

Public Expectation—if the public is optimistic about the near term future, the indexes usually go up. Pessimism drives them down.

Traders Notes

You'll notice that most of the volume and open interest in the stock market index contracts is in the nearby contract months. This indicates most traders are looking at the short–term situation—avoiding the long term which is difficult to trade because the market is so emotionally charged. Personally, we like to trade the S & P 500 because it is very liquid and has a very narrow bid-ask spread.

Summary

At this point, you should have enough information to go "shopping" for your system. It may be computer software that utilizes certain technical tools with which you are comfortable. Or, you may just use this background to help select a broker you'll use as a consultant. In the next chapter, we begin to discuss the specifics of what you will have to do to trade successfully.

CHAPTER 6

SETTING GOALS AND CREATING A PORTFOLIO

Key Concepts

⟹ Specific skills mastered.

⟹ A broker needs to be chosen.

⟹ Account papers understood and completed.

⟹ And, a written plan should be prepared.

So far in this book, we have tried to provide you enough information to allow you to make two very critical decisions:

1. Should you seriously consider investing in the futures markets? Are you financially and psychologically suited to accept the risk-reward opportunities offered by this type of investment?

2.   If you consider yourself suitable, do you have or can you develop a complete trading system?

Now's the time to take the next steps—the "how-to" of it all.

Setting Realistic Goals

The futures industry, more than just about any other, is filled with stories of office clerks becoming millionaires virtually overnight. Some of these stories are even true. But the reality of the situation is that most small individual traders lose money.

For this reason, it is very important that you develop realistic goals. These are road marks you can use to measure your success. Learn to do this often, so you know when you are ahead and when you're falling behind.

Success in achieving goals often depends upon putting them in writing. This makes them more real. More importantly, you have a better chance of reaching written objectives because they don't go away.

At the same time you dictate your goals, also prepare a list of your limitations. What will limit your success or commitment to reaching your futures trading goals? It could be lack of equity, knowledge of the markets, a tested trading system, or time to devote to the market. Or, it could be something you have too much of, like optimism, greed, or self confidence. Or, it could be an equipment limitation—you can't day-trade without tick-by-tick price quotation equipment. You might need a computer to run the trading system you wish to use. Does your current work keep you out of touch with the markets during the day or for other periods of time?

It doesn't matter what your limitations are. You must take them into consideration as you develop your goals.

The primary goal of just about every trader is or should be to take money out of the market. The question is usually how much and how fast. Do you want to double your equity every quarter? Or make 200 or 400 percent or more return on your trading equity?

The more aggressive your goal, the greater the risk you have to take. Keep in mind that one of the keys to reaching financial goals is being in the right market at the right time. You may have to diversify to do this—you may need to trade several markets at the same time.

It was mentioned in the last chapter that an individual trading account with $5,000 in equity had a one in ten chance of being successful after a year of trading. The reason for this is simple. In the futures market, this account could trade only a few markets at a time. Even if the analysis is absolutely right, your timing may be a week or two off. Once the trader loses some money (drawdown of equity), s/he may not be able to get back into the market when the time is right.

For this reason, goals must be tempered with whatever limitations you impose or are imposed on you from without. We'll discuss further how to neutralize some common limitations in this chapter. Another important record you should maintain is a Daily Trading Diary or Journal. A good written record of your trading activity could separate you from the majority of traders who fail.

Why Bother?

This is a common attitude among futures traders. They just don't see the value of chronicling their trading activity. "I get a monthly statement . . . isn't that enough?" is their attitude.

The most important piece of information missing from your monthly statement is the reason you got into the trade in the first place. What did you expect to happen? What was the risk-to-reward ratio? What alternative trades did you turn down in favor of the ones you took? What signals—fundamental or technical—triggered your trading decision? What attracted you to the trade initially?

Remember the proverb, "Those who forget the past are condemned to repeat it." Trading is an extremely personal and emotional endeavor. Our minds interpret the ink blots on the price charts. We learn to rationalize our trading decisions. Some great traders talk about their instincts—they can smell a trade when it is still ten ticks away!

The essence of what these traders are saying is basically believable. But we also know from our experience that writing stimulates thought and clarifies thinking. Researchers, who have studied the papers of some of the world-class traders, have indicated that their trading wasn't by the "seat of their pants." The great traders documented what they did before, during, and after the markets were open.

We learn from our mistakes. Why repeat them? We learn from our successes. Why not repeat them?

The function of the journal is twofold. First, it reminds us why we selected or rejected a trade. It provides an audit trail.

We need this historical record because we all have a tendency to mold the past by our perception of it in the present. If we try to recreate our thinking and our emotional state after the fact, we find ourselves heavily influenced by the results of the trade. This confuses us to the point where we can't be brutally honest.

For these two reasons, you should put your thoughts and emotional reasons for each trade on paper before you call your broker. This is needed even if all you have to go by is a "gut feeling that corn is going higher." Record when you first noticed it as well as what might have triggered it—a news story, a chart formation, etc. Later on, you may be able to piece the puzzle together and make something more concrete of it.

Reliable instincts are as meaningful in commodity trading as they are in any human activity. The price trends and patterns of the futures market reflect the instincts and emotional state of every trader that is getting in or out of the market at a given time. You may be able to instinctively sense where a market is going at times, just like a hunter can sense where game can be found.

Your trading journal helps you hone your instincts. You learn to sort out unfounded hunches from brilliant insights. Fine tune your feel for the market through the use of a journal.

What . . . when . . . where?

This brings up the question of what should be included in a trading diary. When do entries need to be made and where do you keep it?

The diary reflects your trading system. First, answer the question: How do I select trades? What are my key indicators? What are my goals? For example, the first thing many traders do is determine if the trend is up or down for the markets they are tracking. This may be your first entry. You would then do the same for the other signals that you regularly check.

Or, you could have your signals listed and just make a check or sign—an "up" arrow for an uptrend and a "down" arrow for a downtrend, for example.

How often do you need to make an entry or update your journal? There are a couple of ways to look at this. First, do you normally trade for the long or short term? Do you trade slow moving markets, like oats, or speed demons, like the S & P 500? You should make an entry each time you "check" your markets. By this is meant, whenever you evaluate your current position or seriously consider entering or exiting a trade.

How, where or what format is best for a trading diary? We've seen all kinds that work, ranging from hieroglyphic notes scratched on a "Daytimer" by a day trader to an elaborate record maintained on a computerized wordprocessing program.

The what, when, where, and how of keeping a journal is a lot like the question of how long should a person's legs be? Long enough to reach the ground. Your journal should satisfy your needs. It is created only to help you trade more successfully. The worst thing it can become is a chore. If you find yourself dreading the thought of updating it, something is wrong.

Simplicity often makes diaries more meaningful. For example, let's say you receive a weekly charting service, which you update once or twice throughout the week. You could make your journal entries right on the charts as you are filling in the daily trading ranges. Then cut out the charts you use and put them in a three-ring binder. Once a trade is closed, record the results. Then page back through the chart pages and evaluate your performance. On the last page, write a two or three sentence summary. It can be as simple as that.

The key is making your diary simple, painless, and meaningful. Your objective is to learn how you pick a winner and how you can avoid losers.

Selecting a Trading Portfolio

As we mentioned earlier, we'll discuss some ways of overcoming common trading limitations. Your portfolio choice could help you compensate for a shortage of margin money or trading equity.

For example, the amount of margin money required to trade one futures contract varies by commodity. The various exchanges (Chicago Board of Trade, Chicago Mercantile Exchange, New York Futures Exchange, Coffee, Sugar, & Cocoa Exchange, etc.) set the margin requirements for each commodity traded on their exchange. The margin is set based on the size of the contract and the amount of price volatility of that specific market. It can range from a few hundred dollars to several thousand and can change dramatically depending on market conditions.

The purpose of margin money is simply to insure traders stand behind their trades. This is critical since the books on every trade are balanced every day.

Oats is the futures contract with a low margin requirement, usually less than $500 per contract. The Chicago Board of Trade contract specifies 5,000 bushels, and the price per bushel has ranged from less than $1 to just over $4 over the last decade. This calculates to a total contract value of $5,000 to $20,000. The price swings in this contract are usually small on a day-to-day and, even week-to-week, basis. It is a market with low price volatility.

Therefore, a trader who wishes to trade futures with a small amount of equity, let's say $2500, could do well to start with oats. One or two contracts could be traded at a time. It is always recommended to keep at least twice the margin money required in the trading account to cover unexpected price swings.

As an oats trader, what kind of return could you expect? What should your income goal be? Is it worth your while?

We have an in-house trading system, the Wasendorf Trading System. Over the last five years, for example, it has generated a simulated profit of $11,425 trading one contract of oats. This doesn't include a deduction for brokerage commissions and fees, which could vary widely. If you divided this gross simulated profit by five, you have $2,285 per year. To produce this profit, approximately seven trades were conducted each year. If you paid $125 for commissions and fees, you would still have netted over $1400 or about three times the margin money required and your $2500 equity would have increased by about 50 percent. Always keep in mind that whenever someone discusses past performance of a system, a CTA (Commodity Trading Advisor) or a broker, it is not necessarily indicative of future performance.

There were periods of time during that five-year period when our simulated performance record lost money. That's why whomever you trade with will require funds over and above the margin required by the FCM (Futures Commission Merchant).

A complaint we occasionally get about trading oats is that it's dull. If you only make five to ten trades a year, that's less than one per month. Additionally, three or four of these are routine rollovers. That's when you transfer your position from one contract that is expiring to one that is still trading. For example, you could roll over from the June oat contract to the September oat contract. You do this to stay in the most liquid or most heavily traded option. This is done so you can quickly fill an order if you need to—for example, when the trend changes against your position. You can then reverse your position—namely, go from long to short or short to long. Of course you could always choose to get out of the market, called "standing aside."

Choosing a Full Portfolio

One of the keys to selecting a full portfolio is diversifying your risk over as wide a spectrum as possible. The theory is both offensive and defensive. It's offensive in that it is designed to put you in the right place at the right time. By taking a position in several markets, you have a greater possibility of catching a major market move. No one—absolutely no one—can anticipate exactly when a given market will make its next big move up or down. Therefore, the more markets you are covering, the greater the chance you will be successful.

From a defensive stance, by spreading your investment capital over a wide variety of markets, you won't be caught in the wrong market at the wrong time or even the right market at the wrong time. Futures trading is a lot like fly fishing. You're constantly casting your line with the objective of making a big strike. If the trout don't hit, you reel your line in and try again. Futures traders let their profits run and cut losses short. A good, successful trading system, more often than not, has more losing trades than winners. The difference is the overall gain from the few winners exceeds the losses from the many losing trades.

Additionally, experience has taught us the different commodity groups are normally negatively correlated. That means they do not move up and down in unison. When one group is bullish, another is bearish and a third may be moving sideways. For example, if grains prices are high (bullish) and going higher, it puts pressure on livestock producers because it cuts their profit margin. More livestock are subsequently sent to market sooner and livestock prices become bearish, moving lower as the cash market is flooded with animals. Negative correlation can help you from getting caught with all your eggs in one basket.

Therefore, a diversified portfolio would look like this:

Grains:	Corn, oats, soybean oil
Meats:	Feeder cattle, live hogs
Food/Fiber:	Coffee, cotton, sugar
Metals:	Gold
Petroleum:	Crude oil, heating oil
Financials:	Japanese Yen, Dollar Index, Muni-Bond Index, S & P 500 Index

A fifteen-market portfolio, like the one outlined above, requires $40,000 to $50,000 in margin money under normal conditions. In times of extreme stress, such as the U.S.-Iraqi War (January, 1991), some of the margins in these markets were out of reach. During that conflict, crude oil and gold margins exceeded $20,000 each on a per contract basis. The exchanges and the Futures Commission Merchants (FCMs) raise margins during these periods of stress in an attempt to control volatility. The individual trader is often forced to stand aside certain markets because of the inflated margin requirements.

Stock Index Portfolios

Here's another example of how to select which markets you should trade. Let's say you have a decent size stock portfolio or a lot of experience trading stocks. You decide to get involved in the futures market by trading the stock indexes.

To begin with, you have four choices when you decide to trade the stock indexes. Additionally, one of them, the S & P 500, has an option liquid enough for the average trader to utilize. The other three indexes are the Major Market Index (MMI), the NYSE Composite, and the Value Line. It is very important to understand the composition of these indexes in order to attempt to predict how they will react to changing market conditions. Three of them have a broad base of stocks, while the fourth contains only twenty. See Figure 6.1.

You can see from the table above that the Value Line is the broadest based index. It includes both blue-chip and smaller capitalized stocks. About 80 percent are on the NYSE, 14 percent are over the counter (OTC), and 6 percent are from the Amex.

On the opposite side of the spectrum is the MMI. It includes only blue-chip stocks, 85 percent of which are also part of the Dow Jones Index. Therefore, it would be the futures stock index contract that most closely tracks the Dow.

Figure 6.1

Index Composition

S & P 500:	500 stocks, mostly NYSE issues
NYSE Comp:	All NYSE common stocks
Value Line:	Approximately 1650, NYSE, Amex & OTC stocks
MMI:	20 blue-chip, of which 17 are on DJIA

Do the blue chippers perform differently than their little brothers and sisters? Yes, blue–chip stocks usually lead the rest of the market when a bull move begins. Once a bull stampede starts, individual investors rush to buy "under valued" secondary issues that are still affordable. This segment of the market then catches up with the blue-chip segment, as institutional buyers seek out bargains among the lesser issues.

As a major bull move exhausts itself, the prices of the blue chips are traditionally the first to level off. Unfortunately, the prices of the less capitalized stocks often continue to surge. This is where the small investor is just getting into the market and is often the one hurt since it is so late in the move. They end up holding inflated stock as the market moves sideways or down.

The activity of institutional buyers is usually a harbinger of what to expect. Just as their buying of the blue-chip stocks often foretell a bull move, their movement from stocks to cash instruments may warn of a bear market ahead. This lack of confidence in the overall stock market causes a flight to quality; thus, the blue-chip stocks tend to hold their price level longer in bear rallies.

Bull, Bear, Sideways Market

This strategy puts you in the position of deciding whether the next move of the Dow will be to 4,500 or 750. You must also accurately predict what stage of the current move you are in and what to use as an indicator.

Since the MMI most resembles the Dow, it would make sense to go long the MMI at the early stages of a bull or short it just before a bear move. Once the move is well underway, you might want to trade one or more of the other more broadly based indexes.

Since the S & P 500 has a liquid option, you could buy a call at the same time you go long the MMI. Once the small stocks caught up with the blue-chips, you would exercise that option or take profits on it.

A Spreading Strategy

Another alternative would be to spread the MMI against one of the other indexes. A spread is when you simultaneously buy and sell in the same or related markets. This strategy is covered in more detail later in this book. This strategy allows you to take advantage of expected changes, yet you do not have to predict accurately the overall market direction. You are basing your decision on the strength of one contract compared to another or the strength of the blue-chip stocks relative to that of the broader based issues.

This approach may give you more protection in very volatile markets, than taking an outright long or short position. You sell the weaker contract and buy the stronger. Regardless of the overall trend, you can win.

Risk Consideration

There are no risk-free futures trading strategies, including spreads. If for example, your analysis of which contract is stronger is incorrect, the spread moves against you. But, you can close out the unprofitable leg and hold the profitable one. The move must be large enough for you to recover what you lose on the unprofitable side and pay your transaction costs.

What if the markets move only slightly or sideways? If there's no change in the spread between the two contracts, you still must pay transaction costs.

Also, keep in mind that the NYSE Composite and the S & P 500 settle in cash at the opening value on the last trading day, while the MMI and Value Line settle in cash at the closing value. If you're holding a MMI-NYSE Composite spread until expiration, at the opening of the last trading day you would be holding an outright position in the MMI until closing. This might be risky considering expiration day volatility.

The Evolution of Program Trading

Program trading of the stock market can really impact the volatility of the stock indexes. Therefore, we'd like to briefly review how it all got started and its current impact.

By 1960, block trading of stocks had become common. These are characterized as trades of 10,000 or more shares at one time. In the beginning, only one security at a time was block traded. It wasn't until the mid-1970s that block trading occurred in a variety of stocks at one time.

In 1974, the ERISA law was enacted requiring pension fund managers to use "skill, prudence and diligence" to minimize risk. This is sometimes referred to as the "prudent investor" or "prudent expert" legislation.

Like most regulations, it requires managers to "prove" they are being prudent, as well as actually being prudent. How do you prove prudence? You don't put all your eggs in the same basket—you diversify! This led to the first highly diversified index funds which attempt to mimic the performance of the S & P 500 or the NYSE Composite Index.

Enormous amounts of money were flowing into mutual funds at this time. Portfolio managers had to devise a method of moving quickly and efficiently from cash to equities and back, depending on the daily influx of cash and redemptions.

"May Day"

May 1, 1975, brought the end to fixed brokerage fee schedules. Portfolio managers were now free to negotiate commissions. This led to the trading of packages of stocks because the portfolio's performance was now less affected by transaction costs. Brokers were more than willing to provide volume discount packages. When you could hardly move a block of 5,000 shares in 1965, trades of 10,000 shares make up over a half of today's volume on the NYSE. Back then brokers tried to disguise volumes of trades—now they flaunt it. All this impacts volatility.

Five basic portfolio-level trading packages were developed by the major brokerage firms. These are usually referred to as the agency package, open-hand, blind bid, blind-blind bid and incentive trade packages. The cost per share traded ranges from a few cents to a few dollars. The wide range reflects the amount of risk the broker assumes in the trade.

For example, the highest commissions are paid when a brokerage firm is required to guarantee the price in advance. This is done even when the individual stocks and timing of delivery are not identified to the broker. The broker is given a general description of the types of stocks to be traded.

How does a brokerage firm handle the risk of a blind-bid package? This is where the futures and options on futures comes into play. In 1982, index futures became available and a year later index options. This allows the brokerage firm to hedge the transaction. If the package or program trade resembles the S & P 500 and the client is selling, the brokerage firm goes long the S & P 500. Between them, they are neutral or flat the market. When the trade actually takes place, both legs of the hedge are offset. The brokerage fee naturally includes the cost of the hedge.

On the opposite spectrum are portfolio-level trades where the brokerage firm assumes no risk. It simply agrees to handle the transaction whenever the client decides to do it, offering no price guarantee. This is the agency package. The three packages in between include various methods of sharing the risk and rewards between broker and client.

"The Impact"

How does program trading affect you as a futures trader? The most obvious answer is the volatility of the stock market and its related impact on the futures index markets.

A study conducted by the NYSE indicated that the impact of a typical program trading market order was 0.2 percent. This equates to a 6-point move when the Dow Jones is at 3000. But these program trades usually hit the market in waves of two, three, four or even ten at a time. If the average trade is nearly 200 stocks worth $10 million, what's the impact of four of these in a 10- or 15-minute time period? And, the typical trade can double in size, if it is the result of some negative news. That's where some of the 50-point down days come from.

If we look at the NYSE from a longer range perspective, we see a pattern of increased volatility. Between 1983-85, prior to wide-spread use of index arbitrage, or spreading, volatility exceeded 2 percent on thirteen days. In the 1986-88 period, 2 percent volatility days were up to eighty-seven. During the same periods, 3 percent volatility days increased from one to twenty-six and 4 percent volatility days went from zero to fourteen.

Manage the Volatility

There are several important people working hard to curb some of the trading practices that increase volatility. But the movers and shakers of the exchanges are dragging their feet. The portfolio managers are trapped by their success. They have no other way of trading their huge blocks of stocks.

Therefore, you must learn to protect yourself from the risk of increased volatility in the stock market and the index futures markets. The use of trading stops or options as stops can help. Holding an uncovered position, on the other hand, can entail major risk. Now, we'll move from a discussion of your portfolio to the development of trading strategies.

CHAPTER 7

SELECTING THE TRADING STRATEGY THAT SUITS YOUR APPROACH TO THE MARKETS

Key Concepts

➤ The basic concepts of options-on-futures trading, a predefined risk strategy.

➤ Using the 4 major types of spreads, plus straddles and strangles.

➤ Calculating the value of options, breakeven and delta factors.

Before you can complete your trading plan, we need to review some of the basic trading strategies. The most common is simply taking long or short positions in either the futures or options markets. If your analysis indicates the futures contract you are interested in is or going to trend high, you go long. This means you contingently agree to deliver whatever the futures contract calls for (See Appendix 5 for contract specifications) on the date the contract expires at the price specified when your future order is filled.

For example, a June Chicago-Board-of-Trade corn contract calls for the delivery of 5,000 bushels of number 2 corn. Number 2 is the grade which specifies the quality (moisture content, cleanliness, etc.). Let's say your fill price is $2 per bushel or $10,000 total value of the contract.

As mentioned earlier, only a small percentage (2-3 percent) of contracts are actually taken to delivery. Most are offset by taking an equal and opposite position to the one already established.

Therefore, if you "own" (long) 5,000 bushels of corn at $2 per bushel and you sell it (go short to offset your long position) thirty days later at $2, you make 50 cents per bushel or $2,500 for the 5,000-bushel contract, less brokerage commission and fees. If, on the other hand, the market goes against your position and you have to sell at $1, you lose 50 cents per bushel or $2,500, plus the transaction costs. This is a sample of the risk and reward of futures trading.

You could have just as easily taken the opposite side of the trade described above, if you felt corn prices were trending downward. In this case, you would have initially sold (gone short) a futures contract for corn and then later bought it back (offset). When you are short, you're contingently agreeing to accept delivery of a commodity at a given price by a given date. The lower prices go, the more profit you make when you "buy it back at a lower price" (offset).

Option Strategies

Option trading strategies are basically similar to futures strategies, but a call option replaces a long future position and a put replaces a short. Investors, who are new to the futures markets, often start with options because the maximum risk can be defined in advance, while the risk of trading futures is not. It may help to review some of the basic concepts regarding exchange traded options at this time. You may want to incorporate them as part of your trading plan, and it could make a difference in the broker you select to execute your trading orders.

Some Basic Options Concepts

The buyers (sometimes called holders, takers, or longs) of options have the right, but not the obligation to receive a position in the underlying commodity futures contract at a predetermined price (strike price) on or before specific date (expiration date). Unlike a futures contract, which requires the purchase or sale of a commodity if held to maturity, the buyers of options may elect to let the options expire without exercising its rights.

When an underlying commodity increases in value, the premium of the option on that commodity usually increases in value at the same time. Option traders, just like futures traders, can then close out their positions by taking equal and opposite positions. If the options have increased enough in value, the traders will make a profit. If not, they can close out their positions at break even or a loss.

The buyers of options even have a third option which is to exercise the options. This means the buyers convert their option to futures contracts and assume the risk of holding the futures positions.

This defines the rights and opportunities of the buyers of an option. They pay a premium (plus commission and exchange fees) and can take one of the three actions described above. Their risk is limited to the total amount that they initially invest in the options, while the profit potential of the options and the underlying commodity futures contract is unlimited.

Puts and Calls

The two types of options are the "put" and the "call." A call option gives the purchaser the right to acquire a long position in a futures contract at the strike price on or before the option's expiration date. Call premiums typically increase as the futures price increases thus benefiting the call buyer. Calls can also be employed for protection against rising prices. To remember the term "call," you should associate the action of calling something to you. If you call, you'll want to own the commodity in the future because it is increasing in value.

A put option gives the option purchaser the right to acquire a short position in a futures contract. Put options are the type which may be most useful in seeking protection against declining prices because the premium of a put tends to increase in value as the futures price declines.

Rights vs. Writers

The term "right" refers to one of the primary differences between futures and options. With futures, an obligation is created for both the buyers and sellers. The buyers must be willing to take and the sellers must be willing to make delivery unless the positions are offset prior to delivery. In the case of options, unilateral obligation is placed on the "writers" (also referred to as sellers, givers or shorts) of the option—that is, only the option writers are obligated to perform. The buyers of the option may exercise the option, but they may also decide to abandon it, letting the options expire. In the event the options are exercised, the option writers must deliver the underlying futures positions.

In return for assuming these obligations, the writers of the options receive payment of the premiums from the buyers. The premiums must be paid in full, in cash, when the options are purchased. The buyers are paying for specific rights. The sellers agree to grant those rights and are paid for assuming the risks of offering options. To the writers, the premiums are the maximum profit available in the trade. In the case of writing call options, if the value of the options rises, the writer may have to deliver futures positions, or cover their short sale at a higher price, thus incurring a loss. If the value of the options decrease, the short sales are profitable; but, the value can only decrease to zero, thus placing a limit on profits.

The intrinsic value of a call option declines to zero when the price of the underlying futures contract falls to the strike price or below.

Covered and Uncovered Options

As in the futures market, for every buyer there must be a seller. In options trading, option sellers (writers) must be prepared to enter appropriate futures positions opposite to the option buyers, to accommodate buyers if the options are exercised. Option writers may be considered as "covered" or "uncovered." Call option writers are covered if they have long futures contract positions before writing calls. Put option writers are covered if they have short futures contract positions before writing puts. If either one of these covered options should be exercised, the writers would have the appropriate positions to deliver to the buyers of the options and would not have to acquire the position at the current, probably unfavorable, market prices.

Options that are not written against an existing position in underlying futures contracts are called uncovered options. If the adverse movement of the futures contract price is greater than the premium received, the writers of the contracts lose.

Therefore, you have four basic strategies to consider with options. You can

1.   Buy calls

2.   Buy puts

3.   Sell calls

4.   Sell puts

We don't recommend numbers 3 or 4 for the novice trader because of the unlimited risk. Alternative numbers 1 and 2 have the most manageable risk, since it can be calculated exactly in advance.

Options Provide Staying Power

Let's talk a little more about the strategic use of options. Perhaps the most salient difference between options and futures is staying power or the ability to withstand adverse market moves. With futures, both the buyer's and the seller's risk is theoretically unlimited, and each party is in jeopardy of the market moving against their position. Options, on the other hand, have a defined risk. The premium and transaction costs represent the total amount the buyer has at risk. If the options trader forfeits the options or lets them expire worthless, there is no further financial obligation. Due to this unique situation, the buyer is not required to provide margin or face the potential of margin calls regardless of where the underlying futures price moves during the life of the option. No matter how far the trade moves against the position, the buyer can hold the option in anticipation of an eventual turn around in the market that will make his position profitable.

The Premium

Who determines the amount of this payment? Options are traded in an auction type environment (similar to futures) at a registered exchange, with bids and offers made by open outcry. There are, however, some guidelines for determining the option pricing models which mathematically calculate the theoretical value of an option; in addition, computer software programs are also available.

The premium of an option is composed of its intrinsic value and its time value. Intrinsic value is the amount an option would be worth if it were to expire immediately. For example, if soybean futures were trading at $5.60 per bushel and your call option gave you the right to buy soybean futures at $5.25 per bushel, you would have an immediate 35-cent-per-bushel-profit and should be willing to pay at least 35 cents per bushel for that option. This call option with a strike price less than the market price is said to be "in-the-money."

A put option is "in-the-money" when its strike price is above the market price. Using the example above, the right to sell soybean futures at $5.95 per bushel is worth an immediate 35 cents per bushel profit, and this 35 cents is the intrinsic value of this put option.

A call option with a strike price above the current market price is said to be "out-of-the-money." The right to buy soybeans at $6 per bushel when they can be had on the open market for $5.60 per bushel is intrinsically worth nothing, but there may be a processor or soybean crusher (an inventory manager) who wants to assure himself the right to buy soybean futures at $6 in the event the market rallies higher than $5.60.

A future (or time) value may also be bid into the price of this option. There may be a producer who anticipates a sharp decline and wants to insure that he can later sell soybean futures at $5 per bushel even though they are at $5.60 per bushel now. When the strike price of a put is below the current market price, it is also out-of-the-money.

When the strike price of an option, put or call, is exactly at the current market price, it is said to be "at-the-money." With soybean futures at $5.60 per bushel, a $5.60 option still has no intrinsic value. But, there is a high probability that it will gain intrinsic value, given that only a small move in the market would be needed.

The Time Value

The second component that makes up the option premium is time value. Time value is somewhat less specific than intrinsic value. It is based entirely on the future expectations of price movements. By definition, the time value is the amount of the premium that exceeds intrinsic value. However, this definition hardly seems complete. To understand time value, some factors that contribute to the creation of this value should be explained.

In general, the more time until expiration, the greater the time value. Common sense would dictate that all else being equal, the right to buy something is worth more if you have a year to decide instead of only six weeks. The options buyer is asking the writer to pre-price his product regardless of future events. The writer must be paid for this risk—logically, a year's worth of risk costs more than six week's worth. See Figure 7.1.

Other Premium Price Determinants

Option premiums are also affected by short term interest rates—that is, higher rates may result in lower premiums. Options are competing with other instruments for the investment dollar. If the competition's rate of return is lower, options need not be priced as attractively, and premiums will be lower. It is further assumed that the required margin for options will be met using interest bearing instruments, so that there will be no loss of efficiency in the use of investment funds.

Volatility is probably the most obvious and least understood influence on option prices. While there may be many mathematical explanations for volatility, let us again rely on common sense. If soybean futures are at $5.60 per bushel, and

Figure 7.1

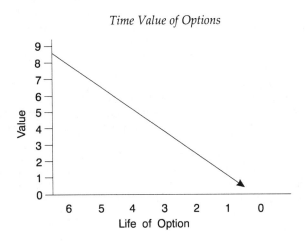

Time Value of Options

Options are wasting assets, because they eventually expire. Their time value continually deteriorates as they move toward their expiration date. To make money or conserve losses, you must offset or exercise options before they expire.

will remain at that price for a year, there is little risk in selling a $6 call option. But if soybean futures trade between $5.25 per bushel and $5.95 per bushel in the same week, there is significantly greater risk associated with the $6 call option.

Once again, the writer of the option must be paid for assuming the risk. The greater the likelihood that the option will trade through the strike price, thus increasing the chance of the buyer exercising the option, the higher the premium must be to accommodate the risk taken by the writer.

The common thread running through each of these components of time value is risk. Anything that increases the writer's risk will increase option premiums, regardless of the source of risk. Any time the amount of risk decreases, option premiums fall.

Price Interrelationships

As we mentioned briefly in Chapter 2, the delta factor is a measure of the change in the price of your option relative to a change in the price of the underlying futures contract. Let's say you have purchased a silver call because you expect the price of silver to rise. You know there is a relationship between what you paid for the option (the premium), the current price or premium being asked for that option, and the futures price of the contract on which you have an option (the underlying futures).

Can you expect a one to one relationship? If the futures price of silver increases 10 cents per ounce, will the premium of that option increase 10 cents?

Change in Option Premium Value Is
Less Than the Change in Futures Price

The delta factor addresses this question. Remember all the factors that impact the premium price: volatility of the markets, traders' expectations, the current price trends, amount of time until expiration of the option, the number of calls versus puts, and whether the option is "in" or "out-of-the-money." You'll learn through study of the options that the change in the option premium will represent only a fraction of the change in the price of the underlying commodity price. Logic dictates there should never be a higher demand for the option on a futures contract than there is for the futures contract itself.

How to Calculate Delta Factors

The delta factor is calculated by dividing the amount of price difference of your option by the amount of price difference in the underlying commodity. For example, if the price of your silver option increased by a nickel when the futures price of silver increased a dime, you would have a delta factor of .50 (.05 divided by .10

= 0.50). This means that you would expect your silver option to increase at half the rate of the futures.

A delta factor of .50 is common when an option is very close to being "in-the-money." The delta factor should never exceed 1. Therefore, the higher the delta factor is, the higher potential there is for profits as the underlying futures contract's price moves.

The opposite is also true. The higher the delta factor, the more expensive the option and the higher the loss can be for buyers. In futures and options trading, always consider the risk-reward ratio.

A low delta factor means that there is less of a cause-and-effect relationship between the option and its underlying futures contract. For example, a delta factor of .20 would mean that, for every $1 increase in the value of futures contracts, the options premium would increase 20 cents.

How Do You Use Delta Factors?

The delta factor is a gauge to help you anticipate what options to buy and when to sell (or offset) the options you own. To begin with, let's say you're looking at three or four different options. You're trying to decide which one to purchase.

You start calculating the delta factors every day or every other day for a week or so. If an option has a very low delta factor, below .25, it may be "deep-out-of-the-money" or in some other way has lost its relationship with the underlying market. You should probably cross it off your list, unless you have a good reason for playing a long shot.

The Importance of Tracking Delta

As you track the delta factors of the other options, you notice one become stronger or outperforming the others. It is increasing in value faster than the others. This is one reason for considering this option.

It is definitely not the only reason. You must consider all the other elements that go into the calculation of the premium, which were mentioned earlier.

Later on, when you've held your option for awhile and have decided to offset it, you'll want to look at the delta factor from a different perspective. Is it getting stronger or weaker? Knowing the trend of the delta factor of your option can sometimes help you make selling decisions.

The Delta Factor as a Planning Tool

The delta factor can also be used as a planning tool. For example, you're considering buying a soybean call. You think between now and the middle of February bean futures will increase by $2 per bushel.

When you calculate the delta factor of the two options you are considering, the first one is .50 and the second one is .60. This means that if your price projection of $2 is correct, the value of the first option will increase by $1 and the second by $1.20. If the second option costs only 10 cents per bushel more, it is probably a better bargain—all other factors being equal—than the less expensive option.

Always keep in mind that delta factors are not stable. They change whenever the price of the option premium and the underlying futures change, which is almost constantly during trading hours. But these prices usually move in tandem, except when the option approaches expiration causing its time value to decay rapidly.

You cannot calculate a delta factor once or twice and expect it to be valid days or weeks later. Especially if your option is in a volatile market. Some traders calculate delta factors daily and then convert them to 3-, 4-, or 5-day moving averages. This smooths out the fluctuations, giving a better picture of the price activity.

If you have any additional questions about options, you might want to peruse Appendix 6, which answers the most common queries. Now that we've discussed the pros and cons of options, let's get back to our discussion of trading strategies.

Spreading Strategies

Spreading simply means trading both the long and short sides of a market at the same time. The spreader attempts to make a profit by anticipating the amount of change in the price movement between two futures contracts or options. The price differential between the two markets is the spread, thus the name.

There are various types of spreads. They can be described by market (exchange), commodity, or delivery month. You can trade "inter" or "intra" types of spreads or combinations of the two. Inter means between two different entities; intra means within the same entity. See Figure 7.2.

Figure 7.2

Spread Types

Long Corn/Short Wheat:	Intercommodity
Long CBOT Wheat/Short MN Wheat:	Intermarket/Exchange
Long July/Short Sept:	Interdelivery
Short CBOT Corn/Long CBOT Corn:	Intermarket/Exchange
Short July Corn/Long Sept Corn:	Intracommodity

Spreads can also be described as bull or bear spreads. A bull spread is usually long the nearby delivery month and short a more distant delivery month. The expectation of the bull spreader is that if the price of the commodity rises, the effect will be felt strongest by the closest delivery month. The bear spreader has the opposite opinion: if prices are destined to decline, the nearby month will be affected more severely.

Also popular for grain futures traders are the crush spreads and new crop/old crop spreads. The former is executed within the soybean complex by spreading soybeans against their products, soybean meal and soybean oil. The term "crush" is derived from the ancient process of crushing soybeans under high pressure to extract the oil. Since the soybean processor purchases soybeans and sells the oil and meal, a crush spread would be long soybeans and short soybean oil and meal. A reverse crush spread would be short soybeans and long both soybean oil and meal.

A new crop/old crop spread may also be described as an interseasonal spread. This type of spread would have one "leg" in one of the delivery months available to market a crop that has already been harvested, and the other "leg" a delivery month available to price the unharvested crop. This is a popular spread when opposing factors are affecting growing crops and crops in storage.

Option Spreading

Spreading opportunities in options are far more numerous than futures because spreading is available between a wide variety of strike prices and expiration dates besides market, commodity, and delivery/expiration date. An option spread is similar to a futures spread, consisting of a long and short position (a call and a put) in one option, with the call and put having either different strike prices or different expiration dates. Spreading can also be used by an investor to reduce the risk inherent in writing either a put or a call option.

Volatility Spreads

Volatility spreads are one of the simplest and most useful options spreads to learn and to use. The spread trader buys a put and a call at the same strike price. For example, let's say corn is trading at $2.52 per bushel. You buy a put and a call at a strike price near or in-the-money, at $2.50.

You do this with the expectation of the corn market becoming more volatile. For example, this situation can occur at the time of the release of an important crop report, such as *Planting Intentions*. You may not be sure if the report will be bearish or bullish, but you expect it to cause a lot of excitement—therefore, volatility!

If this happens, the premium value of both your options could increase. Or if the market takes off north (bullish), your call becomes more valuable. If it goes south, your put premium goes into the money. Your net position should improve.

If the impact of the report is already in the market with prices and volatility unchanged, you lose. You must then decide whether to hold your spread in hopes of future volatility or take your loss. A little added advantage of this spread is that the premium is usually lower than the sum of the premium costs of both a put and a call purchased separately. A put/call spread purchased at the same time at the same strike price is called a special double, and we will discuss it in more detail as a separate strategy.

Time Options

Another popular option spread is the time spread. It involves options with the same strike price but different expiration dates. The prime objective of a time spread is to take advantage of the tendency of the time value of an option to decline at a very rapid rate before finally disappearing just prior to expiration. Typically, a put or call with a nearer expiration date is sold (written), while a put or call with an expiration date that is more distant is purchased. The option sold and the option bought both have the same strike price.

The intent is to sell time. The more distant put or call loses its time value at a slower rate, which limits the risk of such a position by removing the potential for unlimited loss on sharp upside moves.

Price Influencers

The price of the underlying contract is the prime determinant of how much an option spread will profit. If the spread position is established by selling the nearby option and buying the more distant when both options are at the money, the spread will be profitable if the futures prices remain relatively constant. It will tend to lose money if the prices change.

The spread will be at its widest when the price of the futures contract is closest to the exercise price of the option. The spread will narrow as the price moves away from the exercise price in either direction.

Bull Spreads

Option spreads that consist of options having the same expiration dates but different exercise prices are called price spreads. If, for example, we study the silver market and decide that it is going higher, we would purchase a call.

For this example, let's say May silver is $5.50 an ounce and a $5 strike price call has a 43-cent premium, or $2,150. But we really don't want to take that much of a risk. Silver has been somewhat lackluster over the past few months. We feel that it is headed higher; however, we're not sure of the timing. On the other hand, we don't totally want to miss this opportunity.

An alternative would be to write a call with a higher exercise price. In this case, the March $5.50 silver call could be sold for about 14 cents or $700. The spread could be calculated as having a 29 cent debit. Such a spread is called a bull spread and the risk in the position is limited to the amount of the original debit.

Risk limitation does not occur without giving up opportunity. If the risk is limited, so is the profit potential. The maximum profit in a price spread is computed by subtracting the original debit from the difference between the exercise prices of the two options.

In our example, the debit or net premium cost is 29 cents and the difference between the exercise price is 50 cents. You are risking 29 cents to make 50 cents. At the March expiration, a price above $5.50 would peg both options at their intrinsic value. If the price of silver dropped below $5, both options would expire worthless and we would experience the maximum loss of 29 cents.

Bull Spread Rules

The rules concerning option bull spreads that you must keep in mind are as follows:

- A bull spread profits only when the spread widens.

- The maximum profit on the bull spread is the difference between the strike price minus the debit (the amount of the cost of the long side exceeds the proceeds of the short side).
- The maximum loss is the debit, the net premium paid.

Now let's discuss the bear side of spreads.

Bear Spreads

Basically, they are the opposite of bull spreads. We use them when we believe the market is about to plunge.

If you project a declining silver market, you could sell (write) the lower strike price option, e.g., $5 and buy the higher, $5.50. At the time the options expire, any price below $5 would cause both calls to expire worthless, allowing you to retain the premium of the option you wrote.

The maximum loss would occur at any price over $5.50 at expiration. The options would be at their extrinsic value, having only time value. The rules for bear option spreads are as follows:

- A bear spread profits when the spread narrows.

- The maximum profit on a bear spread is the credit (the amount the proceeds from the short side exceed the cost of the long position).

- The maximum loss on a bear spread position is the difference between the strike price less the credit.

Bull Time Spreads

Just as you can trade bullish or bearish price spreads, you can trade bullish or bearish time spreads. A bull time spread would involve buying a deferred month and selling the nearby month.

If on the other hand you were bearish, a bear time spread would entail buying the nearby expiration month and selling a deferred expiration month. For example, buy a July silver call option and sell an October silver call option. The rules cited earlier apply to bull and bear time spreads, as well as bull and bear price spreads.

Straddle Strategies

We will continue this discussion of spreads with a variation called the straddle. It is similar to a spread in that you trade both sides of the market at the same time, but there is a difference. A straddle is a type of spread that entails the purchase of a put and a call (called a long straddle) or the sale of a put and a call (called a short straddle).

Earlier we concentrated on bullish and bearish trading strategies. These are valuable tools when we know (or think we know) where the market is headed. What do we do when we think the market is going to take off, but we don't know which direction? Or even more puzzling, how can we trade a trendless market?

The answer is the straddle. The long straddle, like the volatility spread discussed earlier, is a trading strategy to take advantage of dramatic market moves, even when we're not sure of the direction.

The Long Straddle

In its simplest form, the long straddle involves the purchase of a put and a call that share the same expiration date and strike price. To be successful, a big market move must occur before the options expire.

Let's use the corn market as an example. The primary growing region is the Midwest. In this scenario, it has been in a drought for the past two years. As we head into the planting time, the subsoil moisture has not been replenished.

Last year the crop got by with a series of timely rains. Just enough rain occurred when it was desperately needed. The year before the farmers were not as lucky. What will happen this year?

The U.S. rarely has two down years of corn production in a row. Additionally, the price of corn is very sensitive. When supplies are scarce, the price skyrockets. When supplies are plentiful, the price plummets. When supplies are adequate, the price moves sideways.

This year we think one of two things is going to happen—either there will be plenty of rain or a drought. A full measure of rain will wash out prices. A drought will pop prices to new highs. How do you trade these fundamentals?

If we think the price range could be anywhere from a low of $1.40 to a high of over $3 per bushel, we might decide to use a long straddle. We'll buy a near-in-the-money put and call, at say, $2.40. See Table 7.1.

As you can see, the money is made with this strategy on the extremes. The more the market declines, the more valuable the put becomes. The opposite is true of the call. At some point before expiration, the savvy trader would abandon one leg and exercise the other. The point is you're in good shape to take advantage of a bull or bear run without knowing which will occur!

You lose, of course, if the market trades trendless from the time you enter until expiration of the options. The maximum you lose is the two premiums paid for the put(s) and call(s) and the associated transaction cost. The upside is theoretically unlimited. We say "theoretically" because all bull or bear markets eventually end.

Table 7.1

(In dollars)

Future Price	Call Price	Put Price	Total
1.40	(20.0)	80.0	60.0
1.60	(20.0)	60.0	40.0
1.80	(20.0)	40.0	20.0
2.00	(20.0)	20.0	0.00
2.20	(20.0)	0.00	(20.0)
2.40	(20.0)	(20.0)	(40.0) Max. Profit
2.60	0.00	(20.0)	(20.0)
2.80	20.0	(20.0)	0.00
3.00	40.0	(20.0)	20.0
3.20	60.0	(20.0)	40.0
3.40	80.0	(20.0)	60.0

The Short Straddle

The opposite trading strategy to the long straddle is the short straddle. Rather than going long a put and a call, you short or sell a put and a call. This is the ideal strategy to use when you think the market is going to be flat and lifeless for the duration of the options sold.

Let's use the same corn scenario described above, only we now think the rains will be normal, crop production normal, and the market will trend sideways until our options expire. Rather than buy a $2.40 call and a put, we sell them. See Table 7.2.

You find the short straddle attractive because it allows you to take advantage of the normal decline in an option's time value as it approaches expiration. In this case neither option is exercised, which means you retain the full premium on both sides. The danger is a serious price move, which could be very expensive.

As with all trading strategies, you begin with an analysis of the market. Always be prepared to adjust your position(s) whenever you discover that all or part of your underlying information has changed or is incorrect.

Table 7.2

(In dollars)

Future Price	Call Price	Put Price	Total
1.40	20.0	(80.0)	(60.0)
1.60	20.0	(60.0)	(40.0)
1.80	20.0	(40.0)	(20.0)
2.00	20.0	(20.0)	0.00
2.20	20.0	0.00	20.0
2.40	20.0	20.0	40.0 Max. Profit
2.60	0.00	20.0	20.0
2.80	(20.0)	20.0	0.00
3.00	(40.0)	20.0	(20.0)
3.20	(60.0)	20.0	(40.0)
3.40	(80.0)	20.0	(60.0)

Strangling the Market

The "strangle" is a type of straddle. It differs from the simple straddle we just discussed in that both legs do not share a common strike price and are out of the money. They are similar in the sense that you are trading both sides of the market and you can trade a long or a short strategy.

Another critical characteristic is different: the return curve. With the simple straddle, the maximum return was available at only one price point. Refer back to Tables 7.1 and 7.2. With the strangle, the maximum return is available at several price points. See Table 7.3 below.

Strangles also differ from straddles when it comes to the usual position taken by traders. The short strangles are more commonly used, where you'll usually find straddlers on the long side.

Why Use a Short Strangle?

The basic strategy is the same for the short strangle, as it is for the short straddle or the volatility spread. You seek a market that you expect to trade flat until the expiration of the options. The strangle strategy becomes particularly attractive if there is a history of unexpected volatility in the market you plan to trade, or

Table 7.3

Future Price	Call Price	Put Price	Combined Total
66	1500	($4500)	($3000)
68	1500	(2500)	(1000)
69	1500	(1500)	0
70	1500	(500)	1000
72	1500	1500	3000
73	1500	1500	3000
74	1500	1500	3000
76	(500)	1500	1000
77	(1500)	1500	0
78	(2500)	1500	(1000)
80	(4500)	1500	(3000)

perhaps some seasonal patterns that might come into play. The short strangle, because of the reasons mentioned earlier, insulates you more from this kind of threat than does the short straddle or volatility spread.

The short strangle finds favor with traders over the short straddle because it further reduces risk. To begin with, you are trading different strike prices and they are out of the money. Therefore, the underlying futures contract must move farther than with a short straddle, which has the same strike price and is in or near in the money, before someone will exercise one of the options you wrote.

As with most any futures strategies, less risk means less reward. This is true here since the premium for out of the money options is comparatively lower.

Let's use an example. Your analysis for this scenario indicates the bond market will be stable for the next six to nine months. Therefore, you enter a short strangle by selling a 74 out-of-the-money call and an out of the money put at 72. The underlying futures contract is trading near 73:00. To simplify this example, let's say both options have the same premium, $1,500. The premium you receive would then be $3,000, less any transaction costs. Table 7.3 demonstrates a variety of market price changes and their impact on your investment.

Notice how the maximum income to be gained has increased from one price point on the straddle table to three price points for this strangle–from the 72 put to the 74 call strike prices. Between these two points, both options are still out of the money. When both options expire out of the money, you retain the full premium. This, of course, is the maximum profit you could expect. If one of the legs of the strange expires in the money, then your profits diminish proportionally.

Futures prices can, at least theoretically, increase indefinitely and can decrease to zero. When prices move dramatically against one leg of the strangle, the option represented by that leg is likely to be exercised. This means you'd be assigned an equal and opposite position in the futures market. For example, if you are short a put, you will receive a long futures position if the option is exercised. Since the market is moving against you, it could quickly become expensive.

Calculating Breakeven

For this reason, strangle strategists often calculate their breakeven point. It is slightly different depending on the direction of the market. For example, if prices go over the call strike price, it is likely the short will be exercised. But, it is only when the loss exceeds the net premium received that you become a net loser. You can define the breakeven point by adding the call strike price to the net credit (premium received). Our 74 call strike plus the $3,000 premium, or 3:00 adds up to a 77:00 as breakeven.

The downside breakeven is determined by subtracting the premium from the put's strike price. Once this price is exceeded, you begin to lose money. In our example, you would reduce the 72 put by 3:00 which comes to 69:00.

The Long Strangle

Most of this section was devoted to the short strangle as opposed to the long strangle. Our reason is that a long strategy is rarely used. Everything mentioned about the short strangle is true for the long—only in reverse.

The Long Synthetic

Synthetic means artificial or not genuine. A synthetic element or material takes the place of one that naturally occurs. The most common example might be the invention of synthetic rubber and nylon developed during World War II, when rubber and silk were unavailable in the United States.

In options trading, you can use a strategy that utilizes options only, but creates the same effect as trading the underlying futures contract. The strategy is called the synthetic long or short. Let's talk about the long first.

You create a synthetic long futures position through the purchase of a call option and the sale of a put option, where the two legs of this position share a common strike price and expiration date. Just as the name implies (long), you must be strongly bullish on the direction you expect the market to head.

Here's an example. You do an analysis of the stock market. Your conclusion is that the Dow is headed much higher—you think nothing can stop it. Instead of taking a position in an underlying futures, like the Standard and Poor's 500, you opt to trade a synthetic long. This means you will buy a call and sell a put. For this example, the S & P 500 is trading at 350. We'll assume, for simplicity's sake, that the call and the put are in the money. It costs you two index points to buy the call and you are paid two index points for selling the put. Therefore, you break even, less the transaction costs.

You decide to hold the synthetic long position until expiration. If prices shoot up as you forecasted, the call gains value and the short expires worthless. You win on both by closing out or exercising the call and collecting the premium on the unexercised put.

What happens if prices drop? In this case, you lose double. Your call expires worthless causing you to lose the premium you paid, and the trader to whom you sold the short exercises it. You are required to deliver a short futures position that is in the money.

The third possibility is the market moves sideways. Here you break even, less transaction costs. You keep the two-point premium you received for selling the put and lose the two-point premium you paid for the call. Keep in mind that the transaction costs are doubled on this strategy, compared to just taking a futures position in the underlying futures. The Table 7.4 illustrates the three scenarios described.

Table 7.4

S & P Index	P/L Call	P/L Put	Combined	Futures
356	4	2	6	6
354	2	2	4	4
352	0	2	2	2
350	(2)	2	0	0
348	(2)	0	(2)	(2)
346	(2)	(2)	(4)	(4)
344	(2)	(4)	(6)	(6)
342	(2)	(6)	(8)	(8)

This table illustrates how the synthetic options position (row 3) mirrors the performance of a straight position (row 5) in the futures market. Negative numbers are in parentheses.

Now, both options do not have to be at the same strike price. If the call is in the money and the put is not, you have a deficit since the premium you receive for the put will not cover the call. On the other hand, if the put is in the money and the call is not, you'll have a credit. The only problem with this is that the underlying futures will have to move farther in order for your call to start making money.

Why Use This Strategy?

If this strategy doesn't make sense to you, then you understand an outright futures position would be more logical and the only thing this strategy does is double the amount of commissions that must be paid. If this is true, why would anyone even consider it?

You can use the long synthetic strategy to convert a long call or short put options position to a futures position with the same advantages and risk. Consider that you already have purchased a call option. After a time you decide the market is well supported, and you want to optimize your position by gaining the short put premium. Your resulting position would be a synthetic long.

The Synthetic Short

You can trade a synthetic short, just as you could a synthetic long. For the synthetic short, you buy the put and sell the call. Again, you should use the same strike price and expiration date. This strategy mimics taking a straight short position in the futures market.

The same risks mentioned for the long are experienced if the market goes against you. In this case, you are looking for a bearish price move. If prices go up instead of down, your call will be exercised and your put will expire worthless.

As in the futures market, you must always do your prognostications first. If you call the market correctly, you win the brass ring. If you are wrong, you pay the piper.

CHAPTER 8

USING ADVANCED
TRADING STRATEGIES

Key Concepts

▥➡ The function of the arbitrageur.

▥➡ How to trade futures and options as a team.

▥➡ The impact of hedging on the futures market.

▥➡ Learn the value of trading night markets.

▥➡ The fine art of day trading.

From time to time, special opportunities arise in the markets. You need special trading strategies to take advantage of them. As an added benefit, you may even be able to shelter yourself from some of the risks associated with futures trading by using one of these strategies. But never kid yourself, there is always financial risks associated with trading futures. The initial strategy we'll discuss is called arbitrage.

The Arbitrage Strategy

First, let's define the term "arbitrage." The definition that appears in the National Futures Association's *Glossary of Futures Terms* is as follows:

"Arbitrage—Simultaneous purchase of cash commodities or futures in one market against the sale of cash commodities or futures in the same or a different market to profit from a difference in price."

There is a similarity between arbitrage and spreading (which we have discussed).

The key word is "against." You purchase one position against another. These positions offset each other. Therefore, the risk—compared to holding either position outright—is less, sometimes nominal. If one side or "leg" goes up, the other side normally compensates by declining.

Profits are made from the changes that occur between the two positions. Your risk is not that one of the legs substantially moves against you. It is that no movement at all occurs. When this happens, the trade generally produces little or no profit, yet you are obligated to pay the transaction costs. Since you trade both sides of the market, the commissions and other fees can be twice a regular (one-sided) trade. On the other hand, margins can be less providing greater leverage.

Using Options to "Arb"

The trader who uses arbitrage is called an arbitrageur. The objective of this type of options trade is to find options trading outside fair market values. If an option is overpriced, naturally, you sell it. The opposite—buying underpriced options—is equally effective. But to be an arbitrageur, you do more. If you buy, you sell a similar position to offset the risk. And, if you sell, you buy at the same time.

Let's say you spot a corn call that is substantially underpriced. You buy it. This is essentially a bullish move. As an arbitrageur, you would not let yourself be exposed to the risk of holding a net long position. You would take a short position to balance the risk. Your profit becomes the amount at which the corn call is mispriced. In time, the call moves from an underpriced position to fair market value. That move is where the arbitrageur makes money.

The opposite works as well. An arbitrageur may short an overpriced call, taking a bearish stance. At the same time, he or she offsets the risk of a bull move by entering into an offsetting position on the other side of the market.

Market Purpose

Arbitrageurs serve as price policemen. They make sure that any price that gets out of line gets back in line. Arbitrageurs do this by constantly searching for prices that are over or undervalued. Then they pounce!

Their market activity bids up the prices that are too low and pushes down those that have become too high. Since these arbitrage transactions are for most practical purposes without serious risk, the return is usually low. Little pain, little gain. But arbitrageurs accept the low return because they have little at risk.

Theoretically, anyone who has access to the markets can make these types of trades. But, this is true only in theory. There are two problems. The first is the transaction costs. The return must exceed the cost of the two commissions and the other fees associated with the positions. Often the profit margin cannot withstand normal transaction costs.

Usually, only people who can make money in this game are trading companies or floor traders. They may have their own seat(s) on the exchange(s) and may trade in such large volume that their per transaction costs are low enough to make a profit on these trades. For example, precious metals dealers may arbitrage gold and silver or security dealers actively arbitrage the Treasury bond futures or option markets.

The second problem is the ability to spot accurately those contracts that are over or underpriced. To do this, you must have a reliable pricing model and be in position to act extremely fast. As with the problem involving transaction costs, the professional trader within a specific commodity complex has an edge.

The important point for you to understand is how arbitrage works to keep commodity prices at or near their fair market value. Without arbitrageurs, you could be subjected to unexplained price moves within the various market complexes.

Futures and Options Together

One strategy to consider is called "Trading Futures Against Profitable Options Positions." A scenario might help make this approach more clear. Let's say we believe the silver markets (spot, futures, options) have bottomed. We think silver will begin to stair-step higher over the next few months. From experience, we know that it won't move up on a flat 45-degree angle. We expect it to advance, retrace, advance, retrace, and so on, as do most developing bull markets.

What are the alternatives? We could go alternately long and short the futures markets trying to catch the moves. Or, try the same thing with puts and calls. Another option would be to take a long position in either futures or options and hold it for as long as we dare or until it becomes profitable enough.

Another alternative would be to trade futures against options. One way to do this is to buy a call in or near the money. As the market moves higher, the call increases in value. When the upwards price trend hits an area of resistance and gives a signal that it may retrace, we take a short position in the futures.

Now the key to successfully using this strategy is being ready to take one of three actions:

1. You must offset your short at break-even or near break-even if the retracement doesn't materialize. You might want to consider a tight stop depending on the volatility factor at the time of the trade.

2. You must be poised to offset your short when your retracement objective has been reached, fifty percent for example, an profits on the futures position. You continue to hold the call option.

3. You must be prepared to exercise your call option if the market violently moves limit up against your short position.

Action number one produces a profit on the short futures trade, and you still have the call option intact. If silver prices continue to increase after the retracement, the option becomes more profitable. If they don't, you have your futures profit to offset the cost of the option premium.

With the second action, you either break-even or lose a small amount on the futures side of the trade, perhaps the cost of the futures commission and a few cents per contract on the silver. But, you still have your profit in the call option.

The last action, either breaks even or loses a small amount on the futures side of the trade, perhaps the cost of the futures commission and a few cents per contract on the silver. But, you still have your profit in the call option.

The last action forces you to exercise your call option to offset the short futures position. This puts you out of the market. However, the price at which you bought the call was a lower price than the price at which you went short. The difference is your profit. This may or may not offset the commissions and fees paid to take these positions, depending on how much of a bull move occurred before you went short.

What is actually happening with this strategy is creating a spread position. The approach is to use a call for the long side and a futures contract for the short. The spread, by its very nature, helps manage the risk; it puts you on both sides of the market at the same time. If the market runs away in either direction, the unprofitable leg is lifted and the profitable leg held.

You need to be concerned if the market advances to the point where you think it will retrace and you put on the short, only to see the market trade sideways for a considerable period of time. If this occurs, you could exercise your call option offsetting the short. Hopefully, the profit already accumulated in the call position would be enough to pay both commissions and fees with a little left over for your piggybank.

Put & Call Team Trading

Previously, we discussed the use of options in conjunction with futures positions. Now we'll combine the use of a put and a call into a single, unified trading strategy.

Puts and calls can work well together. A put can be used to hedge or lock in a profit on a call and vice-versa. If an investor has a put and a call in the same market and the market drops, the put is exercised in order to protect the call's profit. But far more important, the put does not interfere with the calls' ability to further profit from a continuation of a bull move. The cost of this protection, without jeopardizing future profits, is still only the premium cost, commission and fees.

As a comparison, a futures long position profit can be locked in by using a short in another contract month which moves in a one-to-one linear relationship. When using futures to hedge futures (an intra-commodity spread), the premium cost of the option is saved, but no additional profits are possible regardless of how high or low the future ultimately trades. This strategy, as we discussed earlier, creates a neutral trading position, where you are holding equal and opposite positions in the same futures market.

A second advantage of the option-hedging concept is the use of a call to hedge a profitable put position. Should the market rise, the call can be profitably exercised. But even more important, if the bearish move continues unabated, additional profits can be generated from the put. The cost of this hedge is simply the premium cost and other transaction costs.

The Special Double

A very unique idea available to options traders is the "special double option," or sometimes just referred to as a "double option." This is a combination of a put option and a call option at a fixed strike price for future delivery at anytime prior to the expiration date. The premium cost of a double is usually close to, but slightly less than, the sum of the premium costs of both a put and a call purchased separately.

The only stipulation of the double option is that only one side of the double can be exercised, but both sides can be traded as many times as desired. All the trading techniques discussed earlier with regard to puts and calls will work equally well with either or both sides of the double. We are specifically referring to the use of an option to hedge another option, options as hedges on futures positions, and options in lieu of stop orders. The only restriction is that only one side may ultimately be declared or exercised.

Naturally, all of the advantages of regular puts and calls are available to the double options trader. These advantages include minimum and calculable risk exposure, tremendous leverage, unlimited profit potential, and freedom from margin calls.

One Big Extra

The double has one additional advantage which places it in a special category far and above other strategies. It frees the holder from his dependence on market direction predictions. The double option, being the combination of both a put and a call, can be profitable regardless of whether the market advances or declines. You may often find it easier to determine a market's volatility rather than the direction it is headed.

Just think about it for a minute. Let's say you notice your favorite commodity beginning to trade in a tight coil or triangle formation. The coil gets tighter and tighter. You know the commodity is poised for a breakout.

But will it go up or down? You're not really sure. All you know for sure is it can't trade much longer without committing itself. This is the opportunity you're looking for to trade a double.

You position yourself on both sides of the market. When the breakout occurs, you close out the losing side and ride the winning side to the next point of resistance. Then decide if you wish to take your profits or not.

Like any trading strategy, it is not without risks. For example, the breakout could fizzle. You could end up holding two worthless options. The key is correctly evaluating the degree of volatility.

If, instead, you had purchased a put only, you would be predicting the market was heading lower—except where the put is used in lieu of a stop to protect a new long position or to hedge a profitable long position. The put buyer is anticipating a substantial drop in price.

Simultaneously, the speculator who purchases a naked call, without the expectation of immediately being short, is anticipating a bull move.

The buyer of a double is looking for a major increase in volatility; but, s/he is not sure if the market will react bullishly or bearishly. Either way, the value of either the put or the call will increase. If the move is strong enough, it will offset all transaction costs and generate a profit.

To use this strategy, you need to be confident of a major increase in market volatility. If not, both your put and call are likely to expire worthless.

Hedging

As a trader, you need to be aware of the concept of hedging because hedgers can have a major impact on prices. Also, bona fide hedgers hold commodities with strong hands—giving you an indication where a market may be headed.

The National Futures Association's *Glossary of Futures Terms* defines hedging as follows:

"Hedging—The initiation of a position in a futures market that is intended as a temporary substitute for the sale or purchase of the actual commodity. The sale of the futures contracts in anticipation of the future sale of cash commodities as a protection against possible price declines or the purchase of futures purchases of cash commodities as a protection against the possibility of increasing costs."

Most traders hedge between cash and futures as a form of price protection.

If a farmer, for example, has 100,000 bushels of corn stored on his farmstead, he is de facto long corn. He actually has possession of the crop. If he thinks corn prices are going to do down, he can do one of three things:

- He can sell the corn on the open market before the price goes down.

- He can take 20-5,000 bushel short futures positions in the corn market. In this case he is selling 100,000 bushels of corn on the market. This makes him neutral—he owns 100,000 bushels of cash corn and has promised to deliver 100,000 bushels at a given price.

- The third alternative would be to buy twenty put options. When and if he decides to exercise these options, he would be neutral—both long (cash) and short (futures) 100,000 bushels of corn.

When evaluating these alternatives, the farmer must evaluate how strong his opinion is, and over how long a time frame he is doing his planning. If he thinks corn prices are going to plummet indefinitely, he should probably just sell the corn and have done with it, thus passing even the risk of storage and spoilage to someone else—the elevator or grain merchant.

If he is happy with his profit margin, the difference between his cost of production and the current futures price, he might find it in his best interest to execute a simple hedge: short the twenty futures positions and deliver the corn when the contract expires.

If his conviction regarding price is not iron clad and if he's not sure corn is going down for the count, he might want to consider the use of put options. They can give him the protection he needs with more flexibility and less cost.

For example, the cost of the puts depend on how near they are to being in the money. He may choose to buy twenty "cheap" out of the money options just to protect himself in case of a crashing bear market. Or, he might buy "in the money" put options with the hope of making some money when the price dip occurs, yet still have the protection of knowing he could exercise them if there is a serious price deterioration.

We use the example of a cash hedger because it is sometimes easier to understand. But this same strategy can be used to protect your futures positions as well.

Let's use a silver example. You go long silver in the futures market, rather than buying a call option. Basically, what you will be doing is reversing your futures and options positions.

As expected, silver makes a major bull move. Your futures position gains just over $1 per ounce, which brings you to an area of very strong resistance. You are confident that the price will go higher; but, you feel you should protect your gains.

What should you do? You could close out your long position and take our profits. This is the most conservative approach. When you think the bull move is about to resume, you could reestablish your long position. This now becomes a risk laden speculative trade. If the market corrects right after you get back in, you get whipsawed. We've seen times when this has happened repeatedly, and the trader gave back all his profits before the next bull leg was made.

A more prudent approach might be to establish a put as a hedge against your profitable futures position. If you bought a put "at the money," you could ride it down during the correction. Then you could sell it at a profit when the bull move began. It would protect your futures profits in case the next bull move never materialized. By exercising the option, you'd close out your futures position at the price level where you had a $1 plus gain. From this, you'd subtract the cost of the premium, commissions, and fees.

If your confidence level was very high that the bull move was going to resume after the retracement, you could calculate exactly what put to buy to breakeven on your futures position. This put would be "out of the money," and therefore, the premium would be lower. You could think of this as a deductible insurance policy.

It's cheaper, but you don't have full coverage. But you do have protection if you are completely wrong—a trading accident that "totals" your position! In the case where silver prices retreat substantially, your out of the money put gains value as it becomes an in the money put.

Puts as Stop Loss Orders

Another way of thinking about this strategy is that the put is, in actuality, a stop/loss order for your futures position. But it has more advantages than a simple stop/loss order. First, an option provides protection at a guaranteed price. You're not at the mercy of the stop/loss order fill.

Secondly, you have more flexibility in deciding when to exercise your option. A stop/loss order is activated when its price is hit, and usually, it becomes a market order. With an option, you can study the market longer before you pick the time you want to exercise it. You have more thinking time.

Lastly, the option gives protection from whipsawing markets. If, for example, your stop order is close to the market and the market makes a brief retracement before continuing its move, your stop could be hit. This would close out your position and your gains. The use of an option gives you more time to access the situation before you have to act.

Do You Want to Add the Night Markets to Your Trading Strategy?

Figure 8.1 graphically explains one of the strongest reasons any currency or stock index trader should give serious thought to the night markets. In late February

1989, the NIKKEI 225 (this is the Japanese equivalent of our S & P futures contract) dove out of the sun like a Zero on a U.S.M.C. Buffalo. The reason involved the tightening of the spread between the U.S. and the Japanese interest rates. Our rates moved higher as did theirs, but theirs moved at a faster pace. This caused their bond and stock market to tumble. The NIKKEI 225 eventually found support at the 33200 level.

Another example occurred in November 1989, when the Berlin Wall was breached. Remember all the TV coverage. The Deutschemark began a strong bull move that evening.

The point is simply this—half the world is working and trading while our markets are closed. In the example of the NIKKEI 225, the Yen gapped lower the next day. An 80-90 point gap, up or down, is not unusual for the Yen. With the Berlin Wall news, the D-Mark went up steadily for weeks. Trends (major moves) begin and end while our markets are closed.

This could be very expensive for you. For example, let's say you're trading a currency and something dramatic occurs after the market closes in the U.S. You don't have to spend a sleepless night waiting to enter or exit the market in the morning. All you need to do is get in touch with your broker. Then adjust your position at the evening session.

Figure 8.1

NIKKEI

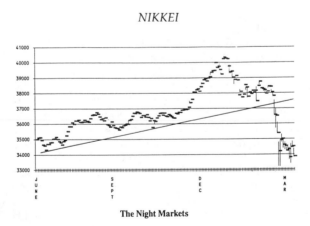

The Night Markets

The Night Markets

Major trend changes can begin while U.S. exchanges are closed. This is very common in the foreign exchange markets. When selecting a broker and developing a trading strategy, you may need to take the "night markets" into consideration.

What Markets Are Available?

Besides the NIKKEI 225, which is traded on the Singapore Exchange from 6:00-9:30 p.m. and 10:30 p.m.-1:00 a.m. CST, you can trade gold, silver D-Mark, Swiss Franc, Japanese Yen, British Pound, and Australian Dollars on Forex. These trade from 2:00 p.m.-7:00 a.m. CST. Don't forget the evening session on the Chicago Board of Trade. You can trade T-Bonds and T-Notes. The hours are 6:00-9:30 p.m. CST.

Whenever you're trading foreign markets, do not neglect to take into consideration the ever changing relationship between the currencies. The tick value of the NIKKEI, for example, is about $4. But, it changes daily depending on the trading activity in the Yen.

This means that it is prudent to use stops. We recommend stops at all times; but, they are twice as important for the night markets.

What about fills, liquidity, and margins? These are not substantially different at night. Fills are just as fast, sometimes even a little faster, at night. The margin for the NIKKEI is usually less than for the S & P. Liquidity is not usually a problem, but that doesn't mean it won't be at some time. Check with your broker.

This discussion of trading strategies is by no means inclusive. All we wanted to do is provide you with an insight into the various options you have, so you can develop your trading plan.

Day Trading

One last alternative strategy to consider is day trading.

This simply means entering and exiting a position during the same trading session. You don't carry any positions overnight or into the next trading session. You get in and out of trades within a single trading session.

Why have traders been cautioned to avoid this type of trading? We think the reason goes back to the old bucket shops of the 1920s and '30s. These were the times before electronic transfer of price quotes (telegraph messages being the exception). In those days, the response time between the trader in the trading parlor and the pits was considerable. You couldn't get tick-by-tick quotes, nor could you telephone a trading desk on the floor. Now you can do both.

Probably an even more important question is why should you even consider it at all. First, the profit motive is valid. You should day trade only if you think you can make money at it.

But there are other reasons as well. In one sense, you reduce risk by not carrying positions overnight. Lately, we've seen an awful lot happening while our markets are closed. Think about what happened to crude oil when the Iraqi-Kuwait war broke out. Anyone who was short crude the morning after the invasion began sure wished they had been day trading the day before. It was the same for those currency traders holding positions when the Berlin Wall was torn down. Events can happen overnight which cause markets to move violently on the following day's open. That's life in the pits. Day traders are unaffected.

Another plus for day trading is that it usually requires lower margins. This makes your money work even more efficiently.

When you are a bona fide day trader, you can simplify your analysis. Fundamental factors are mostly meaningless. You can forget about them. All the technical approaches geared to determining long or intermediate term trends are irrelevant; you only need short term analysis.

Each day is the beginning of the rest of your trading life. You start out when the markets open with a clean slate. Yesterday's problems no longer exist.

The biggest benefit of intraday trading, in our opinion, is the discipline it forces on you. The entire trading cycle—research, trade selection, entry-exit point determination, execution, etc.—takes place in a matter of hours. More importantly, you go through this routine every day, over and over. You have to become organized. There's no time to procrastinate.

Before you call your broker to start a day trading program, there are some drawbacks. The first is the amount of commission generated. You could be trading one lots and have three or four trades in a single session. Also, you need a good source for tick-by-tick price activity. This could easily run $300 or $400 per month, including exchange fees. Then there is the time involved. You should be in front of your quote screen whenever you're in the market. This could be several hours per trading day. If all this weren't enough, there's the normal high risk associated with futures trading. Something you must take seriously.

Day Trading the S & P 500

To give you a better idea of how all this meshes together, we asked Paul Lovegren, a senior futures trader, for his rules for intraday trading the S & P 500. The fact that he had written a set of rules immediately available reinforced the importance of discipline. Let's walk through his list.

1. Select a market with sufficient volume to permit day trading, the S & P in this case.

2. The market selected must have enough daily volatility to offer profit opportunities.

3. Cover your downside risk. A put and a call are held permanently for each unit to be day traded. This is insurance against limit up or limit down days. These options positions can be exercised to exit any position in which you become trapped.

4. Roll options positions when they begin to approach expiration, so you don't suffer total loss due to time decay.

5. Always have a strategy planning session with your broker well before you start trading. During this session, agree on what you both expect the trading range will be for the day. Then decide exactly what you plan to do—for example, get in at the opening, wait until a specific support or resistance level is reached, and react to a given price formation.

6. If your expectations are totally incorrect, avoid that session and start planning for the next one.

7. Always trade with trailing stops and continually adjust them as necessary.

8. Don't enter the market late in the trading session, after 3:30 EST on the S & P, because the market is thin and volatile.

9. Have a definite system to identify the short term trends and your entry and exit points.

10. Be psychologically prepared to reverse your position when the trend moves against your position or a pivot point is hit.

11. Have a cut off point for profits and losses. For example, Paul quits after he makes $1,000 per position during a session. This keeps him from over trading. He also quits after he has two or three losers in a row.

12. Know your break-even to the penny, including commissions.

13. Use quote equipment, or be sure your broker has one, that allows you to access a wide variety of studies, like five-minute RSI, stochastics, premium calculations, moving average bands, trend lines, directional movement, equivolume, Japanese candlesticks, etc.

14. Be geared to making decisions immediately. You don't have time to dilly-dally. If the market goes against you, get out. If your entry point is hit, get in.

Your objective is to make money. Always keep that upper most in your mind. Forget about your ego. Think dollars and think fast. The speed of this type of trading instills the discipline for position trading at some later time. Additionally, all the planning, coordinating and organizing required to day trade is also what is necessary however you trade. That's why we think day trading can build your discipline to new levels, which can help any kind of trading you do. On the other hand, it is not a strategy for the novice trader. Wait and use it after you become very familiar with a market.

CHAPTER 9

PLACING TRADES AND WORKING WITH A BROKER

Key Concepts

⟾ Specific skills mastered.

⟾ A broker needs to be chosen.

⟾ Account papers understood and completed.

⟾ And, a written plan should be prepared.

To implement your trading plan, you need to be able to communicate concisely with your broker. To do this, a firm understanding of the types of orders used in commodity trading is a must. Here's an explanation of the most often used ones.

Market Orders

When the average trader thinks about placing an order in the futures market, he seldom gives much consideration to the type of order that would be most effective in achieving his objective. He just calls his broker and tells him or her to buy this or sell that. In most instances, it is a market order that is issued.

Market orders are orders to buy or sell at the current price as quickly as possible. In the trading pits, they are the first orders to be executed because they can be filled at any price. You use them when you want to get into or out of the market quickly. You're trying to catch a move, and you don't want anything to slow you down. There are no contingencies placed on the order.

When you get the fill back, it may or may not be close to the market price when you placed the order. If the market is on fire, there may be a substantial difference. With orderly markets, it may be right on the money.

When you place a market order, you pass the responsibility to the floor brokers to fill the order as best they can. These brokers are governed by CFTC (Commodity Futures Trading Commission) and exchange rules to give you the best possible service. And, they do. But you don't have any control over the market. You never do. When markets are trading choppy with a lot of volatility and low volume, you may not want to use a market order—you don't know when or at what price you will be filled.

Stop Orders

In special situations, you may want to use stop orders. You place buy stops above the market, if you are bullish on prices. Or sell stops below the market, if you are bearish.

Stop orders become market orders when the price trades, or is bid, at or better than the stop price. What you're trying to do is catch a move, just as prices break out of a trading range or an area of congestion. Once your stop orders become market orders, you take on all the risk of a regular market order. Namely, you may or may not get a fill with which you are satisfied.

For example, prices could spike up or down to hit your stop and then move against you. By the time your order gets filled, it's way above or below the price you were hoping for. That's the risk of market orders.

Stop orders are often used to close out or protect profitable positions. They are called trailing stops, and we highly recommend their use. As your long futures or call options-on-futures positions gain value, you place sell stops just below your positions. You continuously move it up as your trade becomes more profitable. If the market moves against you, your sell stops are hit. They become market orders and you offset your positions. This is referred to as being "stopped out of the market."

You can do just the opposite with buy stops, if you are short futures or holding puts. Just place your stop orders above your positions. You wait for the market to "pick off your stops" and close your positions—hopefully at a profit.

Placing the stop takes some skill and experience. If you place it too close to your position, a slight move in the wrong direction and you're prematurely out of the market. If you put it too far from your position, you can give up too much of your profit before it is hit.

To select the right position for your stop, you need to get a handle on volume and volatility. What have the daily trading ranges been recently? Is the volume high enough to smooth out the markets?

MIT Orders

The opposite of stop orders are the MIT (Market If Touched) orders. These are sometimes referred to as board orders and possess two of the characteristics of stop orders:

• They are activated when their price is hit.

• Once hit, they become market orders.

The difference is that buy MIT orders are placed below the current market price. (Remember, buy stops are placed above the current price.) Sell MIT orders go above the current price. (Sell stops go below the current price.) MIT orders can be used to establish new positions or close out existing ones. MIT orders are not allowed on the Chicago Board of Trade, but can be used on the Chicago Mercantile Exchange and other exchanges. You need to check the exchange rules before you make your decision to use them.

Limit Orders

If you don't like being left to the mercy of the market when your stop or MIT order becomes a market order, you can use a limit order (sometimes called price orders). These are orders that are used to buy or sell at specific price levels.

Buy limit orders are placed below the going market price. They can only be filled at or below the limit price. Sell limit orders are placed above the current market price and can only be filled on, at, or above the limit price.

Keep in mind when you use any order, other than a straight market order, they have a lower priority. This means that market orders get filled first. In fast moving markets, you may not get filled at all. Or the market may not move to a point where your stop, MIT or limit contingency allows your order to be filled. This may keep you out of the market—which may or may not be a good thing.

Stop Limit Orders

A variation on limit orders are stop limit orders. Buy stop limit orders are activated when the futures contract trades or is bid at or above the stop level. But these orders cannot be filled unless the price level subsequently stays at or moves below the limit level. Sell stop limit orders are activated when the commodity is offered or trades at or below the stop level. These orders are not filled unless the price subsequently remains at or moves above the limit level.

Now, the stop price and the limit price need not be at the same price level. For example, and order might state: "Buy 90:16 stop 90:20 limit." This order would be activated when the price hit 90:16, but would only be filled if the price remained below 90:20.

Stop limit orders are sometimes used to give protection in fast moving markets. They let you place orders within price ranges.

Time Limit Orders

Besides putting conditions on the price of your orders, you can also put time restrictions on when your orders can be executed. These contingencies tell the floor brokers when your orders are to be activated.

Kill or Fill (KOF) is an example. These orders must be filled immediately or they are canceled. Traders use them when they spot a trading opportunity. But since they are not market orders, they do not have top priority. On the other hand, floor traders try to accommodate these orders.

Another common type of time limit order deals with placing your orders in the opening or closing trading range. "Market on Open" orders must be filled within the open range, just as "Market on Close" orders must be filled within the closing trading range.

You may want to place standing orders. These are called "Good Till Canceled" (GTC). Theoretically, these orders will stay in the market until filled. You risk the danger of losing track of these orders—only to have one filled just when the market turns against you. We do not recommend GTC orders under normal conditions.

Another type of time limited order lets one order replace another. These are called "One Cancels Other" (OCO) orders, where a new order replaces one already in the market.

Priority of Orders

Floor brokers in the trading pits fill the order they have in their books in the following order of priority:

- Market Orders

- Stop

- Limit

- Limit—Price, Stop, Time. Also, keep in mind that all orders are assumed to be day orders unless otherwise specified. Therefore, if your order is not filled during a trading session, you would have to reenter it when the next trading session begins. Some markets, bonds for example, have two trading sessions each day. Orders entered in the day session may not automatically carried over to that evening's session, depending on your FCM's trading rules. You may have to reenter your orders in the evening session if that's what you wish to do. Or, reenter your orders in the next day's trading session.

"Good Till Canceled" or "Open" orders do not always do what the name implies. Many exchanges will not accept them. If an order is not filled during a session, it becomes an "unabled." An unabled order is simply one that cannot be filled during a specific trading session or within the given price/time limit.

Your orders may also be characterized as "out of range." This means that the orders are out of the normal trading range for that commodity. The trading range reflects the daily trading limit. For example, the daily trading limit for corn is 10 cents per bushel. If your order is more than 10 cents above or below the opening price, it would be out of range. Most exchanges will not accept out of range orders. With options on futures, there are no daily price limits.

Take note also that grain orders use a different nomenclature than other futures contract. Grain orders must be stated in thousands of bushels, rather than numbers of contracts. For example, if you'd like to buy ten corn contracts, you'd tell your broker to "go long 50 corn." Since corn trades in 5,000 bushel contracts on the major exchanges, you would be long ten corn contracts. When you decided to offset this position, if you placed an order to go short ten corn, you only offset two of your ten contracts. You still would be long eight contracts. This could be a very expensive error.

The Mid America Exchange in Chicago trades "mini" contracts in many commodities. For example, the mini corn contract is for 1,000 bushels of corn, rather than 5,000. This is another important alternative the novice trader should consider.

Rely on Your Broker

It pays to find a knowledgeable broker with a strong order desk behind him or her. This way you can explain in plain English exactly what you wish to do and let the broker convert it to the trade jargon. For example, you can place what amounts to "Good Till Cancel" or out of range orders with your broker. The broker, and his order desk, tracks them for you and puts them in the market each day until you get a fill, or when they are within range. Your broker should also constantly review your positions with you, so none get entered without your knowledge. This way you won't lost track of a GTC order or get an unexpected and unwanted fill.

Develop a Written Trading Plan

At this point, we strongly recommend you prepare a written trading plan. It doesn't have to be formal or extensive, but it should answer the following questions:

Trading Plan Checklist

1.   Am I psychologically and financially suited to trade in the futures markets?

2.   What are my goals?

3.   What are my limitations?

4.   How will I keep a trading diary?

5.   Will I trade futures, options on futures or both?

6.   What commodities and contracts will I trade?

7.   How will I do my analysis?

8.   What trading system will I use?

9.   Do I have hard and fast money management rules?

10.   What trading strategies will I use?

11.   What type of orders do I plan to use?

12.   What do I need from my broker?

Once you have answers to these questions—again, we strongly recommend putting them in writing because it clarifies thinking—you're ready to begin the broker selection process.

Selecting a Broker

To begin with, there are professional commodity brokers, and there are futures order takers. You must decide which you need. This also determines whether you trade through a discount or full service brokerage company.

The per trade cost at a discounter ranges between $20 and $35. In most cases, the trader places a toll-free telephone call to the order desk at the discounter headquarters. An order clerk takes the order and relays it to the order desk at the appropriate exchange.

To utilize this type of service, you need a lot of experience. The order clerk is not in a position to assist you in choosing or evaluating a trade. Their function is strictly to execute orders. In most cases, they will not even provide current price quotes or other information—like highs, lows, trading ranges, trends, market news, etc.—you may want at the time you are placing your order. This discount cost matches the service, as a general rule.

Discounters serve full-time traders who have the time and money to generate all the information they need to trade. Full service firms are set up to work in tandem with both experienced and inexperienced traders who need assistance in gathering and interpreting information about the supply and demand situation of the commodities being traded.

How Do You Spot a "Good" Broker?

First off, the key word is "good." It means good for you, your trading style, your personality, and your needs. If you require no assistance in selecting trades, tracking them, money management, technical and fundamental information, order placement, exchange floor reports, etc., you should seriously consider using a discounter.

One of the best places to develop a list of what you want from a broker is to review your list of limitations. Your broker should become your partner; you make money together. The broker must earn his or her commissions.

There are at least four common limitations most individual traders must overcome. The first is time—time to follow the markets and to sort out the important information from the false rumors that clutters the pits. The second is the flow and cost of information available about the markets. As fast moving as the futures markets are, you often need tick-by-tick price quotation equipment. Additionally, you need immediate access to the wire services and other forms of news. Therefore, you require some expensive and sophisticated equipment, which most individuals cannot justify as part-time traders.

Next is the experience that only comes from trading the markets day after day, year after year, facing bull markets and bear rallies, spotting the major moves early, and avoiding getting whipsawed by false breakouts.

Last of all, there is just an enormous amount of background information you need at your fingertips to trade and avoid making expensive errors. You need to know all the specifications of the contracts you're trading, the hours the markets are open, what days they are closed, if they are closing early for some reason, how to place orders, when important government reports that will impact markets are to be released, what rumors are sweeping the exchanges—and it goes on and on.

To look at it from another perspective, here are some serious errors that could happen if you get into the futures markets without enough knowledge or assistance.

- A farmer has hedged his corn. He had 100,000 bushels in his bins and had sold 100,000 on the Chicago Board of Trade. When he went to offset his short futures position, he told his broker to "buy 20 at the market." Since each corn contract is 5,000 bushels, he thought he was offsetting the 100,000 bushels he was short. But grains are is traded differently than all other contracts, as mentioned earlier. The number refers to each 1000 bushel unit. His broker did what he was told and bought "20 at the market" or 4 contracts. Since he had sold his 100,000 actual bushels of corn on the cash market, the farmer was still short 80,000 bushels. He was at extreme risk. For every cent the corn market goes up, he loses $800.
- Something as seemingly simple as placing an order to be filled within the closing range can prove expensive and risky. For example, there is a case of the trader waiting to place a market order in the last fifteen minutes of trading to fulfill a trading strategy. Because of a clock running late, the order was received on the floor too late. The customer had to take the risk of holding the position overnight and exiting in the morning. His broker could have used a MOC (market on close) order, if he fully understood the situation.

Therefore, develop your list of what you are going to look for in a broker before you begin to interview (usually by telephone) broker candidates. And, we do mean candidates. Use all the skills you learned over the years in hiring employees or vendors, selecting schools for yourself or your children, and other critical buying decisions. Make a "T" list on all candidates after you talk with them. Refer to Table 9.1.

If you do this for each broker you interview, the selection process becomes much easier. Review the "Trading Plan Check List" as you develop your "T" list.

Our experience with working and training hundreds of brokers over the years has shown us the following are some characteristics common to "good" brokers.

Table 9.1

Broker Selection "T" List

Broker's Name: _____

Firm: _____

Phone Number: _____

My Needs and/or Limitation	Pro	Cons
1. Live time quotes	X	
2. Market Experience	10 years	
3. Reliable Trading System		?
4. Track Record		Unclear
5 Personality	Excellent	
6 Reliability	Good	
7 Commission		$72/rt
8 Reference	Check out	
9 Firm		Unknown
10. Trade Presentation		Unorganized
11. Type of Trader	Technical	
12. New Services		Limited

My overall impression is:

_____

_____

Note: You customize the "T" list depending on what your needs and/or limitations are. This list is for illustrative purposes only.

- Availability—Good brokers are available to their customers whenever they are needed. This often equates to long hours from covering the early grain markets to the evening Treasury Bond sessions. When they aren't personally available, they see to it that an assistant or associate is. You're never out of touch. Ask prospective brokers about how "reachable" they are. Then, when you open an account, test them (call them at 8:00 a.m. and again at 8:00 p.m.) before a market emergency occurs.

- Responsiveness—You need a broker who'll help you overcome your limitations and satisfy your needs. Therefore, this person must be responsive. In the interview process, ask him or her to send you some obscure piece of information such as, "When is the Federal Reserve releasing the next beige book?". Find out in advance how the broker performs. Ask how fast you'll get fills? Try to discern how hard he'll push to respond to your needs.

- Honesty—Naturally, you must trust and have confidence in your broker. You can often learn a lot about sincerity when you ask about the risk of futures trading or a specific trade. If the broker evades or glosses over the high risk involved, beware. You should receive a serious, no holds barred discussion from prospective brokers about the unlimited nature of the losses that can be sustained in futures trading. Regarding the buying of options, the risk is limited to the cost of the option (premium) and the transaction costs (brokerage commission and fee)—but, you can lose 100 percent of this amount. Most options expire worthless. Few traders make money in options. If he tells you this is a serious investment with high risks, it's a big plus.

- Dealing with Losses—Under the stress of losing other people's money and the pressures of trading, many brokers come apart. The first sign is often a lack of communication with the losing client. This is almost impossible to detect in the early interview stage of the selection process; but when you start to trade, you should become sensitive to it. If possible, ask for some reference of past customers you can call. Ask them how the broker performed when the account was in a drawdown? The best brokers don't let it bother them because losing money is a large part of futures trading.

- Trading—Find out how they trade. What system do they use? Are they fundamentalists, technicians or a combination? Have them "sell you a trade." Just ask them what their trade recommendation for today is? You want to learn how well they present an opportunity to you. Is it well thought out? Convincing? Have they done their homework?

- Discipline—Good traders and brokers are very disciplined. They spend hours studying the market and refining their system. Bad brokers will try to emotionally sell you the "hot trade of the day." Probe to get a feel for the daily routine of prospective brokers. Do they keep a trading diary? What do they do each day that assures that your positions will be reviewed?

- Experience, Knowledge, Track Record—If you know more or have traded more than a prospective broker, who's going to help whom? Find out what they have done, what they know, and how that's going to make you more successful.

The question of a trading track record is tricky as you'll see in Chapter 10. Most brokers do not have one. If they do not take total discretion in an account (Power of Attorney that permits them to actually trade the account as if it were their own), the customer approves each trade. Therefore, the broker is merely a consultant and the customer is the trader. The broker cannot use these accounts to create a track record, as per CFTC regulations.

Next, there are some very stringent regulations imposed by the Commodity Futures Trading Commission (CFTC) regarding track records. These regulations make it difficult and expensive for a broker to prepare a track record. This is another reason most brokers do not have one. Personally, if a broker shows or offers a track record that is not part of a full blown disclosure document, that has been reviewed by the CFTC, you should be very suspicious. We'll talk more about this in Chapter 10.

These are just a few of the areas to which you must be sensitive as you select and work with a broker. Always remember that it is your money that's being invested in the market; you're the one who is financially responsible.

Opening an Account

Let's quickly review the different types of commodity futures trading accounts you can open and the basic forms you'll be asked to sign or acknowledge understanding of. Some of this will vary slightly from one FCM to another FCM (futures commission merchant), but there should not be too much variation.

Types of Accounts

Here are definitions of the most common types of accounts.

Individual Account—An individual account represents the account of one customer as an individual.

Sole Proprietorship—A sole proprietorship is the same as an individual account, except that the account is in the name of a sole proprietor.

Joint Account—A joint account represents an account established in the names of two or more people. Joint accounts require information on all parties to the account.

General Partnership Account—Basically, a general partnership is a business arrangement between two or more individuals or business entities, each of whom is a general partner conducting a business in the name of a partnership. Each general partner can make decisions on behalf of the whole partnership. The business of the partnership is usually conducted pursuant to an organizations agreement in accordance with the law of that state. A general partnership can be established to conduct a full-time business, such as commodity merchandising, or for a specific investment or trading activity, such as futures trading. An important aspect of a general partnership is that each general partner is liable for commitments and debts incurred in the partnership.

Limited Partnership—Limited partnerships are primarily established for investment, rather than for general business activities. They are usually established and operated pursuant to an organization agreement in accordance with federal and state law. An important aspect of a limited partnership is that the limited partners are not involved in the management of the partnership, and each limited partner's liability is generally limited to the amount of the individual's investment in the partnership. We'll discuss these in more detail in Chapter 10.

Corporate Account—Corporate accounts are those accounts established by a corporation. The information for individuals does not have to be completed; however, corporate information must be submitted. Additionally, the corporate resolution must be completed and signed by at least two officers of the corporation allowing the corporation to trade futures and options on futures. The account papers must indicate who is allowed to trade on behalf of the corporation. In addition to this document, the corporation must submit either a personal guarantee or a copy of the firm's most recent audited financial report.

Trust Account—A trust property is controlled by one person for the benefit of another. For example, a father may create a trust (and be the trustee) for property held for the benefit of his minor children. Or a pension fund could hold funds for the future benefit of members of that fund. In order for a trust to trade futures, the trust agreement must specifically authorize it. A copy of the trust agreement is usually requested with the account papers.

Now let's discuss what you'll be asked to sign. The package of forms you'll receive are generally called the account papers. Each FCM prepares their own, but all papers must meet the requirements of the regulatory agencies (CFTC and NFA). For this reason, there is a strong similarity between all the forms you'll see.

One of the first things your broker is charged to do, by the National Futures Association in its Compliance Rule 2-30, is obtain information about you. The broker must be able to prove to the NFA that he "knows" you. Specifically, your broker needs

- Your true name and address.

- Your principal occupation.

- Your current estimated annual income and net worth.

- Your age.

- Your previous investing experience.

The purpose of this information is to assess your suitability to trade futures. You will be asked to answer a series of questions and/or fill out some sort of financial statement. In addition, you'll need to supply information about your previous investing experience.

The next part of the account papers includes a variety of risk disclosures. The purpose is to make you fully aware of the serious risk involved in investing in these types of investments. The following is a sample of what you'll see.

"Non-Cash Margin Disclosure Statement": This statement is provided to you so that you understand and acknowledge that in the unlikely event of the FCM's bankruptcy, funds not held in segregation (i.e., held as T-Bills), will be returned to you based upon your pro-rate share of all property available for distribution.

"Commodity Account Letter & Customer Agreement": The commodity account letter and customer agreement should be read carefully. It highlights the following areas:

Order entry, margining, commissions and fees, commodity options, delivery and short sales, security interest, liquidation, foreign exchange rates, customer representations and warranties, market recommendations and information, communications, credit, recordings, term of the agreement, and miscellaneous provisions.

The customer must sign this acknowledgement indicating that it has been read and understood. All parties to the account must sign and date this agreement.

"Lending Agreement": The Lending Agreement comes into play when a customer makes or takes delivery, which is unusual. If the balance in the customer's account is not adequate to pay for the delivery and the delivery creates a deficit in the customer's account, a signed Lending Agreement allows for the FCM to use the commodities or evidence of ownership of the commodities as collateral for a loan, the proceeds of which are used to pay for the delivery until redelivery of the commodity and/or payment in full by the customer can be completed.

Figure 9.1

Futures Industry Structure

United States Congress
   Commodity Futures Trading Commission (CFTC)
     National Futures Association (NFA)
       Exchanges
         Futures Commission Merchants (FCM)
          Introducing Brokers (IB)
           IB Branch Offices

Once your account is approved, it must be funded before trading can begin. This is usually done by bank wire or check. Therefore, if you're anxious to trade, send funds with your account papers. Now, we'll look at an alternative to calling all the trades yourself.

"Permission to Cross": The permission to cross agreement allows the FCM to inadvertently take the opposing side of any trade that may have been placed on behalf of a customer. Simply stated, the clearing firm is allowed permission to inadvertently take the opposite side of your order. The CFTC requires the FCM to get your permission to take the opposite side of trades. Since the FCM handles so many trades each day, it asks for your blanket approval because it doesn't have any practical way of keeping track of all the possible conflicts of interest.

"Options Disclosure Statement": The Options Disclosure Statement informs you of the risks associated with trading options, as well as describing the different types of options traded.

"Transfer Form": The Transfer Form should be completed if you are transferring your account from one FCM to another.

"Pre-dispute Arbitration Agreement": The Arbitration Agreement allows for the filing of an arbitration conducted by a self regulatory or other private organization rather than pursuing the matter through civil court litigation. The Arbitration Agreement does allow you to request a Section 14 Reparations Proceeding before the CFTC. You have 45 days from the date of such notice to decide. NFA rules prohibit the signing of this agreement to be a condition of opening an account.

"Risk Disclosure Statement": This statement discloses to you the various risks associated with futures trading. CFTC Regulation 1.55 requires that each customer receives and signs a copy of this statement before an account can be approved to trade. If an account executive ever plays down the importance of this document, you should be concerned. It's important you read and understand what you are getting into.

Once you complete the account papers, you send them to your broker. They are reviewed by his supervisor. This is usually at the Introducing Broker level. From here, it is sent to the New Account Department at the FCM for their approval.

CHAPTER 10

GIVING TRADING DISCRETION
TO SOMEONE ELSE

Key Concepts

➠ Using the Modern Portfolio Theory to structure an investment portfolio.

➠ How various types of discretionary authority can be used to reach your trading objectives.

➠ Step-by-step procedures for the evaluation of any type or class of investments with an emphasis on managed futures programs.

Over the years, we have run into investors who wish to diversify their overall investment portfolio with the addition of a position in the futures markets. Research studies by several experts indicate this may give a portfolio more balance and stability and even increase the return.

The pioneers of this approach were such notable financial theoreticians as Harry Marowitz, John K. Lintner, and William R. Sharpe. Many of their ideas and research evolved into what is currently known as the Modern Portfolio Theory (MPT). The MPT can be simply stated as "don't put all your eggs in one basket."

What these gentlemen (and several others) did was carefully quantify the concept. They also developed sophisticated methods of structuring and evaluating the performance of portfolios.

Modern Portfolio Theory

Both active money managers and academicians subscribe to this theory. It states it is the duty and obligation of the prudent investor to seek "combinations of assets" which yield the maximum return with the lowest associated risk. The key phrase is "combination of assets."

With this as their goal, and access to virtually unlimited computer time, several renowned business schools began to crunch numbers. They loaded their mainframe with historical data detailing the performance of all major classes of assets: stocks, bonds, real estate, commodities, cash equivalents, etc. Then they played "what if" games. They arranged and rearranged their experimental port-folios. They constantly changed the asset mix and evaluated it against historical returns generated over the last ten years, last twenty years, etc.

Negative Correlation

They did develop some extremely useful information. For example, they popular-ized the concept of balancing a portfolio with negatively correlated assets. This simply means that when a certain asset class goes up due to a given set of economic circumstances, other asset classes go down or remain the same.

Now this may not sound like much, but it is. If you can quantify the positive or negative reaction of various investment opportunities to given sets of economic data, you can begin to build sample portfolios that can withstand various types of adverse conditions.

What's the single most serious, long-term disease that your net worth faces? Most investors will probably say inflation. Many economists attempted to develop a portfolio resistant to inflation.

The most prominent researcher of the group was a professor from Harvard University, Dr. John Lintner. He used data from July 1979 through 1982, comparing fifteen futures portfolio managers and eight public futures funds to stock and bond portfolios. At Boston University, Zvi Bodie and Victor Rosansky took a longer term view, 1950 through 1976. Jack Barbonel, Phil Lipsky, and John Zumbrunn studied the period of 1960-82, while Scott Irwin and B. Wade Brorsen's (Purdue University) analysis covered 1963 to 1983.

A common conclusion of this number crunching was that the stock market and the futures market are negatively correlated. This becomes particularly critical during periods of inflation. Inflation pushes prices and interest rates higher. The cost of doing business increases while sales decrease—stock prices suffer and the market drops.

At the same time, inflation pushes prices higher. Futures investors profit from bull markets, particularly in the physical commodities. Inventory managers, fearing higher prices, buy more which fuels the fires of inflation.

The recommendation resulting from much of the work on the subject was to spread your risk by reducing the volatility—while at the same time enjoying an increase—in the return from your total investment package. A common theme was to put from 5 percent to 15 percent of your investment portfolio in futures.

While many investors showed interest in doing this, most were not willing, able, or interested in making the commitment necessary to trade a futures account directly. As we are sure you have learned from the preceding chapters, there is a lot of homework to be done before you make your first trade. For this and other reasons, investors have sought the help of various professional (and even non-professional) traders to assist them. This is accomplished by signing over to the trader, called a third party controller, the authority to trade the account. The authority used is usually a limited power of attorney.

Types of Discretionary Accounts

There are a wide variety of trading approaches that can give your associated person (broker) or a third party advisor varying degrees of freedom to act in your behalf in your futures trading account. For example, you can give your broker price or timing only discretion in a trade(s). This allows your broker to decide at what price level or time s/he will enter your order in the market. This type of discretionary authority does not require giving power of attorney. But it must be to your, (the customer's) benefit, not the broker's convenience.

Let's review an example of how this works. You are very busy or will be out of touch during a particular day, yet you want to place some trades. You discuss the situation with your broker the night before. You decide on the futures market, month, quantity, side (long or short/put or call), and strike price in the case of options that you wish to trade. You let your broker pick the time or the specific target price or range. Situations like this occur, for example, when you want to get a feel for the day's market before you commit. You might tell your broker to go ahead and place your order if the market opens higher tomorrow. This would be a time only discretion order.

Or, you might want to wait for a certain trading range. You instruct your broker to enter the market if the commodity you want to trade hits a certain price. "Buy me 5 December S & P's if it trades over 322." Personally, we recommend that when you use price only discretion, you limit your broker to a trading range.

There is another type of discretionary trading that also does not require you to sign a limited power of attorney. This is called a guided account.

With a guided account, a third party, who must be registered with the National Futures Association (NFA) as a Commodity Trading Advisor (CTA), suggests all trades. He explains his thinking. You, the client, must accept or reject the trades.

Another possibility is turning over your account to a third party who isn't required to have a formal disclosure document. To do this, you'll be asked to sign a limited power of attorney and a written statement explaining why this third party account controller is not required by the CFTC to provide you with a disclosure document. There are four reasons a disclosure document is not required by an account controller:

1. If the controller advised less than fifteen people over the last twelve months and does not generally hold him or herself out to the public as a CTA;

2. If he or she is a dealer, broker, processor, or seller in cash market for the commodity to be traded or provides advice incidental to the conduct of his or her cash market business;

3. If the person is properly registered in another capacity and whose advice is solely incidental to his or her business;

4. Or, if the person is a relative of the person doing the trading.

Other than these four exceptions, all third party advisors are required by the Commodity Futures Trading Commission (CFTC) to provide their clients with a formal disclosure document. Additionally, clients must sign a written acknowledgement that they have read and understood the disclosure document. The purpose of the disclosure document is to make you aware of all the pertinent facts, i.e., the amount of risk involved, explanation of the trading system, fee schedule, past performance, etc.

Before we go too much further, we need to call your attention to the fact that your broker may be exempted from the disclosure document requirement based on exception number three listed above. An individual broker, who is not registered as a CTA, would be considered someone who is "properly registered in another capacity and whose advice is solely incidental to his or her business." The section about the advice being incidental means that a broker cannot trade all or the majority of his accounts on a discretionary basis. Also, brokers must have two years experience in handling accounts before they are allowed to take discretion in other people's accounts.

Brokers who don't have two years experience and want to take discretion in accounts can do one of two things. First, they can petition the NFA for a waiver of this requirement. We have seen this tried several times, but we've never seen the NFA approve any. The other option is to register as a CTA. If a broker takes this route, a disclosure document must be prepared. In it, the broker's experience must be revealed. Therefore, it behooves you to read all disclosure documents carefully before investing. Being registered as a CTA doesn't mean that the person can trade profitably or even ably.

Other than the discretionary options mentioned, you can select to invest in a managed account program. There are basically two types: individual and limited partnerships. With an individually managed account, the CTA takes complete control of trading your account and trades it using his/her system. The size of the portfolio or the diversification possible depends upon the amount you put in the program. While some CTAs will trade amounts as low as $5,000, most require $50,000 or more. Many are asking $100,000 to $200,000, so the accounts have some staying power and can spread the risk over ten to fifteen markets.

Your other choice is a limited partnership, which comes in two varieties: public or private. The basic difference between the two is the size, meaning the amount of money that can be raised by the CPO (Commodity Pool Operator) and the number of investors that can participate. Private offerings are somewhat more restricted by the CFTC than public.

Over $12,000,000,000!

Limited Partnerships have become popular in the last decade. The amount under management is estimated at over $12 billion. This growth has occurred, in our opinion, because of some benefits intrinsic to this form of investment. For example, an individual can invest a little as $5,000 and receive the following:

- Diversification into a wide variety of markets, far more than one could with most individual futures portfolios. This gives your account more stability, putting it in a better position to take advantage of major moves.

- Leading CTAs to manage your account. You might not normally have access to this caliber of traders.

- Lower than normal commission rates. Most funds because of their enormous volume trade at or near discount rates.

- Freedom from margin calls. The fund or the limited partnership is responsible for all margin calls.

- Defined risk—your initial investment is usually all you are obligated for, but be sure to carefully read the particular prospectus for the investment you are considering.

- Interest income from funds held in Treasury Bills by the fund or limited partnership.

Best of all, your upside potential has no restrictions. Many of the CTAs that manage these types of investments have very impressive trading histories, which will be detailed in the disclosure document.

Word to the Wise!

We can't stress how important it is to read, study, and understand the disclosure document or prospectus for any fund or limited partnership you are considering. It explains your rights, risks, and obligations. Be sure to understand what you are signing and the risks involved.

When you begin to do your research on an investment opportunity, the first thing you usually hear about is its past "rate of return" or expected ROR. Brokers of all classes of assets hype this number. If a product has a high ROR, it is supposed to overcome all other obstacles.

Personally, we evaluate investments differently. ROR is important, but it's not number one. The key issue is risk management. This is especially true of any investment involving the futures markets.

Let's say, you invest in a limited partnership (LP). The first month your LP has a 50-percent drawdown of equity. Month two it appreciates 50 percent. Are you back to break-even? No, you are still behind. To recover from a 50-percent loss, you need a 100 percent gain. If the fund began with $1,000,000 and lost $500,000, a 50-percent gain brings it to $750,000. Only doubling its remaining equity can make it whole again. Study the table below to get an insight into the effect loss of equity has on a LP.

As you can see, the greater the loss, the greater the effort it takes to recover. A substantial drawdown could take months to recover from, if recovery is even possible.

Loss-Recovery Table

% Loss	% Needed for BE
5	5.26
20	25.00
30	42.86
40	66.67
50	100.00
70	233.33
90	900.00
100	Impossible

Risk Management Ranks Number 1

We've seen a lot of CTAs attempt to recoup from a severe set back. They are no different than anyone else. By this we mean they often try too hard and succumb to the pressure.

For this reason, the first attribute to look for in any CTA who is going to manage your money is his or her risk management skills and experience. You want to know what downside volatility can be expected on average? How deep are the drawdowns of equity? How frequent? What was the maximum consecutive draw-down, and how long did it take to recover? In trading futures, there will always be months where you lose money. But if you can't quickly recover, you dig a hole that is near impossible to climb out of.

Consistency Ranks Number 2

We get a queasy feeling when we evaluate a limited partnership that rocks up and down. Up 32 percent one month, down 26 percent, up 22 percent, down 17 percent, up 19 percent, down 13 percent. We may be making money; but, we're too anxious to enjoy it.

When we invest, we want consistency. The last thing we want is to get a statement from our brokers telling us our investment zagged twice in a row when it should have zigged. Steady and reasonable gains are more comforting than wild, uncontrolled energy.

How do you measure consistency? You chart out the monthly gains and losses of the CTAs you are considering. Are the monthly and annual gains impressive? Are the losses controlled and reasonable? A loss of 10 percent to 15 percent is not a problem if it is quickly recovered. But wide swings can leave you in a state of uncertainty, which is the last state an investor enjoys visiting.

Now . . . ROR!

Once you're satisfied the investment vehicle you are evaluating manages risk and performs consistently, you begin to pay more attention to its rate of return. Keep in mind that the ROR means nothing until you're satisfied with steps one and two.

The importance of ROR only comes into focus when you consider what you must give up or are expected to withstand to receive it. This is called the "efficient frontier." It is the amount of risk, measured in standard deviation, that can be expected to obtain a given amount of reward, measured by the mean (average) return.

We have an acquaintance who used to say he would stand in front of a fast moving train for $2,000,000 cash. He meant it! But most of us draw a line regarding how much risk we can or will accept for any expected reward.

How to Measure Volatility?

One of the easiest methods to determine the amount of the volatility you'll be facing is to draw a simple bar chart. On a blank piece of paper, draw a straight line across the middle of the page. Let this represent zero percent change in the monthly rate of return. Now, plot a bar for the positive rates of return above the line and the negative months below. You find these figures in most disclosure documents on the "Performance Summary Page."

Study the chart you create. How wide are the swings from positive to negative? How often are there consecutive drawdowns of equity? How deep are the drawdowns?

Another important aspect of this study is the length of the study. You need to know how the CTA(s) performs in bull and bear markets. Some traders and systems do better in one or the other. Certain trend following systems, for example, do better in bull markets because they last longer than bear markets. Once trends are established, the trend followers jump aboard and ride them for all they're worth. You can't always do this with bear markets. Markets can turn around, and the moves are over before some trend following systems can take advantage of them.

Markets moving sideways or in channels up or down present unique problems. Trend following systems are virtually useless. Discretionary traders who pick and choose each trade tend to do better in these markets.

You can also plot the CTA's month-to-month performance, using the VAMI (we'll get to this shortly) table from the disclosure document on a chart with a long-term commodity market index. The index used should match as closely as possible the portfolio the CTA trades. For example, if the trader deals primarily with the physical markets, use an index such as the Wasendorf Composite Index. If the portfolio is only meats, metals, or grains, use one of its sub-indexes. Long range charts are ideal for this purpose. If the CTA is into all commodities, including gold, you might want to use the CRB (Commodity Research Bureau) Index.

This combination of the CTA's performance and the composite index value of the futures markets provides an important insight into how the trader handles the up and down sides of the market. You want to know if the performance drops substantially when there is an abrupt change of direction of the market. Or does the trading system quickly adjust? Ideally, the line representing the track record increases each month, no matter if the index is going up or down.

The acronym VAMI, mentioned earlier, stands for "Value Added Monthly Index." The Commodity Futures Trading Commission (CFTC) requires this figure to be calculated for each CTA's track record that is printed in a disclosure document. As you probably know, the CFTC reviews all disclosure documents prior to the time they can be offered to the public. Its review does not in any way equate to an endorsement. More importantly, it examines the documents to see that its regulations are heeded—not to evaluate the chances of the offering generating a profit!

The CFTC is the investors' watchdog. It tries to root out disclosure documents that may mislead the public. This is the thinking behind the VAMI. It is required by the CFTC so an investor can easily compare one offering against another over a given period of time, that is, which $1,000 unit increased the most?

The CFTC requires the CTA to re-index the VAMI to $1,000 at the beginning of each year. Therefore, you may want to calculate your own cumulative VAMI for track records over longer periods of time.

As you evaluate past performance, always keep in mind that it is not a reliable forecaster of future performance. That's why you want to look at as long a period as possible—3 years, 5 years, or longer. The period of time should include bear and bull moves. Again, that's why you chart the VAMI against a commodity price index.

All VAMIs are calculated using the same formula, as prescribed by the CFTC. The formula is:

VAMI for Period "Z"

Z = (1 + rate of return of period Z) × VAMI for Prior Period

Therefore, the VAMI for any particular period increases or decreases based on the rate of return for that period. Calculating the number can become complicated when there are a lot of monthly additions and withdrawals. If all the withdrawals take place at the beginning of the period and all the additions at the end, they can skew the rate of return to the downside. The opposite is equally true. It is hoped that over a reasonably long period of time this evens out.

The Sharp Ratio

The Sharp Ratio is another way of evaluating trading programs.

It is a method of determining the rate of return of an investment, after making an allowance for risk. You do this by subtracting the current rate of return (ROR) available from what is generally considered a risk-free investment, such as Treasury Bills, from the average annual ROR of the investment you are considering. This is used as the numerator. The denominator is found by dividing the standard deviation of the average annual ROR of the investment into the remainder of the subtraction operation.

The product of the division generates the Sharp Ratio which can be used to evaluate one investment opportunity against another. It doesn't matter if they are in the same class of investments or not. You can calculate the Sharp Ratio on a monthly or annual basis, depending on the data and time available. We like to do this on a monthly basis and then graph the data points of the various investments being evaluated. You should be looking for a Sharp Ratio that is very consistent and increasing.

As you refine your analytic skills, keep in mind that there is no fool proof formula to foretell the future. VAMIs, Sharp Ratios, and Charts, are not guaranteed; their sole purpose is to improve your odds of picking a winner. Futures investing is an investment in what we expect or hope to happen sometime in the future.

Sterling Ratio

Another evaluation tool is the Sterling Ratio. It is a measure of the risk adjusted return you might expect from an investment. Think of it as the amount of return you should obtain per unit of risk you are willing to accept. The more risk you take, the more you should receive for living with that risk.

With the Sterling Ratio (SR), the higher it is, the better. A ratio of two is theoretically twice as attractive as one.

Here's the formula for the Sterling Ratio:

Average annual return for last three calendar yrs. divided by largest average cumulative. Losses for last three calendar years plus 10 percent.

Notice that we are evaluating the average annual return for the last three calendar years and divide this figure by the largest average cumulative loss for each of the last three calendar years plus 10 percent. Now this extra 10 percent is added to the average cumulative losses because quarterly and monthly returns tend to underestimate the actual maximum loss periods.

Let's look at an example. Suppose we are attempting to evaluate two Commodity Trading Advisors (CTAs). The first one has an Average Annual Return (Return) for the last three calendar years of 30 percent. His average cumulative loss (Loss) for the 3-year period is 20 percent. The second CTA has the same return, but his losses are lower, 15 percent. What are their Sterling Ratios (SR)?

	CTA No. 1	CTA No. 2
Return	30%	30%
Loss	20%	15%
SR	1.00	1.20

Here is how the calculation of the SR looks for CTA number 1: thirty divided by the sum of twenty plus ten (or thirty). For CTA number 2, thirty was divided by the sum of fifteen plus ten (or twenty-five). From this analysis, CTA number 2 appears to be 20 percent better than CTA number 1.

Look Beyond the Ratio

You must pay particular attention to when drawdowns occur. For example, if we are analyzing two CTAs with the same returns and losses as used in our example.

Advisor number 2 looked good. However, if we examine carefully the CTA's track record in his disclosure document, we may, indeed, discover that CTA number 2 had an average loss of 15 percent per year; but, it was 30 percent over a 6-month period of time—Oct, Nov, Dec, Jan, Feb, and Mar. The "calendar" year split the 30-percent loss into two 15-percent losses.

Now, a couple of things usually happen when a CTA loses money for six months straight. First, some investors lose faith and jump ship. This, combined with the losses, reduces the CTA's equity base. The lower the equity, the harder it is for the CTA to recover (see Loss-Recovery table). Secondly, when a CTA is losing money and clients, he often loses confidence.

Therefore, it is our contention that using calendar years as part of this formula seriously flaws the results. But this is not the only problem.

Let's look at another example. This time CTA number 1 has an average annual return of 30 percent and maximum average cumulative drawdown of 20 percent. CTA number 2 has the same. Therefore, the Sterling Ratio is the same for both, namely 1. That makes them equal . . . right?

Which CTA would you be most interested in if the average loss of the CTAs were as follows: number 1 has an even loss of 20 percent each year; CTA number 2's average drawdown of 20 percent is composed of 10 percent, 20 percent, 30 percent? Both average 20 percent, but CTA number 2's losses are increasing each year. CTA number 1's losses are fairly consistent. Or what if CTA number 2's losses are 0 percent, 20 percent and 40 percent or 0 percent, 0 percent, and 60 percent? Volatility likes this can mean trouble—a fact that is not reflected in the Sterling Ratio.

Where did 10 percent come from?

We also have problems with the arbitrary 10 percent added to the losses. If you add 10 percent to an average loss of 15 percent, you increase it by 67 percent. If you add it to an average loss of 35 percent, you only increase it 29 percent. This, of course, substantially changes the Sterling Ratio.

	CTA No. 1	CTA No. 2
Return	25%	50%
Loss	15%	35%
SR	1.00	1.11

CTA number 2 is more volatile, yet has a better Sterling Ratio. It appears to us the more consistent traders are penalized by the arbitrary 10 percent assessment to loss column.

When your broker begins to brag about the Sterling Ratio of the CTA, please take the time to go beyond the ratio. Find out how it is put together. How stable and consistent is the CTA? That's what counts.

CTA Batting Averages

Since we had some problems with the Sterling ratio, we look for an alternative. We found one was devised by a Commodity Pool Operator (CPO), Nick Vintila, that, we think, overcomes some of the short comings of the Sterling Ratio. It's called the CTA Batting Average. Here are its formulas:

> Long-Term Batting Average equals the Compounded Annual ROR divided by Greatest Cumulative Drawdown Ever Experienced by the CTA.

> Short-Term Batting Average equals the Compounded ROR Over the Last thirty-six Months divided by the Greatest Drawdown Experienced by the CTA over the Last thirty-six Months.

What are the differences?

There are several important differences between the CTA Batting Average (BA) and the Sterling Ratio (SR). To begin with, BA utilizes a Present Value Future Value calculation in the numerator, rather than a simple average. In our opinion, this much more accurately reflects the ROR.

The denominators of these equations are even more important. In the SR, you use the Maximum Average Drawdown. It is based on a calendar year. This can be very misleading if a drawdown continues over more than one calendar year, as was pointed out earlier.

With the BA, the Greatest Cumulative Drawdown for the Last thirty-six Months, or the entire track record, is used. This may seem somewhat unforgiving; but, we want to evaluate the worst case scenario. If this drawdown occurred over thirty-six months ago, it does not affect the short-term batting average. Then we can compare the long-and short-term batting averages. Has a CTA improved or regressed? Having two views is also an important feature not available with the SR.

The BA also provides a new view each month. The numbers used are rolling constantly. You don't have to wait for the end of the year to recalculate the ratios. This allows you to do two important ongoing analyses.

1. You are alerted sooner to up or down trends in performance. This gives you time to react.

2. You can evaluate your CTA's performance in given market conditions shortly after they occur. If a major bull or bear market develops, how is your CTA performing? Can he trade a trendless market? By recalculating the BA on a monthly basis and charting it on an index that reflects the CTA's portfolio, you'll know. You may want to switch location of your funds between CTAs depending on the long term trend of the market.

You also note the BA does away with the arbitrary 10 percent added to the denominator of the Sterling Ratio previously discussed. We didn't want to discriminate against conservative and consistent CTAs.

We personally like the BA approach because a CTA with large drawdowns cannot hide them in an average. For example, let's go back to the CTA with a 0 percent, 0 percent and 60 percent drawdowns over a 3-year period. Using the Sterling Ratio, these averaged to 20 percent. With the BA, you would use the 60 percent loss.

When evaluating CTA track records, cumulation of losses is a key concept. The more equity lost, the more difficult it is for the CTA to recover.

Another aspect we like about the BA approach is being able to see if the CTA's performance is affected by changes he makes in his trading system or the amount of money under management. CTAs will often tell you that they "fixed" their system. By studying performance on a rolling basis, you can substantiate these claims.

How does a CTA's trading react to a big influx of equity? Comparing the results of BA with the additions to equity on a month-by-month basis answers that question. Performance often drops when large amounts of equity are added if the CTA's back room and/or system isn't up to the challenge.

"It Pays to be a Little Paranoid!"

This is an old saying in the futures business. It simply means there is no perfect method of determining who will out perform whom in the futures market. You must use all the tools available to you and make your own decision. For example, there are more ways than one to calculate the return on investment. The various approaches produce different answers.

The real ROR question is often not what the return computes to but how was it calculated?

Let's look at an example. You want to evaluate the performance of a commodity trading advisor (CTA). From his disclosure document, you calculate the following VAMI (value added monthly index) figures.

Period	VAMI Value	% Increase
End of 1988	$2,928.00	
End of 1989	$8,766.00	299.38
End of 1990	$8,882.00	1.32
End of 1991	$12,828.00	44.43

A $1,000 unit invested in this particular CTA increased in value from the inception of the fund to $2,928 at the end of 1988. The next year, 1989, was a big year for the CTA with an increase of almost 300 percent. 1990 turned out to be a rather flat year and 1989 brought an increase of over 40 percent.

Now, how should we calculate the overall return for the three years in question? The simplest method is to add the returns for the three years together and divide by three.

299.38% + 1.32% + 44.43% = 345.13%/3 = 115.04%

This would give us an average annual return of just over 115 percent.

Option number 2 would be to first calculate the total amount of gain. You would do this by subtracting the initial amount from the ending amount, or $12,828 less $2,928. The remainder is $9,900. You would then divide this remainder by the beginning amount, or $9,900 divided by $2,928. The result is 338.11 percent or the 3-year period. On a per year basis, it is 112.70 percent, which is 338.11 percent divided by three.

What happens if we use a more sophisticated technique? Let's say you decide to do some time-value analysis. You want to determine the compounded annual rate of return.

With the present value of $2,928 and the future value of $12,828, you decide to calculate the ROR over three periods, representing the years. This produces a figure of 63.63 percent as the compounded annual rate of return.

If you wanted to do this same calculation on a monthly basis, you would use thirty-six periods, rather than three. This would generate a monthly compounded return of 4.19 percent. To annualize the monthly return, you would multiply it by twelve resulting in a figure of 50.27 percent.

This gives us four different ROR figures, using the four formulas. Once you select a method for a specific class of investment, always use the same one. If someone, a broker, for example, provides some RORs to you, make sure you find out which method was used to calculate them. If necessary you may have to recalculate the figure so it is consistent with your other data.

For evaluating CTAs, we prefer to use method number 3. This provides what we think is the best measurement.

Once you have an annual compounded ROR for the CTAs you are considering, you can evaluate them against an index of other CTAs. Figures on the performance of public and private funds can be obtained from the *Managed Accounts Report* newsletter or *Futures Magazine*. This provides an insight as to how an individual CTA compares to other CTAs. It is similar to evaluating the performance of your stock portfolio with the S & P 500 Index.

The Impact of Additions and Withdrawals

The annual rates of return (ROR) just discussed are the composite of twelve monthly trading periods. You need to take a closer look at how these periods are put together in order to have confidence in the ROR figures you calculate.

As mentioned earlier, one of the stickiest tasks any accountant or statistician has is accounting for additions and withdrawals when calculating performance. This is because of the timing of these transactions. Let's say an account receives an additional $10,000 of equity on June 15th. Should it be included for the entire month, half or not at all? What if the addition comes in on the first or the thirtieth?

You face the same problem with withdrawals. Money coming out of an account on the first of the month may make more of an impact on that month's return than a withdrawal on the last business day of the month. The commodity trading advisors (CTAs) will theorize that if they had the money all month the return would be higher.

The point is simply this, when you attempt to calculate a ROR, you divide the gain or loss by the amount of equity. Much depends on how the denominator (or amount of equity) is determined. If you assume in your calculations that the funds always come in at the beginning of the month and always leave at the end, you'll skew the ROR to the down-side. The opposite is also true.

Historically, here's how Commodity Futures Trading Commission (CFTC) has done it. The monthly ROR is determined by dividing the net monthly performances (gain or loss) by beginning equity. For example, let's say a Commodity Pool Operator (CPO) has a fund of $1,000,000. He gives his three CTAs one-third each and holds back $100,000 in reserve. The CTAs use the $300,000 as their beginning equity for the first month.

If CTA number 1 generates $18,000 in profits the first month, his ROR would be $18,000 divided by $300,000 or 6 percent. This changes his beginning equity for the second month to $318,000. If $5,000 is gained for the second month his ROR would be 1.6 percent ($5,000/$318,000).

Losses are calculated the same way. Let's say in the third month, the CTA takes a $6,000 loss. The beginning equity for the month is now $323,000, which is divided into the loss of $6,000. Therefore, the monthly ROR is a negative 1.8 percent.

This method works well, especially for small accounts that have very few additions or withdrawals. But once you get into a situation where there are a lot or large movements of money in and out, these ROR figures can become less meaningful. They can become very distorted, especially when the changes in total equity exceed 15-20 percent in a given month.

The entire process can become even more distorted when you're evaluating composite performances. This could be the track record of all the accounts traded by one CTA or the composite trading records of several CTAs advising a single fund. The reason is simply the large number of additions and withdrawals that it would probably include in multiple and long term track records. To overcome this problem, the CFTC now requires additions and withdrawals to be time weighted over the period of time the CTA has access to the funds.

An Alternate Method

Since we were not entirely comfortable with the method described above, as accurately giving us a satisfactory picture of the ROR, we looked for an alternative. You could, as Mr. Vintila whose was mentioned earlier does, base your monthly performance calculations on a $1,000 unit. For example, if you opened a $60,000 managed account, you would have sixty $1,000 units.

Therefore, if your account was worth $64,000 at the end of the first month—barring any additions or withdrawals, each unit would be worth $1,066.66. This is an increase of 6.66 percent for the month. A loss is determined the same way, always calculated on a per unit basis.

What about withdrawals? Let's say you needed to withdraw $16,000 after month one. You would divide that amount by the unit value to figure how many units you were withdrawing. It would be $16,000 divided by $1,066.66 or fifteen units. You now have forty-five units with the same value of $1,066.66 each or $48,000, which is $64,000 less the $16,000.

In the next month, you make $3,000. You add this to the beginning value of $48,000 and divide by the forty-five remaining units ($51,000/45) for a unit value of $1,133. Next, you subtract the original $1,000 and divide by 1000 to convert to a percentage. The return is therefore 13.33 percent for this month.

The most important consideration is that you are dealing only with funds in your account. In our opinion, this provides more validity. Equally important is our feeling that it makes it easier to compare one CTA with another.

A Milking Stool

Solid investment programs are built like old fashioned milking stools. The three legs are rate of return (ROR), risk control as measured by volatility, and consistency of performance. So far, we covered the first two. Now let's discuss the third.

Why do we care about consistency? Can't a high enough ROR overcome all other obstacles to success?

Actually, a high rate of return often covers up the true picture. You need to analyze the ROR figure to determine when the gains were generated.

Consider two CTAs who have posted RORs of 300 percent over a three-year period of time, 36 months. CTA number 1 had an ROR of 100 percent each year, while the second CTA gained 300 percent in one of the years and broke even the other two.

Now, if you just happened to be investing with CTA percent 2 during his "hot" 12-month period, you'd be extremely happy—an ROR of 300 percent! But what if your timing wasn't so perfect? Would you rather have had your money with CTA number 1 for any twelve months during the 36-month period? It almost comes down to choosing between trying to be very lucky or learning how to discover advisors who produce consistent returns.

Time-Interval Analysis

Another statistical technique, suggested by Mr. Vintila, is called Time-Interval Analysis (TIA). A CTA's track record is broken down into time intervals of 3-, 6-, 9-, 12-, 18-, and 24-month periods. TIA takes the position that calendar years are not any more important than any other 12-month periods. If you open an account in March and by the following April it's losing money, it's not any consolation that the CTA performed well from January to December. TIA gives you a higher number of observations at which to look compared to having only using calendar performance statistics.

Therefore, you quickly learn two things: the CTA's volatility and consistency. If you run TIA over 3-, 6-, 9-, 12-, 18-, and 24–month periods, it tells you immediately if the CTA has been more consistent when given twelve months, instead of one or three months to trade.

For example, if a CTA has a 12-month track record, you could calculate ten 2-month time intervals, seven 6-month intervals, four 9-month, and one 12-month time interval

Time Intervals	3-Month	6- Month	9-Month	12-Month
1				
2				
3	1			
4	2			
5	3			
6	4	1		
7	5	2		
8	6	3		
9	7	4	1	
10	8	5	2	
11	9	6	3	
12	10	7	4	1

Each time interval is determined by rolling one month forward and dropping the last month, similar to moving averages. The ROR is calculated based on the VAMI.

Next, you take the results of the various time intervals and create bar charts. The midpoint of the charts is zero ROR. All intervals with positive RORs are charted above the midline and all negative intervals below. This technique provides a very graphic picture regarding a CTA's consistency.

Pay particular attention to the 12-, 18- or 24-month interval futures. You're trying to find out how consistent the ROR is over long periods of time. Hopefully, this period of time would include both bull and bear market moves, plus periods where the market moves sideways or is choppy.

Ideally, the ROR will be consistent no matter what the market is doing. By doing this analysis, you'll find out exactly when the money was made and over what period of time, i.e., at the beginning of his career as a CTA or consistently throughout his entire career.

You'll easily be able to see if you need to be lucky and guess when to invest or whether you can invest anytime because the performance is consistent.

"Give Me Another Three Months . . ."

When you have money in a managed account or a fund and you're unhappy with the current performance, you may be trying to decide when and if to cash out your investment. At that time, your broker or CTA may ask for another few months to get things going. If this happens to you, you can easily compare the 1-month, 3-month, or 6-month time intervals and immediately see what you can expect.

Does this CTA perform well over the short term?

If you calculate the percentage of profitability over the different time intervals, you will know if it makes any sense to put off your decision to liquidate.

Once you get serious about investing in a fund or an account managed by a CTA, we suggest you do some research. It is commonly referred to as "due diligence."

What Do We Mean by the Term "Due Diligence"?

In a legal sense, it means undertaking a study of a person or an entity to uncover as much background as possible. The root word "diligence" carries the connotation of perseverance and determination—an unwavering drive to uncover the essence of the subject being studied.

When we talk about preparing a "due diligence report" on CTAs, we mean we are going to learn as much as possible about these traders, their systems, and their performances. A study of this sort is done to make sure their track records can be relied upon as an accurate representation of their trading. Additionally, a due diligence study provides valuable insights into how certain CTAs will help us reach our investment goals. We also want to learn if they are compatible with us and our goals. Can their staff (back room) respond to the challenge of trading more funds?

Let's go over some of the activities that are involved in executing due diligence on CTAs. One of the best places to start is the disclosure document. This instrument should contain all the information that is pertinent to investors who are considering investing in a particular CTA or a fund. If we are looking at a fund or limited partnership, the document is called a prospectus. In addition to information about the futures traders, the document also includes the risk disclosure statements required by the Commodity Futures Trading Commission (CFTC). It also includes background on anyone or entity—such as the organizer (Commodity Pool Operator, CPO) and clearing firm (Futures Commission Merchant, FCM)—that will play a major role in the investment.

Your goal in examining the disclosure documents is to read between the lines and to validate all salient points. Keep in mind that the offering documents are written by attorneys who are paid to interpret the facts of any case or argument in light of their clients' best interests.

The unfortunate part of this situation is that these documents have grown longer and more complicated each year. We assisted with the preparation of one not too long ago. Once it was approved by the attorneys, we ran it through a computer program that evaluated its level of reading difficulty. This particular one, which appeared to us to be "average," required a post-graduate education to understand, according to the computer program. Personally, we feel very strongly that the investing public would be better served if the CFTC stressed simplicity and understandability, as well as risk disclosure in these documents.

Prior to being made available to prospective investors, these offering documents are sent to the CFTC for review. The CFTC reserves twenty-one days to make comments and order required changes. If the promoter of the offering doesn't hear from the CFTC within this time period, they can begin the selling process. This process may include reviews by the Secretaries of State of the various states in which it is to be sold, depending on the specific type and size of the offering. Many of these investments are considered a security during the selling process. Therefore, they are under the jurisdiction of the Security Exchange Commission or each state's Secretary of State at this stage. Once they begin trading futures, the jurisdiction is passed to the CFTC and the National Futures Association (NFA).

The CFTC and state and federal regulatory bodies can still require changes or additions to these documents even if the 21-day review period by the CFTC has expired, and the offering document has been printed. Therefore, from time to time, you may find additions or changes pasted or bound into an offering document.

What to Look For

There are various levels of due diligence investigations. Take the examination of a CTA's track record as an illustration. We once worked for a firm that conducted professional due diligence studies. They would send out accountants who would "test" the CTA's track record, just as you would test a company's accounting records.

They would randomly select specific periods of trading for review. The CTAs would be asked to produce the order tickets (the NFA requires members to retain each order ticket for five years) covering the period. These would be checked against records of the range the market traded on that day to make sure the trade was possible. The accountants would track the trade until it was closed, calculating the profit or loss for all trades for the period. This would then be compared with what was presented in the performance tables.

The analysis of the rate of return and how it was calculated is another example of a less intensive, but equally important, level of investigation.

But there is much more in the offering document than the track records. For example, review the backgrounds of all the principles: CPO, general partner(s), advisors, clearing firms, etc. Do they have enough experience to satisfy you?

As you study the offering document, write down your questions. Don't hesitate to call or write the administrators of the investments (their addresses and phone numbers are in the front of the documents) with your questions.

Another important area covers the conflicts of interest. Are they acceptable? For example, if the advisors receive per trade commissions, as well as a management and/or incentive fees, will they have the tendency to over trade?

The fees involved critically affect performance. Think of them as drawdowns of equity. It is money paid out of the trading equity and can no longer be used to generate profits. If the fees are unreasonable, they drain the equity. Reasonable fees are needed to compensate all those involved for the work and risk assumed in bringing the investment to market.

"If it sounds too good . . ."

Do your homework before you invest. Most investments that sound "too good to be true," are! You are the only one who can make the decision to invest. Take care that you have looked over the entire offering very carefully.

Diversifying CTA Trading Systems

When you or the investment vehicle you are considering uses more than one CTA, consider the concept of using CTAs that have diversified trading systems. Just as the prudent trader diversifies his portfolio, the prudent investor does not invest in CTAs that use similar trading systems.

The reason is simple. If all the CTAs in a fund are trend followers and the trend takes an abrupt change of direction, they all get caught in the move. If one CTA is a trend follower and the second a contrarian, the trend change just described may not impact the investment as severely.

There are several other ways of looking at diversification with regard to CTAs managing futures trading accounts. Futures portfolios should normally be diversified as to the markets in which they are traded. The risk involved in trading all of one's equity in one or two markets is great.

The second test for diversification among multiple CTAs sharing management responsibilities for a managed account program is called "negative correlation." Analysis of the long term trading results of the different CTAs indicates they do not incur drawdowns at the same time. This gives the program balance.

Your objective in creating diversity in a group of CTAs is to understand how their systems trade the market. Then mix and match systems. If, for example, an adverse condition, that could severely restrict one type of trading system takes hold of the market, not all the CTAs managing your funds would be affected. What would happen to your investment in a fund if it was managed by a group of strict trend followers, and the markets traded trendless for six months to a year? It's not a situation which allows you a good night's sleep.

CTA Selection Summary

Let's quickly review the steps you should take when you select a trading advisor.

Step Number 1

> Locate a group of commodity trading advisors (CTAs) that interest you. Since futures trading is very speculative and involves such a high degree of risk, you naturally expect a high return for assuming the risk. Therefore, the first number we often look for is the rate of return.
>
> As discussed earlier, there are several methods of calculating ROR. We prefer using the compound annual rate of return method. This was the formula that utilized the present value and the future value to determine the ROR over the length of the track record in years.
>
> Secondly, avoid or at least be very wary of track records that are shorter than three years or are hypothetical. Simulated or hypothetical performance tables are often generated to test trading systems developed through "paper trading." These track records have certain limitations, such as eliminating the human emotional factor that comes into play when a trader is actually risking his own or his clients' money. Any offering memorandum, such as a prospectus or disclosure document, reviewed by the Commodity Futures Trading Commission (CFTC) requires hypothetical performance records to be clearly stated as such and to carry a special disclosure statement. Be sure to read it.

Step Number 2

> If you didn't get anything else out of this chapter, we hope you at least reached the conclusion that a high ROR is not the most important factor to consider when selecting CTAs. In our opinion, a stable and consistent performance record is more important than an occasional astronomical ROR figure. We'd be much more comfortable with a trader who produces a 40-percent or 60-percent return year in and year out to one who produces a 100 percent or 200 percent one time with equally high drawdowns.
>
> Remember the Loss-Recover Table from this chapter. To recover from a 70-percent loss, the CTA needs a 233.33 percent gain or a 900 percent gain to

recoup a 90-percent loss. Whenever the equity is seriously depleted, chances of success geometrically decline.

We discussed the pros and cons of various methods of evaluation—ROR, VAMI, Sharp Ratio, Sterling Ratio, CTA Batting Average and Time-Interval Analysis. You'll have to go back to review the various techniques and decide which one or ones you find most meaningful. As you know, we lean heavily toward the Batting Average.

Step Number 3

Once you isolate CTAs that have acceptable trading records and whose performance is stable and consistent, you can move on to the more time consuming analysis. We recommend starting with the analysis of the numbers because it is the easiest data to obtain. You'll find it in each CTA's disclosure document, which is printed and distributed to prospective clients. Be sure to check the date on the cover, so you're dealing with current numbers. The CFTC requires the CTA to update his disclosure document every six months.

Step number 3 involves due diligence—learning as much as possible about the integrity, trading acumen, and operations of the CTAs under review. You'll want to check with the National Futures Association (NFA) Information Center (1-800-621-3570) to see if they have ever disciplined the CTAs. You can request references from the CTAs, for example. Ask for client, as well as professional, references.

Next you want to learn about their trading system. For example, if it is a trend following system, how well does it adjust to trend changes? How has this impacted the ROR?

We'd also recommend you interview the CTA and/or Commodity Pool Operator (CPO) in the case of a fund, limited partnership, or pool by telephone or in person. What kind of person will you be dealing with? Can s/he be trusted? Is s/he and will s/he be responsive to any questions you may have?

Also, take a look at his or her back room if possible. The back room is where the paperwork for the trading takes place. Are the orders handled efficiently? Is s/he well equipped with people, computers, quote equipment, etc.? If your investing in a fund that will give a CTA another $500,000 or $1,000,000 to trade, can s/he absorb the increase in volume? How has s/he managed volume increases compared to ROR in the past?

Fees are a critical area to study at this point in your investigation. Are they in line with industry standards? Keep the Loss-Recovery table in the back of your mind. Money paid out as management fees is not any more available to trade than equity loss trading. Exorbitant fees can cripple traders as fast as a large drawdown.

Step Number 4

By now, you're down to a short list of CTAs that have passed all your tests. Who do you choose? As always with futures trading, we recommend you diversify. Select more than one CTA or invest in a fund that uses more than one. Match your CTAs so they are negatively correlated.

Step Number 5

You must develop an ongoing monitoring procedure. One of the best we've seen is the time-interval analysis previously described. The worst thing you can do is take your eye off the target—of increasing your equity.

All of the above is the minimum you should do when selecting a professionally managed futures trading program. But it is not a foolproof way of making money. The best CTAs experience drawdowns. You may well have your money with them when they do. Only invest what you can afford to lose. The high rewards associated with futures trading are matched with the high losses that can also be sustained. Some of the analytical tools described in this chapter can also be used to study your personal trading performance.

CHAPTER 11

YOUR RIGHTS AND RECOURSE AS AN INVESTOR IN THE FUTURES MARKETS

Key Concepts

➠ Advantages of investing in a federally regulated industry.

➠ Knowing the CFTC and NFA regulations gives you some protection against swindlers.

➠ How you sort out the ethical from the unethical commodity broker.

➠ Fifteen questions to ask before you invest.

➠ Communicating with your broker—one of the keys to successful trading.

➠ Three cardinal sins committed by brokers, and what you can do about them.

If you understand your rights before you become a participant in the futures market, you'll have a far better chance of being successful then if you plunge into it without fully understanding of the risks. Over the years, most individual traders have been net losers. But the opportunity to make a 200 percent or 300 percent or more return on one's money in a few months, weeks, or even days brings a steady flow of investors to the pits.

But if you do lose, who's fault is it? Should you accept the blame no matter what? Or is your broker, the IB, the clearing firm, or the exchange completely or partially responsible? If so, what can you do about it?

What we'd like to do first is walk through the sales process most investors experience. As we do, we'll point out your rights. Additionally, we'll provide insights into how you can evaluate what you are being told, how you can protect yourself against swindlers, and what action you can take if you ever feel you have been cheated or mistreated. Then we'll discuss your rights in relationship to the FCM and the exchanges.

The first point to keep in mind when you are considering futures and/or options on futures (also known as exchange-traded options, as opposed to some metal options that involve the cash metals market that are unregulated) is that the futures market is regulated by the National Futures Association (NFA). It is an industry supported organization authorized by Congress via the Commodity Futures Trading Commission (CFTC).

No person or firm can engage in any business involving the buying or selling of futures contracts for the public without becoming an NFA member, or associate member. In other words, to conduct any futures business you must be an NFA member, and members can only do business with other members. An exception is the associated person (AP), who deals with the customer. These are commonly known as commodity brokers.

Most APs work for introducing brokers (IBs). The IB introduces the person or firm that wishes to trade to the futures commission merchant (FCM). The FCM is the entity that enters orders into the market through floor traders. The floor traders are the ones that do the actual trading in the pits of the exchanges.

The FCM is also responsible for what is known as the back room operation. This is the accounting involved in maintaining the trading account of each person or entity that is trading. Each exchange has a clearing operation to balance each day's trading.

Our point is simply this: if you are approached by anyone regarding an investing in the futures market, that person must be a member or an associate member of the NFA. To check a person's standing, i.e., a salesman (broker) or firm (IB) that sent you a letter about opening an account, with the NFA, all you need do is make a toll-free call to the NFA (1-800-621-3570) and ask.

If the person or firm is not registered with the NFA, tell the NFA's representative exactly what was sent or offered to you, and the NFA will investigate. Don't do any business with a salesperson or firm until you clear up, to your own satisfaction, this point. The type of investment being promoted may sound like it should be part of the futures industry, but isn't, and it doesn't require NFA registration. If the product is not federally regulated, you may have more difficulty getting satisfaction if something goes wrong.

If the person or firm soliciting you is NFA registered, s/he must adhere to all NFA and CFTC rules and regulations. Let's review the guidelines the NFA has set down for promotional material. By knowing these rules, you'll know if the firm that is soliciting your business is in compliance. If their advertising clearly violates these dictates, you should consider yourself forewarned. Also, if you ever have problems with the firm, you can use their disregard of NFA rules in your complaint against it. The specific NFA rule governing promotion is 2-29.

The NFA has a very broad definition of promotional material. It includes the following:

1. Any text of a standardized oral presentation, such as a sales script, or any communication for publication in any newspaper, magazine, or similar medium, or any broadcast over television, radio, or other electronic medium, which is disseminated or directed to the public concerning a futures account, agreement, or transaction.

2. Any standardized form of report, letter, circular, memorandum, or publication, such as a newsletter, which is disseminated or directed to the public.

3. Any other written material disseminated or directed to the public for the purpose of soliciting a futures account, agreement, or transaction, such as a seminar or class.

In general, you can consider just about all communications with you, the public, as promotional activities or promotional material.

The NFA has three general prohibitions which apply to all communications with the public. They are:

1. Fraudulent or deceitful communications.

2. High-pressure communications.

3. The statement that futures trading is appropriate for everyone.

Rule 2-29 requires anyone selling futures trading to provide a balanced discussion of the profit potential and the risk of loss. Whenever the possibility of profit is mentioned, it must be accompanied by an equally prominent statement of the risk of loss.

To make this determination, the NFA analyzes the overall impact of the promotional material. They take into consideration the number of times each word is used, size of type, and the amount of time or space devoted to each. But these are not their only considerations.

Remember, the mention of profit can take many forms and is not limited to the word "profit." Charts and graphs showing the growth of an account, for example, are considered statements about profits.

Cautionary statements, that are required to be made about hypothetical results or actual past trading is not indicative of future results, do not count when evaluating balance. These are separate and distinct requirements.

The question of balance is particularly important in video and other oral presentations. For example, a sixty-second commercial with only five seconds discussing loss or superimposing a disclaimer at the bottom of the screen is not acceptable to the NFA.

This holds true for telephone sales as well. The AP can't talk about profits for ten minutes and then say, "Past performance is not indicative of future results," and let it go at that. The AP would be in clear violation of Rule 2-29.

High-pressure sales tactics are a serious breach of the NFA's customer protection program. The NFA considers the following as the principal characteristics of high-pressure selling:

1. Exaggeration of profit potential.

2. Exaggeration of past results.

3. Exaggeration of the qualifications of an AP.

4. Exaggerating the need for urgency in making the investment decision.

5. Constant badgering of the prospect.

6. Belittling the prospect for not investing.

7. Emphasizing profits that have been missed.

8. Using courier services to deliver and pick up account papers.

9. Down playing the importance of the paperwork as mere regulatory red tape.

10. Lack of service to the customer after the sale.

We mentioned the term "hypothetical results." Let's clarify what it means. These are records of the results of trading that actually did not take place. It was constructed from computer simulations or some other mechanical method.

When presented with a trading track record of a broker, CTA, or system, the first thing to do is to check to see if they are labeled as hypothetical. It must be done in a manner that any reader would be able to immediately and clearly understand.

Next, NFA Rule 2-29(b)(4) requires any hypothetical results (including graphs) to be accompanied by a cautionary statement from CFTC Regulation 4.41(b)(1), which describes the limitation of hypothetical results. This statement must be printed **exactly** as follows (all caps):

HYPOTHETICAL OR SIMULATED PERFORMANCE RESULTS HAVE CERTAIN INHERENT LIMITATIONS. UNLIKE AN ACTUAL PERFOR- MANCE RECORD, SIMULATED RESULTS DO NOT REPRESENT ACTUAL TRADING. ALSO, SINCE THE TRADES HAVE NOT ACTUALLY BEEN EXECUTED, THE RESULTS MAY HAVE UNDER-OR-OVER COMPEN- SATED FOR THE IMPACT, IF ANY, OF CERTAIN MARKET FACTORS, SUCH AS LACK OF LIQUIDITY. SIMULATED TRADING PROGRAMS IN GENERAL ARE ALSO SUBJECT TO THE FACT THAT THEY ARE DE- SIGNED WITH THE BENEFIT OF HINDSIGHT. NO REPRESENTATION IS BEING MADE THAT ANY ACCOUNT WILL OR IS LIKELY TO ACHIEVE PROFITS OR LOSSES SIMILAR TO THOSE SHOWN.

The creator of the track record must be able to demonstrate to the NFA the basis for the hypothetical results and keep records to prove how it was calculated.

Real and hypothetical results should never be mixed on the same track record. The NFA believes this is confusing and misleading.

Are the rules any easier if actual, rather than hypothetical, results are used?

The person promoting the track record must be able to prove the results using actual account statements. The accounts selected must be representative of all the accounts the person controls. A CTA can't just show you his best account. The NFA will check equity runs and do all the detail work needed to compare the accounts used to all accounts, if and when they audit the CTA.

If different types and sizes of accounts are traded, using a representative account becomes more difficult because the NFA will want an explanation of the selection and how it compares to a "typical" account. Some of the differences taken into consideration are size, margin rates, trading strategies, markets, and commis- sions.

Beware of advertising that uses a lot of high-powered adjectives, such as the largest or best or fastest firm in the futures industry. If superlatives are used, the user may have problems with the NFA. The NFA's position is simply this: such claims may be regularly used in other industries, but they cannot be used by NFA members without detailed documentation.

In the eyes of the NFA, the use of qualifiers, such as "one of the fastest" or "one of the largest," does little to alter the need to document the claim. The point is simply this: Whatever is said in sales and advertising must be proved if ques- tioned by the NFA.

When it comes to promoting exchange traded options, there are additional considerations. The NFA takes exception to the use of the term "limited" risk when referring to options. The broker must make it clear that the risk is limited to the entire amount of the premium plus transaction costs. The term transaction costs means the commission and fees. Fees means NFA, exchange, and FCM fees.

If a broker is promoting a third-party controller (a CTA), he may use some promotional material prepared by the CTA. This does not reduce the broker's accountability in any way.

The NFA looks at the responsibility to police the industry as a two-way road. In other words, if a broker is promoting a CTA and his sales literature is misleading, the broker will be held responsible along with the CTA, if the NFA gets involved in a complaint.

Every party that prepares or uses promotional materials is responsible for compliance with NFA Rules 2-29. Additionally, the supervisory organization is responsible.

Live TV or radio interviews done by APs or CTAs do not fall within the strict definition of promotional material. But the registered person doing the interview is always subject to the three general prohibitions: fraud, high pressure, and inappropriateness of futures trading for all investors. On the other hand, if the show is paid for by the NFA member and this fort is not disclosed, the NFA will call it fraud. Shows that "pretend" to be news are strongly discouraged by the NFA.

"Commodity Traders Consumer Reports" newsletter and other independent sources that rate CTAs are often used as promotional materials. The person using the material still has a lot of responsibility. He or she is responsible for the accuracy of the report and that proper disclosure is made regarding the limitations of the results and rating.

This means that rates of return must be calculated in a manner consistent with CFTC Regulations (4.21(a)(4)(ii)(F)). The user must be able to show to the NFA that the calculations comply with the rules. Lastly, all the data available to support any numerical information must be available to the NFA if they request it.

We think the overall position of the NFA is very clear. From time to time, interpretation of borderline cases can cause consternation between a broker and his customer.

If you are solicited by a broker who is using some type of advertising that delivers an unbalanced presentation of the enormous profits to be made from the futures market with little or no mention of risk, you'll know at least two important facts. First, the material is in violation of NFA Rules 2-29. Secondly, beware of whoever is presenting the materials. If their initial overture is so out of tune, the rest of their song will probably be as well. The next refrain most likely will be a high-pressure sales presentation. Consider yourself forewarned and keep your distance.

Advertising, which is balanced and informative, can be very helpful to you both in deciding if you are suited for futures trading and if you want to learn more. As you absorb these type of messages, you'll learn how much risk you'll be accepting and have a more complete picture of profit opportunity.

Once attention is aroused, most buyers begin the next stage of the sales process, which is the search for more information. Investing is serious business. Therefore, as our interest in a product or service grows, we want to learn as much as we can about it.

At this stage, you often see a big difference between the ethical broker and one who plays fast and loose. The former will spend time with you, send you information, such as newsletters, and be sincerely interested in learning about your investment needs. The wheeler-dealer's objective is to raise the prospects' greed level to such a fever pitch that you send money immediately. This is high-pressure sales. There's no time for thought and reflection. You'll hear lines like this:

- "An opportunity this good only comes by once in a blue moon!"

- "If you don't get $2,000 to me by noon tomorrow, you'll miss your chance to turn it into $10,000 in the next two weeks!"

- "Gold is going sky high—tomorrow!"

From ethical brokers, you'll hear description of opportunities won and opportunities lost. The legitimate AP will tell you that sooner or later another good, solid trading opportunity will appear. You'll also be provided with a balanced presentation of the risk, something you won't hear from "deal-peddlers." Remember the old adage: "A futures trade that sounds too good to be true probably is."

In their booklet, *Before You Say Yes*, the NFA lists fifteen questions that can help you distinguish qualified investment sales people from swindlers. The following is a paraphrased version of those questions:

1. What is the commission rate? Other costs?

2. What are the risks?

3. Can you send me a written explanation of the risk involved?

4. Can you send me copies of your sales literature?

5. Are you selling futures contracts sold on the regulated exchanges?

6. Which governmental or industry regulator supervises your firm?

7. Specifically, where would my money be held?

8. When and where can we meet in person?

9. How and when can I liquidate my investment if I so desire?

10. Will you send me your entire proposal in the mail?

11. If a dispute arises, what are the means available to resolve it?

12. Where did you get my name?

13. Would you mind explaining your proposal to my lawyer?

14. Would you give me the names of your principals and officers?

15. Can you provide references?

Experience has shown that the dishonest sales people usually resist or are not prepared for this type of interrogation. Their "marks" are impulsive buyers who make entirely emotional decisions. The answers you get are vague and evasive. For example,

Question:	How much are commissions?
Response:	They're never a problem.
Question:	If I have a complaint, what can I do?
Response:	Don't even worry about that, I'll take care of you personally.

By gathering a lot of information and taking some time making your decision, you can protect yourself from the majority of swindlers—but not all. The very best mimic legitimate sales operations, but most can be uncovered if you do your homework and control your emotions.

Step 3 of the typical sales process is the evaluation of alternatives. Only the most experienced investors take the time to do this. Most people, if they decide to trade, go with whomever pursues them. At this point, you should want to refer back to the earlier section on selecting a broker in Chapter 3. Select one that provides synergism to your trading effort. One who will help you overcome your limitations. Use the due diligent approach suggested later in this section. As far as checking on a specific broker, call the NFA on their toll free number. Tell them you want to check the status of an AP and ask the following questions:

1. Is Mr. Broker currently registered?

2. With which firm?

3. How long has he been registered?

4. Has the NFA taken any public disciplinary action against him?

5. Has he been registered with any firm that has been cited for compliance problems?

6. Is there anything else you can tell me about him, since I'm considering investing with him?

This toll-free call takes about five minutes and tells you if the AP in question has ever had problems with the NFA. You'll also get some facts about his (her) experience which you can compare with what you've been told.

Additionally, you can call the Compliance Department of the CFTC (202-254-3067) and find out if the broker has any customer complaint pending or previously filed against him(her). If so, you'll be given a docket designation and a telephone number to call to get the status and explanation of the complaint.

Another source to check is the NFA Manual. It includes a section, which is well cross referenced by broker name, detailing the disciplinary hearings conducted by the NFA. It is published by Prentice-Hall Information Services (1-800-562-0245). Your public library may have it or might order it for you. It costs about $78 per year and is updated periodically throughout the year.

Once you decide who you think the right broker is, you make your selection by completing the account papers, which we've already reviewed in Chapter 3. Your broker should ask you to read them carefully and fill them out in your own handwriting. The reason for you to do it in your own hand is so the broker is assured that you saw them and had the opportunity to read them. The broker will ask you if you understand them and have any questions. The account papers describe the risks you are assuming. You have no one to blame but yourself if you ignore them.

If the broker offers to fill them out for you ("I'll just get them typed up for you"), consider this a warning signal. The easier the broker makes it for you to fill out the account papers, the less likely you are to study them. They are worth the time and effort it takes to understand what you are signing because they define the risk you face in great detail.

The last phase of the sales process is called the post-purchase period. What happens after your account is opened and funded?

Most accounts begin trading at this point. To place a trade, you communicate with your broker (he calls you or you call him). The broker has your order relayed to the order desk of the proper exchange, which passes it on to the pits. Once filled, it moves back through the chain culminating with your broker calling you with your "fill."

A written confirmation is mailed to you the next day from the FCM's back office. On a monthly basis, you receive a summary report of your trading.

At this stage of your relationship with your broker, what should you be protecting yourself against? The first thing is simple, clerical errors on the part of the back room (accounting) of the FCM. We can't tell you how many riffs occur because customers paid no attention to their per-trade and monthly statements. Carefully examine the statements for the following:

1. The commissions charged your account are those to which you and your broker agreed. Time and again, we've heard customers argue with the broker because of an error on a statement that is weeks or months old. First off, the broker has very little or nothing to do with the preparation of the statements. They are generated at the headquarters of the FCM and, depending on its policy, the FCM may or may not send a copy to the broker.

2. The fill price is the same as the one your broker gave you.

3. Any money you deposited in your account has been properly credited.

4. The trade you made is the same as the one on the statement, particularly if you are on the side (long or short) that you want to be.

5. The mathematics are correct, and all debits and credits have been properly applied.

The broker does get a preliminary run of all the trades he makes each day. His responsibility is to check it and to make the FCM aware of any discrepancies. The corrections may or may not get made before the trade confirmation is mailed to you. A correction is then mailed, which you would receive the following day. In these cases, your broker would normally alert you, but you must double check to see the error is corrected. If it doesn't get corrected, contact your broker, and he'll see the corrections are made.

Communications Are the Key

The glue that holds the customer-broker relationship together is good communications. The most professional brokers set up guidelines early on so you know what to expect and what is expected from you. Here is an example:

1. Time of day you are most easily accessible.

2. Whether you are to call in or whether your broker will call you.

3. What steps will be taken if you can't be contacted, i.e., should your broker put stops in the market, close out positions after 4, 8, 12, or 24 hours of not being in contact, etc.

4. What steps will be taken if the account goes into debit. Do you plan to wire money into the account? Transfer from another account? Overnight a check?

5. How trading emergencies will be handled.

6. What hours you are available and who to contact when you are not available.

7. Normal office hours, plus any evening hours your broker is available.

8. You may need to provide your broker with your home phone number, if that's the only way for him to stay in touch with you.

9. Your broker needs to know who to contact if you are not always near a phone; this person should be able to reach you quickly. For example, farm wives are often in radio contact with their husbands during planting and harvesting.

10. You need to make provisions for unusual situations, such as when you are traveling or taking a vacation.

The point is simply this: don't get out of touch with your broker no matter what. If a situation arises where you are going to be out of touch, either put stops in the market or close out the positions or even the account. Do not risk trading when you cannot be reached quickly, if the market situation warrants it. If your broker doesn't mention this, be sure you do.

The Three Cardinal Sins

There are three very serious offenses of which brokers are accused that you should be aware of. They are misrepresentation, unauthorized trading, and churning.

Misrepresentation, which we discussed to some extent in the section on promotional material, usually evolves around the broker not telling the prospective client enough about the risk of futures trading. For example, one day a customer opens his mail to find a $2,000, or $5,000, or $10,000 margin call. The customer was told by the broker that this would never happen because stop/loss orders were to be used religiously. Unfortunately, the futures market being traded made limit moves against the client's position for a day or two and no trading took place, so the stop orders could not be activated. When the smoke cleared, the customer was seriously in debt. The customer had not been warned about the possibility of limit moves.

Another common type of misrepresentation is representing a hypothetical track record of a trading system or showing a track record without noting that commissions have not been deducted. When they are, the track record is negative or substantially less attractive.

The second cardinal sin is unauthorized trading. This occurs when a broker places trades for his customer's account without the customer's authority, knowledge, or consent. Often this is a breakdown of communications. The broker "thinks" he knows what the client wants to do. Or he "thinks" he talked it over and got approval. Or worse yet, the broker deliberately placed trades, without talking to the customer solely to generate commissions.

For this reason, you must carefully review the trade confirmation and monthly statements. Do you remember discussing and approving each trade?

The professional broker guards against this eventuality by tape recording all orders placed by customers. Some firms have tape equipment that records every conversation. The order desks of the exchanges, for example, record all conversations. Check with your broker in the beginning to learn if he uses taping equipment. When there is a question, ask him to play back the conversation. You may want to tape your conversations with your broker. If you do, be sure to tell him/her.

The last cardinal sin is churning or over trading an account. This is measured by calculating the commission to equity ratio over a specific period of time, usually a month. For example, let's say $1,000 in commissions are generated in an account with $10,000 in equity during the month of January. The commission to equity ratio would be 1:10 or 10 percent.

How high is too high? When has your broker violated NFA rules?

First, if you are calling all the trades, there are no grounds for complaints. You can trade as much as you want as long as you maintain the proper level of equity.

If on the other hand, you have turned over trading discretion in your account to your broker by signing a limited power of attorney, your broker's supervisor, the FCM, and the NFA may be checking the trade volume. There is no set ratio figure that automatically triggers a churning violation. But once the monthly commission to equity ratio gets into the 15 percent to 25 percent range, regulators and supervisors take notice. They may require an explanation of why the ratio is so high.

There are some legitimate reasons. For example, let's say you have agreed to have your broker trade a certain day trading system. These are very short term positions that are opened and closed during the same trading session. No positions are carried over night. Day trading systems, because they are so short term, often generate a lot of commissions. Customers also like them—if they are making money—because they do not assume the risk of holding a position overnight.

If, on the other hand, the broker is churning an account just to bolster his income, he could face disciplinary action from one or more of the regulators. The customer could file a complaint as well in hopes of recovering commissions and equity.

Managing Your Complaint

Futures trading is a very complex and fast moving investment. There are thousands of things that can go wrong—most accidentally, but few may be on purpose. Nevertheless, there are procedures to deal with them all.

Naturally, the simple complaints, involving obvious errors on statements, can be resolved with a call to your broker. But what do you do if you feel you have suffered some serious loss or damage at the hands of your broker? What recourse do you have?

The possible eventuality of this ever occurring is one of the strongest arguments for only investing in federally regulated investments, such as futures. With these types of investment vehicles, there is a wide array of options open to you.

The first step, as always, is discussing the problem with your broker and his supervisor. If you get no satisfaction, you can turn to the regulators for help.

The first level in the futures industry is the NFA. Call them on their toll-free number. Explain your situation and they will outline your options. One of the questions they'll ask is whether you signed the "Pre-Dispute Arbitration Agreement," included with your account papers.

You were not required to sign it, but if you did, it binds you and your broker to accepting arbitration of disputes by the NFA. This can be to your advantage, particularly if you are a small investor, because it reduces the expense and time of litigation. You won't have to hire an attorney and you can request non-industry arbitrators on your panel. You'll get a square deal, particularly if you are in the right. The only negative aspect is that you may be waiving further rights to sue in a court of law.

If you didn't sign the "Pre-Dispute Arbitration Agreement," you can still turn to the NFA for help and take advantage of their arbitration facility. Or, you can file a complaint with the CFTC. If you are considering this approach, contact them for a copy of their free booklet *Questions & Answers About How You Can Resolve a Commodity Market-Related Dispute*. They have basically three reparation procedures:

- Voluntary

- Summary

- Formal

The voluntary procedure is used for claims under $10,000. It is administered by judgment officers appointed by the CFTC. Both parties have an opportunity to uncover facts ("discovery") and present their arguments in writing. There is no oral hearing. Decisions are final, and no appeal is permitted. A non-refundable $25 fee is required.

The summary procedure is similar to the voluntary, but it allows for both a limited oral presentation and a written presentation, which takes place in Washington, D.C. Further, you can appeal the decision to the CFTC and to a court of law if you are still not satisfied. It handles complaints of $10,000 and less and requires a $50 non-refundable filing fee.

The formal procedure is designed to handle major complaints, over $10,000. A court-like hearing is conducted in one of 20 locations throughout the United States before an administrative judge. You can be represented by an attorney if you wish. Appeals to the CFTC and the courts are possible. A $200 non-refundable fee is required to file.

Besides the NFA and the CFTC, you can take a complaint to the American Arbitration Association, or file a civil suit. If you think your broker or his firm has committed a criminal offense, you can contact the Federal Bureau of Investigation (FBI), or if the U.S. mail was involved, the Chief Postal Inspector of the United States Postal Service.

If you invested in a limited partnership or a fund, you may be able to appeal to your local state attorney general or the Security and Exchange Commission. Other places with which you may check are the Better Business Bureau and the Federal Trade Commission.

For help deciding your most effective alternative, you should probably sit down and discuss it with your attorney. Please keep in mind two very critical considerations:

1. Your most effective protection results from systematically conducting due diligence research when selecting a broker. Act with reason—don't get caught up in an emotional response to the potential the futures markets may offer.

2. In our opinion, sticking to investments that are federally regulated usually give you a better dispute resolution process than unregulated investments.

Over the many years we have been in this business, the most beneficial arbitration has been done, in our opinion, between brokers and clients. Once it goes beyond this stage, the costs and complications seem to outweigh the results. Our advice is to work hard at this level to keep the lines of communication open. Efforts in this area pay dividends in better trading, fewer errors, and more enjoyable trading.

OVERVIEW OF SOME OF
THE ACTIVE MARKETS

Key Concepts

➠ Avoid non-liquid markets.

➠ Become aware of all fundamental/technical factors that have an impact on prices of the markets you trade to avoid being financially hurt by an unexpected event that could adversely affect those particular markets.

The following is neither an exhaustive list nor an exhaustive summary of the markets available to futures investors. We have limited our discussion to markets we feel have now, and will have in the future, enough trading volume to make them acceptable for traders new to the futures markets.

Non-liquid markets—those that are lightly traded—cause serious problems for experienced and inexperienced traders alike. These should be avoided because their thinness causes minor trading activity to result in a disproportionate amount of price movement, referred to as volatility. Additionally, the low volume can, at times, make it difficult to open or close positions. You can be unwillingly trapped in these markets or have them unexpectedly move violently against your position.

There is only space available to mention the key fundamental and technical factors. We touch on the basic information you may need to know to trade successfully. The professional trader learns his/her markets inside out to avoid being blind sided by an unexpected market event. Use the following information as a starting point.

Overview of the Corn Market

Corn is a member of the feed grains family, which includes corn, sorghum, oats, and barley. Corn is the single largest member of the group, accounting for over 80 percent of the total U.S. production of feed grains.

The crop year for corn begins October 1st of every year and ends September 30th of the following year. Since corn is a commodity that can be stored for a reasonably long period of time and can be moved long distances, keeping track of the amount available worldwide is important. For this reason, United States Department of Agriculture (USDA) releases regular projections of production and disappearances (usage).

Fundamental Factors

The key issue is usually pipeline supplies. How much corn is in farm and commercial storage (that is, left over from the previous crop years)? How much is expected from the current crop that's still in the ground? These numbers are then compared to what is expected to be used. The supply-demand equation looks like this:

Beginning Stocks + Production + Imports = Total Supplies

Feed, Seed, Residual + Food + Export = Total Usage or Demand

Total Supplies – Total Usage = Ending Stocks or Carryover

In the United States, the import figure is not significant, since we produce so much. However, the export figure can make or break a market.

If there is an abundance of inventory, this hangs over the market and depresses prices. If stocks are scarce, prices soar.

Supply Side

Water is the key to the production of corn. It takes 5,000 gallons of water per bushel. Eighteen to twenty-four inches of rain are required during the growing season to produce 100 to 175 bushel yields. For every pound of dry matter (leaves, stalks, ears, etc.) produced, 372 pounds of water are needed. Normal rainfall during the growing season provides half of the needed moisture—subsoil moisture is critical.

Water can be a problem at planting time and at harvest. In Iowa, and other Midwest states, wet fields in the spring can delay planting. If it is substantially delayed, farmers may switch to soybeans. Heavy rain at harvest can knock down stalks, slow harvest, and reduce yields. There's usually no such thing as a "normal" year—either you get too much or too little rain.

One of the most critical periods occurs when the plant pollinates. This usually lasts for about ten days around mid- to late-July in the corn belt. During this period of time, corn needs moisture—either rainfall or subsoil. Additionally, the temperature cannot be excessively high. A week of 100-degree-plus temperatures during pollination substantially reduces yields.

Demand Side

Approximately 70 percent of the U.S. corn crop is used domestically. It is consumed as feed for livestock, food, alcohol, and seed. Feed is by far the most important. Alcohol may get a boost from gasohol production.

Demand depends quite a bit on the financial conditions of livestock producers and the cattle cycle. Are animal numbers increasing or decreasing? Are herds expanding or contracting? Demand for feed can be estimated when you can get a good fix on these numbers.

The price of wheat must also be taken into consideration. Farmers will use wheat as a substitute feed when it is economical to do so.

The next big demand consideration is export. Although the U.S. only exports about 30 percent of its crop, this represents approximately 75 percent of the world's feed grain trade. Most countries produce their own feed, primarily, in the form of silage. Only a handful of countries grow enough corn to be a real force in the export business. Of these countries, none are considered a steady and reliable supplier. They export only when they have a particularly abundant crop.

Price Forecasting

Accurately analyzing corn prices using fundamental analysis is nearly impossible! Keeping track of impact of the worldwide weather patterns on yields alone is a Herculean task. Further, you must accurately forecast cattle and hog numbers as well as usage for alcohol, seed, and food. There have been several attempts to develop econometric models to manage all the variables, but none have proven terribly successful.

Technical analysis has been more successful. For example, seasonal patterns are reliable. Price highs are usually made in late July or early August, lows come in November or April. Several reasonably reliable long- and short-term cycles have been isolated.

Chart analysis also works pretty well. Head and shoulder formations, for example, can be traded with an acceptable amount of confidence. The price activity of corn also responds to other predictive formations, such as flags and triangles. Once a solid trend is established, you can work the trend line for all it is worth. Corn is a very popular market and almost always has plenty of liquidity.

Overview of Live and Feeder Cattle Markets

Cattle

The production of beef requires the breeding, raising, and fattening of cattle. This industry has a unique vocabulary that you need to understand.

Cow—A mature female that has had a calf.

Heifer—A female that has not yet produced a calf (and is under three years of age).

Bull Calf —A male calf, not yet castrated.

Steer—A castrated male.

Bull—An uncastrated male, capable of reproduction.

Yearling—A calf that has been fed on pasture for approximately one year.

Another unique aspect of beef production is its cycle.

- There are fourteen to eighteen months between when a heifer calf is born and when bred.

- The gestation period of a calf is nine months.

- There are approximately seventeen to nineteen months between when a bull calf is born and when it can be slaughtered as a fed steer.

- It takes over two and one-half years from the time a cow is bred until a steak is in the butcher's case from its offspring.

A lot can happen from the beginning of the production cycle to the end. The cattle go through several stages and hands.

There are three distinct sectors to the cattle industry. The first is the ranch, called the cow-calf operation. Calves and feeder cattle are produced here.

Sector two is the feed lot. The feeder cattle are fed out in preparation for slaughter. When ready for market, the feeder cattle are called fat cattle.

The packer is the third segment of the industry. It converts the live cattle to beef and byproducts.

Supply Side

The cow-calf operation produces calves. It is the driving force that moves the cattle business. A typical breeding herd in the United States consists of seventy-five cows, with one bull per twenty cows. Depending on the climate and rainfall of the ranch, it may take from five to 200 acres to support one cow-calf unit.

The herd is usually bred in the summer with the calves born in the spring (a 9-month gestation period). The calves are weaned after 6-8 months, when they weigh about 300 to 500 pounds.

The weaned calves are two-way cattle. They can either go directly to the feedlot for fattening or they can be put on grass for another six to ten months, until they weigh 650 to 800 pounds. The decision is made based on cattle prices, production costs, and economic conditions. Additionally, the cow-calf operation must hold back up to 20 percent of its heifers as replacements for cows that become barren.

The feedlot sector takes the calves from the cow-calf operator and fattens them for slaughter. Usually steers are fed until they weigh 1,000 to 1,200 pounds and heifers until they weigh 850-1,000 pounds.

There are basically two types of feedlots: commercial and farmer. The most common distinction between them is that the commercials have a larger capacity. They can feed 1,000 or more head at a time. Anything less is classified as a farmer feedlot. The commercial feedlots tend to be more efficient—better rates of gain per head, higher gains per day, and shorter feeding time.

The last sector is composed of the packers. They purchase the fed cattle, slaughter them, and sell the beef and just about everything else (hide, trimmed fat, bones, blood, and glands). The carcass, which is approximately 62 percent of the live weight, will yield about half steaks and roasts. The rest will be hamburger, except for about five percent that becomes stewing beef, on an average.

Demand Side

After the packer, the beef enters the retail food chain. Beef is almost exclusively produced for human consumption. A small amount is used in dog food. Beef has a lot of serious competition, such as pork, chicken, fish, and other types of meat and poultry. Several vegetable products, soybean fillers, and meat substitutes, for example, attempt to compete directly or indirectly.

Fundamental Analysis

Because of the lengthy production cycle and the limited ability to store beef, one popular approach to analyzing price is the Pipeline Method. Users of this analytical tool estimate the supplies at hand in each of the various sectors of the industry. They attempt to anticipate the decisions of the managers of each sector. Will cow-calf operators hold back more than 20 percent of their heifers this year to increase the size of their herd? Which way will two-way cattle go?

The basic source of information on the status of the pipeline comes from quarterly reports issued by the United States Department of Agriculture (USDA). They are called the *Cattle on Feed Reports* covering the top thirteen cattle feeding states or about 85-90 percent of all cattle on feed. Since the typical length of feeding is approximately two quarters, you can anticipate slaughter numbers. USDA also publishes data on fed cattle, slaughter and beef production which can be compared to earlier forecasts.

The Cattle Cycle

The size of the cattle herd has a distinct, long-term cycle. There have been eight cattle cycles identified since 1896, averaging twelve years in length. They have ranged from nine to sixteen years in length. On an average, the national herd expands for seven years and contracts for five. The primary reasons for the cycle is the length of the production cycle and heavy investment (land, equipment, cattle) required to enter and stay in the business.

Seasonality

There are no set planting or harvesting time periods for cattle, as with other agricultural products. But there still is a seasonal cycle. Most calves are born within forty-five days of April 1st and weaned within forty-five days of October 1st. The 350-500 pound calves are usually kept on grass until they gain 250-350 pounds. Then they are sent to the feedlot to gain two pounds a day for the next 210 days. At that point, the steer is twenty-six months old, weighs 1,150 pounds, and is ready for slaughter.

Price Determinants

There are several factors that impact the price of beef besides supply-demand equations already discussed. Feed costs account for approximately 30 percent of total production costs. Low corn prices stimulate production, particularly putting additional weight on fat cattle which increases beef supplies, lowering prices.

Since cattle production is capital intensive, interest rates can stimulate or stifle production. Weather can also impact production. Particularly hot or cold weather reduces weight gain. Taste, fashion, and sales promotion can influence consumers.

Is eating beef the healthy "thing" to do? Will TV spots increase usage or switch consumers to the "other white" meat?

Trading and Technical Analysis

The length of time required to make major changes in the cattle cycles causes the market to develop long-term trends which are ideally suited for technical analysis. This can also result in the market trading for long periods of time within narrow ranges, making it is difficult to trade it profitably, except on a very short-term basis.

Overview of the Wheat Market

Wheat

Like sugar, wheat is a universally grown crop. It is grown all over the world and is harvested year round. Carvings found in Egypt indicate wheat has been cultivated since at least 1000 B.C.

Wheat belongs to the grass family. Its kernels grow in compact heads on the end of hollow stalks making it easy to harvest. The former Russian Empire and China are among the largest producers. But, they consume what they produce and are often net importers.

Approximately 60 percent of the U.S. production is exported. Canada is also a major exporter. From time to time depending on crop conditions, other countries—France, for example—can make a major impact on world pricing. Since most countries consume the wheat they grow, the production of the exporters must be watched closely. Also, the wheat price analyst needs to be aware of the amount of supply available worldwide. Since wheat is primarily a food, prices are elastic. The price is very responsive to changes in the supply-demand equation.

Wheat is unique, as far as the price analyst is concerned, in that the type of wheat available is an important consideration. Wheat produced in the United States, consistently the world's largest exporter, can be classified as common and durum wheat. Common is further classified as by color (red or white) and by hardness (hard or soft). It can also be classified by the time of planting (spring vs. winter). The U.S. crop is about evenly divided between spring and winter wheat.

Supply Side

Winter wheat is planted in the fall, lies dormant over the winter (ideally with a snow cover that prevents the erosion of soil/seed and to provide moisture for germination in the spring) and is harvested between late May and June. Spring wheats are planted as early as possible and harvested in late summer.

Hard red wheats, which are the majority of the U.S. production, are valued worldwide because of their high protein content. They also contain a large quantity of strong, elastic gluten which is ideal for bread making. These wheats are produced in dry climates, like the states of Kansas, Nebraska, Oklahoma, and Northern Texas.

Soft red wheat is produced in areas with high rainfall: the Great Lakes, Atlantic Coast, and Eastern Texas. Its primary use is for making pastry, crackers, biscuits, cakes, and similar products. It has a lower protein content.

The last major type of wheat produced in the U.S. is durum. It is grown in North Dakota, South Dakota, and Minnesota. Durum wheat is used for making a semolina which is particularly suited for pasta.

Demand Side

Worldwide demand for wheat is caused by the need to feed billions of people every day. Most countries consume all they produce. In the U.S., demand also comes in the form of export. This can be either commercial export or government export programs.

Food is a very politically sensitive subject. A well fed country is usually a politically stable country. The opposite is also true. For years, the U.S. government exported large amounts of wheat in hopes of stabilizing client countries. Therefore, politics can play an important role in demand.

As mentioned in the section of this series on corn, wheat can be used as a feed substitute for corn in livestock enterprises. But the quantity of wheat used for this purpose is very insignificant. The impact, if any, is on the price of corn and is usually short-term.

Price Forecasting

Worldwide weather is the dominant factor affecting wheat prices. Refer to the supply-demand equation printed in the section on corn. Particular attention must be paid to the large, importing countries, such as China.

Government policy is the second most dominant determinant of wheat prices. If a shortage occurs in a controlled society, to what extent will it go out on the open market to replace the short fall? Or will the government tell its people to tighten their belts? How will the foreign policy of a major exporter, like the U.S., have an impact on pricing?

Other important determinants are:

- Exchange rates (a strong dollar hurts U.S. exports).

- Level of carry-over stock (the higher the level, the lower prices will be).

- Availability of storage and transportation (these have a short-term impact on prices).

- Changes in production and consumption patterns (these produce gradual changes).

Seasonality

Prices tend to decline into harvest months as supplies become plentiful and increase toward the end of the year.

Technical Analysis

Wheat is a very popular futures contract. It usually has plenty of liquidity and responds well to basic technical analysis.

Overview of the Oat Market

Oats

Oats are cereal grasses that grow well in cool, temperate climates. They are found all over the world. Farmers have always found them useful because they actually do best in poorer soils. Even in areas with an abundance of high quality ground, you'll find oats grown on the lesser fields.

Supply Side

The Commonwealth of Independent States is the world's largest producer, followed by the United States, Germany, Canada, and Poland. Production on a global basis has been on the decline since the 1970s. The U.S. production is currently at its lowest since the 1880s. Oats have been displaced by higher value crops. The U.S. has even "stooped" to the point of importing food quality oats in recent years. Given our capacity to grow just about any crop we choose, it is almost a national embarrassment.

Oats are a lot like wheat—the producing countries consume just about all they produce. Less than 5 percent of the world's production finds its way into export channels.

In the United States, the major producing states are South Dakota, North Dakota, and Minnesota. We primarily grow white oats; although, some red and grey are grown. Oats are planted in early April or late May and are to be harvested between mid-July and late August.

Demand Side

The single largest use of oats (approximately 95 percent) is as livestock feed. Worldwide, most oats are consumed by livestock on the farms on which they are grown. They are a particularly excellent feed for horses, breeding animals, young stock, and poultry because oats have the highest amount of protein among the cereal grains. They are also high in carbohydrates, which provides energy.

The decline in oat acres and production in recent years has been the result of a decline in the number of horses and mules employed as work animals.

A small amount (less than 5 percent) of oats are processed into food for humans. These are made into oatmeal and other food products. Recently, results of clinical tests indicate oat bran can be used in human diets to reduce the amount of cholesterol in the blood. This may increase food consumption. It, however, won't be significant to the overall world production. Also, a small portion of each year's crop is held back for seed for the following year.

Seasonality

Like most crops, oat prices tend to weaken as we move into harvest when supplies are plentiful. This puts the lows in the July-August time frame. After harvest, prices usually increase with the high being hit most often in January.

Price Determinants

Oats, as previously stated, are primarily used as feed for livestock. Therefore, the number and mix of livestock and poultry on feed is the primary price determinant. Analysts must pay close attention to all of USDA's livestock and crop reports because oats compete with other grains—corn, sorghum, and even wheat—as feed.

Here's a partial list of reports you'll want to monitor if you trade oats: Planting Intentions, Prospective Planting Report, Monthly Crop Production Reports, Monthly Eggs, Chickens & Turkeys Report, Quarterly Hog & Pigs Report, Livestock and Meat Situation, Cattle on Feed, Weekly Roundup of World Production & Trade, U.S. Export Sales, Stocks in All Positions, Grain Market News, Feed Market News, Wheat Situation Report, and others. Additionally, you'll want to review various state agricultural reports, particularly those of North and South Dakota.

Another important fact to keep in mind when you do your analysis and begin to compare oats to other feeds, is that oats are lighter than other feeds. A bushel of oats weighs only slightly more than half of what a bushel of corn weighs. This equates to its feed value, which is slightly more than half that of corn.

Therefore, a cattle feeder would have to buy more oats than corn to feed the same number of cattle or poultry. It's not a one-to-one comparison. In general, if you compare oats to corn by weight, oats sell for about 85 to 90 percent of the price of corn.

As with any crop, weather is an important price determinant. However, oats are a hearty crop. They are less vulnerable to bad weather than most. This is documented by the fact that so much of it is grown in North and South Dakota, states which are not known for their pleasant climates.

Carryover of stocks from one year to the next is another critical factor when forecasting price levels. Refer to the supply-demand equation in the corn overview. The higher the amount of carryover, the lower prices will usually be. Also, keep in mind that you must compare the oat carryover figures with those of other feed crops, particularly corn. If one is high and the other low, feed users will switch to the more plentiful, usually less expensive, feed.

We cannot neglect Uncle Sam when we attempt to determine future price levels. He has a heavy hand in the process. You must know if there is a government program affecting oats, how it works, and its expected impact.

Traders Notes

The speculative use of the oats futures contracts are very similar to that of corn, but there are some important differences of which you should be aware. Because of the enormous size of the corn crop and the tremendous amount of hedging that goes on, moves are usually slow and ponderous. It often takes "forever" to get a major trend change in corn underway. This market can absorb large jolts, like when the foreign countries unexpectedly enter the market to buy several million metric tons.

Oat futures contracts are much thinner. They are much more responsive to trading activity. Many traders use this characteristic to their advantage by using oats as a leading indicator of the grain complex's direction.

If oats make a major change in trend, the traders then position themselves to take advantage of this in the corn and wheat markets. But if you trade oats, remember a thin market is often very volatile and dangerous. On the other hand, the margin money required to buy a futures contract in oats is usually the lowest of all the commodities.

Overview of the Cotton Market

Cotton

Cotton is an ancient crop, first cultivated in China over 5,000 years ago. It worked its way west via Persia and India over routes traveled by Alexander the Great. The first weaving techniques were introduced into Spain in the 13th century. From Spain, the science of making cotton spread to the Netherlands and to England, where it flourished in the 17th century. The first cotton mill in North America was established in Rhode Island in 1790.

It was a good old Yankee ingenuity that really gave the industry a boost. In 1793, Eli Whitney invented the cotton gin. This machine alone increases productivity fifty fold. The gin removes seed from the fiber, which is woven into cloth. For the first time, enough fiber was available to supply a commercial textile industry.

Supply Side

On the supply side, of the supply-demand equation(refer to corn overview), are 75 countries throughout the world growing cotton. Most use all their production internally. The three dominant producers are the United States, China, and the Commonwealth of Independent States. Turkey and Egypt are also major suppliers of raw cotton.

There are many different varieties of cotton; but, the one that is traded internationally is called upland. Upland cotton is evaluated using three characteristics: grade, staple, and micronaire.

Grade is based on several factors, such as color, foreign matter, and preparation. Color refers to the whiteness or brilliance of the raw fiber. Low-grade cotton has a spotty color. Foreign matter is the amount of dirt, bark, leaf particles, and other impurities that combine with the cotton during harvesting. Preparation means the roughness and uniformity of the cotton fiber.

The second characteristic used to evaluate cotton is the length of the staple or fiber. Short staple cotton is under 13/16 inch; medium to long from 13/16 of an inch to 1 3/32 inches, long is from 1 1/8 to 1 5/16 inches, and extra-long staple is over 1 3/8 inches. Upland cotton has medium to medium-long staples.

The last characteristic is called "mike," which is short for micronaire. The mike rating is made by a scientific instrument that measures the airflow through cotton. Immature and overly mature cottons have lower values than "perfectly" mature cotton.

Cotton requires a 180-day, frost-free growing season. Hot weather with evenly spaced rains is preferred. In recent years, irrigation has been substituted for natural rainfall. Nowadays, cotton is grown in the United States in three regions. The first is along the Mississippi from Louisiana to Southern Missouri, the Delta. The second is the High Plains of Texas and Oklahoma. The San Joaquin Valley of California is the third major producing area. Some cotton is also grown in the Rio Grande Valley of Texas, as well as Arizona and New Mexico. In the original cotton-growing region of the Southeast (the Carolinas, Georgia, and Alabama), cotton has been replaced by other crops.

Demand Side

Approximately half of the cotton grown in the United States is used in the manufacture of clothes. The other half is used for household or industrial uses. This division allows for a fairly stable demand pattern.

Synthetic materials have had an impact on demand in this country. Americans like the convenience of clothes that do not require a lot of ironing. Since the development of rayon in 1930 and the more recent introduction of polyester, synthetics have grown in popularity because of their low cost and resilience. This has not yet happened on a worldwide basis. But it may in the future.

The demand side of the supply-demand equation is also impacted by the importation of textile and finished garments from the Far East. Competition from Korea and China, using cotton grown in that part of the world, reduces the demand for U.S. grown cotton.

Price Determinants

Cotton is a crop that is produced once a year. Although it is grown in 75 countries, most countries use all their production internally. Therefore, the cotton price analysts need only track the production of the five key producers mentioned earlier.

Additionally, while demand changes are, naturally, very significant, they usually occur slowly and in somewhat predictable patterns. Supply changes, on the other hand, occur abruptly and without warning. Now, let's discuss some of these supply-demand factors.

Weather—As with any crop, weather is critical, particularly during the growing season. For example, rain and cold temperatures can delay planting in the spring. Late planted cotton can be caught by an early frost. A wet, cool fall can cause the cotton boll to rot. If rain washes the insecticide off the plants, insects—particularly boll weevils, boll worms and thrips—will do plenty of damage. Too little moisture reduces yield, too much reduces fruiting and causes late maturity.

Government Programs—During the last sixty years, government programs have had as much impact on production (supply) as the weather has. Government protection of cotton began in 1929 with the Agricultural Marketing Act, which established loan rates. Later, price support programs priced the U.S. crop out of the world market, and cotton carryover grew to 17 million bales in the mid-1960s. More recently, the PIK (Product-In-Kind) and ARP (Acreage Reduction Program) have muddied the price discovery process.

Fashion—The demand for permanent press clothing hurt the demand for cotton. This fad has appeared to have reached its bottom, and now there seems to be a demand for more "natural" fabrics, particularly jeans made from cotton.

Inventory and Carryover—The amount of cotton available at any one time is a critical element. Cotton ginners, brokers, millers, and shippers all hold inventory, not to mention our Commodity Credit Corporation.

Seasonality—Prices usually reach lows in late fall during harvest. Highs normally come between May and July. The crop year officially begins August 1st of each year.

Trader's Notes

As mentioned in the beginning, there are many types of cotton. When evaluating demand, make sure the need is for the type of cotton you plan to "buy" on the futures exchange. For example, on the New York Cotton Exchange, the contract calls for 100 bales (50,000) pounds of "low-middling, 1 1/16 inch premium mike." You would hate to go long only to find out the market is demanding extra-long staple cotton—as you watch your long go into debit.

Overview of the Gold Market

Gold

Like silver, gold came into common use around 4000 B.C. It was first found in nugget form and later mined. Although it has been in constant use since prehistoric time, over one-third of the amount produced since the beginning of time has been mined in the last thirty years. The reason is simply the advances made in mining technology.

It stretches, but it's inelastic!

One of the unique characteristics of gold is its malleability—an ounce can be formed into wire over one mile in length. That's one of the reasons it has been a favorite metal of jewelers over the centuries.

However, from a supply-demand perspective, it is quite inelastic. This means that demand is somewhat insensitive to supply price. For example, if the supply drops, demand may not be greatly affected. Gold is not like food. With food, if supplies disappear, prices soar. If gold supply decreases, consumers (particularly industrial users) simply go without or find a replacement, i.e., platinum, palladium, or silver.

Gold has some other supply-demand considerations that an investor must be prepared to evaluate. First, gold is usually used in applications that allow for reclamation. It's so valuable that steps are usually taken to plan the recovery of whatever gold is used. This is particularly true in industrial applications. Therefore, disappearance as we know it in other commodities, like soybeans, corn, cattle, copper, etc., is not a serious factor.

Supply Side

New gold comes from mining. South Africa is by far the leading producer, followed by the Commonwealth of Independent States. The rest of the world trails far behind.

The supply side of the supply-demand equation is distorted by hoarders. Central banks maintain the largest stockpiles. For example, central banks in the top fifteen industrial countries store over eighty-five times the world's total annual production. If just 1 percent of this supply comes to market in any one year, the annual supply of gold would double.

As mentioned earlier, South Africa and the Commonwealth of Unified States are the major producers. But both are somewhat unreliable suppliers. They do not always bring their gold production into the market place in an orderly manner. Both countries are politically unpredictable, and gold is one of the most politically sensitive commodities.

Another unstable hoarder of gold are the OPEC members. They release gold reserves based on the price of a barrel of oil. If petroleum prices drop, they must sell gold to pay debts. If petroleum prices rise, they'll buy gold to add to their hoards.

Individuals, particularly individuals in countries that have experienced serious monetary problems, have learned to hoard gold. Germany, for example, has experienced the total destruction of its currency four times in the last 100 years. France is not far behind. Citizens of the U.S. are supposed to have enormous stock stashed away. The problem for fundamental analysis is that no one knows for sure how much is hidden away and what it would take to bring it back into the marketplace.

Demand Side

Decorative uses, primarily jewelry and objects d'art, account for about 60 percent of demand. Other major uses include electronics, dentistry, coinage, medicine, and chemicals.

Unfortunately, for commodity analysts, demand doesn't project price since it is an inelastic commodity. Additionally, there are several substitute (metals mentioned earlier) that can dampen a demand driven market.

Marketing of Gold

Like silver, the bullion price is "fixed" each day in London. Five major brokers get together twice each trading day and set the price. The brokers are N.M. Rothschild, Johnson Matthey, Sharps Pixley, Mocatta & Goldsmid and Samuel Montager. Other very important marketing centers for bullion are Zurich, Hong Kong, and Singapore. Chicago and New York City dominate the futures market in gold.

Fundamental Analysis

The problem involved in analyzing the price of gold is isolating the pressures that impact gold. Gold is a commodity which is used in a variety of ways. But it is more. Humans have a sentimental attraction to jewelry made from this metal.

Governments use it for coinage or to pay foreign debt. It has a monetary value. Individuals respond to this by hoarding it to stave off the effects of inflation or to protect them in times of financial crisis.

The vast majority of above-ground gold is controlled by governments. Therefore, it becomes a tool of their foreign or domestic policies. President Roosevelt, in 1933, made the possession of gold illegal and confiscated bullion held by U.S. citizens. Iran and Iraq sold gold to support their war. South America uses it to bribe other countries to lift sanctions.

Technical Analysis

Just as gold is one of the most popular of possessions, it is also a commodity on which analysts love to do price projections because "everyone" follows gold.

Let's look at its seasonal pattern first. The high is most often around February and the low is in place around August. The reason for this is the migration of workers to and from their farms. Supplies from South Africa are reduced when they are out planting their fields in February, (our winter, their summer). Supplies increase when they return to the mines in August (our summer, their winter).

The silver-to-gold ratio is a simple, technical trading system. You simply calculate the number of troy ounces of silver it takes to buy one ounce of gold. At present, the "normal" ratio is around sixty to one. When it drops below fifty to one, gold is too scarce compared to silver and should be bought. When above seventy to one, buy silver.

Gold markets often trend. The basic bar chart formation analysis, discussed in Chapter 2, can often be used successfully.

Overview of the Copper Market

Copper

Copper, known as the "red metal" since antiquity, was first used by man for the manufacture of weapons, armor, and tools. Because of its malleability, man quickly learned to blend it with other metals to produce more rigid materials, such as bronze and brass. Since prerecorded history, copper has always been one of man's most widely used metals. Even today, copper is one of the most actively traded metals on an international basis.

Supply Side

Let's look at the supply side of the supply-demand equation. Copper enters the supply stream from two directions: newly mined and reclaimed.

Copper mining utilizes the open pit method. Large amounts of earth are dug and run through a three step process: milling, smelting, and refining. The milling procedure crushes and grinds the earth dug from the open pits. It is then moved through a flotation device that separates the copper ore from the earth, resulting in a copper concentrate.

Intense heat is applied to the copper concentrate in the smelting step. This produces a copper that is 99 percent pure. The last stage is refining. It is a electrolytic technique that removes just about all of the remaining impurities, bringing the copper to a purity level of 99.9 percent. This is the most commonly traded grade on futures markets.

Newly mined copper primarily comes from four areas: the western slopes of the Andes mountains in Chile and Peru, the South African countries of Zaire and Zambia, and the USA and Canada in North America. These countries account for approximately two-thirds of the world's mining production. In the United States, Arizona produces the most cooper.

One of the most popular characteristics of copper is its ability to resist corrosion, which makes copper an ideal metal to recycle. The scrap or secondary production of copper has been an ever increasing source and must be taken into account when doing fundamental price analysis.

Demand Side

Copper is an industrial metal. Therefore, the demand for copper comes primarily from developed countries. Its industrial uses stem from its ability to conduct heat and electricity, resistance to corrosion, strength, ductility, and malleability. Copper is often alloyed with copper and nickel.

The two largest consuming countries are the United States and Japan. Japan is not a major producer. The electrical industry is the largest single user. Copper, because it conducts electricity well, is used as wiring and in electrical components of all sorts. The growth of space and telecommunications industries in recent years has boosted usage even more. Extensive use of copper can also be found in the housing, automobile, and plumbing industries. A considerable amount of copper is used for jewelry and coinage.

Price Determinants

Since much of copper is mined in undeveloped countries and consumed in developed countries, it must be exported from its source to where it is needed. This means that foreign exchange rates and transportation play an important part in the price discovery process. Secondly, no single nation has a monopoly on either the mining or refining of copper. It is truly a worldwide commodity. This fosters competition which impacts pricing strategies.

As mentioned earlier, copper is a commercial metal used heavily in construction, automobiles, and electrical appliances. For this reason, the supply-demand equation is sensitive to economic trends within the developed countries. If housing starts or new car sales plunge, you can expect copper prices will follow as demand slackens. Actually, copper prices usually lead the way as users cut back on inventories.

Thus, during economic hard times, look to short the copper market. But be sure to evaluate the situation on a global basis. If not, you could be caught in a situation where prices stay firm because demand is still strong in some parts of the world.

When evaluating economic or business cycles, you need to pay particular attention to the strength or velocity of change. Demand for copper feeds on itself and becomes stronger and stronger as demand builds momentum.

Politics in both the source and consuming countries must be monitored closely. For example, strikes by mine workers can restrict supply, which would drive prices higher. Political unrest in undeveloped countries is common and can spill over into the copper mines or slow down the movement of copper to the consumer nations.

In the developed countries, political programs that promote housing, construction, or manufacturing of electrical components foster demand usually translates into higher copper prices. Governments can also influence demand with their monetary policy. For example, programs that encourage development of industry and promote jobs usually have a favorable impact on prices. They also directly control the amount of copper used for coins. If they lower interest rates, it will often impact housing starts, which will eventually be felt in the price of copper. Finnally, don't forget the defense industry which is a major user.

Copper inventories on all levels can be a damper or spark to prices. Heavy inventories hold prices down; shortages instigate bull markets.

Seasonality

Copper does have a seasonal pattern related to its uses in the housing and automobile industries. These industries build inventories which cause copper prices to peak during February through April. The trough usually comes in late summer and early fall.

Traders Notes

Because copper futures contracts have a long history, are heavily traded, and are known for making long trending moves, they are very popular among speculators. It trades somewhat similar to lumber, which is also a commercial commodity and influenced by interest rates and housing starts.

Overview of Petroleum and Petroleum Products

Petroleum and Politics

Historically, the petroleum market has been a reasonably stable market, with steady prices and a reliable distribution system. Since the early '70s, a lot has changed. The primary disruptions began in 1973 and 1974 with the formation of OPEC (the Organization of Petroleum Exporting Countries) and the oil embargo. Prices shot up; lines formed at gas stations.

The major significance of these developments was a shift of power away from the major oil companies (The Seven Sisters) and into the hands of the producers. OPEC never congealed into a unified force. Big players, like Saudi Arabia, cheated on the agreed quotas. Additionally, some producing countries refused to join.

In other words, chaos often reigns in this market causing both super opportunities and high risk for investors. The Iranian crisis of 1978 and 1979 continued these trends, as did the Iraq-Iranian War and the Iraq-Allied (Desert Storm) War of 1991.

Supply vs. Demand

The two largest producers, the Commonwealth of Independent States and the United States, are also net importers. That gives control of supplies to the major exporters, namely Saudi Arabia, Iran, Iraq, Kuwait, Libya, Nigeria, and Algeria. This group of producers must carefully balance output to usage.

For a time, the producers believed usage would never be a problem. They could charge what they wanted and the world would pay. But high prices convinced even United States citizens that enough was enough. Eventually, in 1983, conservation efforts left consumption in the United States unchanged for the first time in its history. This led to an oversupply of crude oil and lower prices. The oil cartel weakened.

Seasonality

Demand has another twist when it comes to petroleum. Gas for automobiles is most in demand in the summer, while heating oil demand peaks in the winter. These two factors compliment each other as far as demands for raw crude, refining, and storage capacity are concerned.

The basic process of a refinery is distillation. Crude oil is heated until it vaporizes. The vapor or gas is then cooled to a liquid form. This process separates ("cuts" or "fractions") raw crude into several petroleum products (compound in the raw crude vaporizes at a different temperature).

The lighter the compound, the lower temperature at which it vaporizes. The following are the "fractions" that compose crude oil, in order from lighter to heavier: butanes, gasolines, naphtha, kerosene, heating oil, and residual oil.

Two other critical considerations are the types of crude available to a refinery as well as the distillation process a refinery uses. There are sweet and sour crudes. The lower the sulfur (less than 0.5 percent by weight) the sweeter it is. Sour crude contains over 1 percent sulfur. This characteristic has become very important because of pollution standards.

Density is the second critical characteristic. Low density or light crude is more desirable because it produces more of the more valuable products, namely gasoline, and jet fuel.

The origin of the crude is also a critical factor. It accounts for such characteristics as viscosity, pour point, color, flash and fine points, and metals content.

Every refinery is designed to efficiently process a certain type of crude. If the right crude is not available for the way the refinery is set up or the end products needed, the price for the "right" crude may shoot up on the spot market while other crudes go begging for a home.

Price Determinants

As if balancing the supply-demand equation between producers, processors, and consumers was not enough, there are several other factors that must be taken into consideration by the futures price analysts:

Weather—Unseasonably warm or cold weather during the winter (heating oil season) can play havoc with projections.

Conservation—How seriously are consumers reacting to pressure by the government and other bodies to conserve energy.

Politics—Threats of war, blockades, etc. send prices higher. Peace and cooperation among nations drives the price down.

OPEC—The solidarity of OPEC sends prices up while squabbling leads to lower prices.

Stocks—Plentiful stock piles and pipeline supplies reduce prices; shortages send prices skyrocketing.

New sources—Discovery of new reserves damage price prospects. High prices can open closed or inefficient wells.

Crude oil and its by products can be stored for reasonably long periods of time. One would expect the deferred contracts to evenly reflect the cost of storage and insurance as is usually true in the grains. However, because of the seasonality of both gasoline and heating oil (the two main by products), this is not true. Also, the petroleum is a very regionalized business, with each area of the country having different demands.

Trader's Notes

The petroleum markets lend themselves to hedging. Oil companies need to hedge future production; refiners hedge their requirements for crude and production of gasoline/heating oil; jobbers buy contracts of gasoline futures to hedge their needs.

Inter-contract (crude oil vs. gasoline, crude vs. heating oil, gasoline vs. heating oil) and intra-contract (buying one month and selling another) spreads are very popular. More sophisticated speculators arbitrage between the New York and London futures markets. The important thing for the investor to note is that these are usually very liquid markets.

Overview of Interest Rates

Interest Rates

Simply put, interest rates are the cost of money. Just as you must pay (buy, rent, lease) to have the use of any other tangible product or service, you must pay a price to have the use of money. Also like any other product or commodity, the cost of money varies with changes in the supply-demand equation.

Interest rates impact every commodity traded on the futures market directly or indirectly. For example, low interest rates make it easier for farmers or manufacturers to expand. This gives us more corn, soybeans, cattle, etc. Farm prices are driven down by abundant supplies. When manufacturers expand because of low interest rates, their earnings increase. This enhances the value of their stock, and the futures contract in the S & P 500 moves higher. These are examples of how interest rates influence the commodity markets.

Interest rate changes have a direct impact on the debt instruments traded on the exchanges. When interest rates go up, debt instruments go down and vice-versa. Thus when you trade debt instruments, you are taking a position on whether you believe interest rates are going up or down. By debt instruments traded on the futures and options on futures exchange, we are specifically referring to such contracts as Treasury bonds, bills, notes.

Fundamental Factors

Understanding exactly where we are within an economic cycle is probably the single most important fundamental factor. Studies have verified the fact that interest rates follow the level of general economic activity. When the economy is expanding, the demand (and, therefore the price) for money increases. In periods of recession, the supply of money exceeds demand causing interest rates to fall.

Additionally, you must take "herd psychology" into consideration. Once a period of expansion is well underway, the demand for money continues after the actual expansion has subsided. Momentum carries demand, as reflected in high interest rates, forward. The same is true in the late stages of recessions. Interest continues to decline, even as expansion is beginning.

The fact that the transition in the economic cycle—from boom to bust and back again—precedes major changes in the interest rates emphasizes the need to closely monitor the economy. In *Business Conditions Digest*, a monthly publication of the Department of Commerce, you'll find three important indexes. They are the

Index of Leading Indicators, the Index of Coincident Indicators, and the Index of Lagging Indicators.

As mentioned earlier, interest rates must pick up momentum, meaning demand for money, before they make a major impact on the indexes. For this reason, they most closely follow the Index of Lagging Indicators. But for purposes of forecasting, you'll want to monitor the other two indexes because you need to wait 3-6 months for a trend change in the economy to be verified. For trading purposes, you use the old grade school race starting sequence: "On your mark (check the Leading Index), get set (verify with the Coincident Index) go (trade the Lagging Index)."

Bank Reserves

There is a strong, well documented correlation between interest rate trends and the level of free/net borrowed bank reserves. When reserves go down, so do interest rates. A move from free or low net borrowed reserves to higher net borrowed reserves coincide with higher interest rates. Therefore, the reserve position of banks is an indicator of the supply-demand situation. The Bank Reserve Position Report is issued each Friday by the Federal Reserve.

The Fed

The Federal Reserve has three valves it can manipulate to control bank reserves and, in turn, interest rates. The first is the discount rate. When the discount rate is increased or decreased, the reserves of bank members are reduced or expanded respectively.

The second valve is the reserve requirement, which is the percentage of various deposits that banks are required to hold in reserve. It, like the discount rate, is seldom used, except in emergencies.

The dominant tool used by the Federal Reserve is the open market option. This is the purchase or sale of government securities. If the Fed wants to drive interest rates down, it buys government securities from dealers. This injects funds into the system, increasing supply. If it wants to push interest rates up, it sells government securities, thereby draining funds from the system, reducing the supply of money in the market place.

Some interference or government control over the economy may be unavoidable in this day and age. But when this power is used to artificially control inflation, it only compounds the demand for the area under control. Eventually the economy is distorted more than if it were left to freely react to economic pressures.

Forecasting Price Trends

Tracking the economy and the Federal Reserve is your first step. The real challenge lies in determining correctly the impact on interest rates of these two forces. Will a certain action taken by the Federal Reserve to reduce or slow down interest rates throw the economy into a recession?

The United States, and the world economy for that matter, is like a battleship. It takes a good bit of ocean and a few hours to turn it around. It always has a lot of momentum, and this must be taken into consideration. In other words, when you are dealing with interest rates, time and patience are critical virtues.

Technical Analysis

Debt instrument futures are very popular among both institutional, as well as individual, traders. This has given rise to much research on the technical side. Particular attention has been paid to price chart formation analysis and cycles. You must study these two areas thoroughly.

Overview of the Foreign Currency Futures Markets

Foreign Currency

When the Smithsonian Agreement came apart in March of 1973, it set all currencies floating freely. This event really gave momentum to the futures markets that began in 1972 at the International Monetary Market (IMM), a division of the Chicago Mercantile Exchange. The initial markets traded were the British Pound, the Canadian Dollar, the West German Mark, the Japanese Yen, the Swiss Franc, and the Mexican Peso.

Skeptics of the foreign futures exchange (Forex) markets didn't see any need for it because there was already a well established bank forward market for foreign currencies. But the bank forward market had some drawbacks. First, access to it was limited to large banks and corporations with excellent credit. Small firms and retail speculators were barred.

Secondly, only large denominations of $1,000,000 and over are traded on the bank forward market. Additionally, the market was set up primarily for traders to take or make delivery. It's expensive and difficult to liquidate a position before expiration of the contract.

Since futures contracts negate all these drawbacks, they immediately found a place in the foreign currency market. Volume has steadily grown over the years.

Arbitrage and Hedging

Developers of the foreign currency futures contracts made it easy for banks and other commercial users of the bank forward market to arbitrage between it and the futures market. This increased volume in the beginning when it was dearly needed. It also helped keep the price range of some of the thin futures currency markets in line with the more liquid bank forward market. In time, the banks took the lead and began arbitraging for their commercial clients. Thus keeping additional profits for themselves.

Another group of U.S. commercial firms that is a major user of the foreign exchange futures markets are the agricultural firms. They need to hedge their foreign exchange exposure since the very large grain deals often take several months to complete.

The "commodity" discussed in this group is money. Therefore, there isn't any real supply-demand equation in the classic sense. Granted, countries can increase or restrict the supply of their currency from time to time. But the value or demand for a currency depends more on other factors.

Price Determinants

Foreign exchange rates or the price of money is commonly expressed in its relationship to the United States dollar. Foreign currencies are quoted on the futures market in the number of U.S. dollars that must be paid for one unit of the foreign currency.

Therefore, to determine the value of another currency to that of ours, we must compare the financial or economic situation of that currency to ours. We must assess the impact of a variety of trends, factors, and events on the relationship of the currency being compared to our dollar. Now let's look at a few of the most important influences on this relationship:

> Balance of Payments—This is a measure of the number of dollars flowing out of the United States compared to the inflow of foreign currencies into the U.S. Over the years, this concept has become more complex as economists have tried to measure different types of inflows/outflows. For example, we now look at the flow of merchandise, services (together these are the balance of trade), direct investments, stock issues, bank claims/liabilities, and government assets abroad. Each measure tells us something different about our financial situation.
>
> We are in a deficit position when more money flows out of the United States than flows in. A balance of payment surplus is the opposite.
>
> As a rule of thumb, a surplus causes the dollar to become stronger relative to foreign currencies (the dollar value of foreign currencies declines) because there are fewer dollars in foreign countries. A deficit, on the other hand, causes the dollar to weaken compared to foreign currencies (the dollar value of foreign currencies increases) because there are more dollars in foreign countries.
>
> Interest Rates—High interest rates in the United States compared to foreign countries usually attracts capital. Money flows into the country. The dollar becomes stronger. Bankers call this worldwide pool of money that flows to the best deal as "hot money."

Economic Growth—The strength of the U.S. economy has been a two-edged sword for the dollar. A strong U.S. economy has often created a weak dollar because it has sometimes lead to balance of payment deficits, thus weakening the dollar.

At other times, a strong U.S. economy has been seen as an indication of political stability in an unstable world. This perception has lead to a strong dollar.

Inflation—High inflation rates in the U.S. makes our products more expensive relative to foreign goods. This increases imports and decreases exports. A deficit and a weak dollar result. But at other times, inflation has created higher interest rates leading to an inflow of capital and a stronger dollar.

Political conditions—If the political instability is in foreign countries, wise investors move their funds into the U.S. This strengthens the dollar. The opposite can also be true.

The price determinants discussed must be carefully evaluated because the impact can be either positive or negative for the relationship between the dollar and the other currencies. You must learn to read the psychology of the market as the events occur.

Trader's Notes

The rapid growth of the futures contracts in the foreign currencies testifies to their usefulness and popularity. But some of these markets are still somewhat thin. This can be very dangerous. Also, avoid trading Friday afternoon after the London markets close because of the lack of liquidity at this time.

Overview of the Coffee Market

Coffee

The fist common usage of coffee has been obscured in antiquity. Most scholars of the subject believe it was probably first used in ancient times in Ethiopia. From here, its popularity spread to the Arabian countries (Egypt and Turkey). Around 1600, its use spread through Italy to the rest of Europe. In North America, by the time of the American Revolution, coffee houses were common. Great Britain and her possessions do not consume much coffee. The U.S. has become the world's largest consumer.

Arabica vs. Robusta

There are basically two types of coffee. The most popular and most in demand is arabica. It is a mild coffee grown mainly in Brazil, Colombia, and other parts of

Latin America. Arabicas make the richest blends. They are grown at altitudes of 2,000 feet and require forty inches of rain per year.

Robusta comes from Africa. It is a much hardier plant. Robusta is more resistant to disease and insects; however, it lacks the flavor and aroma of arabica. Robustas are often used to make instant coffees. Five hundred to 2,000 feet of altitude are required to grow robustas, and they can stand greater weather extremes.

Young coffee trees begin bearing at about four years of age and continue for about twenty-five years. Each tree produces enough beans (on an average) to make one pound of marketable coffee each year. The trees begin the process by producing a white flower that becomes a "cherry." The cherries are originally green and turn red as they ripen. At harvest, the berries are hand picked and consist of sweet pulpy fruit usually covering two flat beans.

Once picked, the fruit can be processed into coffee beans by one of two ways. The most commonly used method is the wet method, in which the bean is washed in fermentation tanks after the outer pulp has been mechanically removed. This improves flavor and color. The berries are washed again, then dried to remove the inner skin. The second processing method is the dry method. The berries are dried naturally in the sun to remove the pulp. This method requires a lot of dependable weather.

Once the initial process is complete, the beans are sized and graded. Then they are packed into heavy bags (132 pounds each) for storage or shipment. Most beans are moved to New York, New Orleans, San Francisco, Le Havre, or Antwerp for roasting, blending, and packaging for the customer.

Supply vs. Demand

The United States is the world's major consumer of coffee. Yet coffee is not consumed to quench thirsts, nor does it have any nutritive value. Its popularity depends on its use as a stimulant (caffeine). It tends to be emotionally addictive. Millions and millions of people "need" a cup of coffee to get going in the morning.

This makes a very inelastic demand situation. Prices have to increase drastically to make an impact on demand. Therefore, the short term demand can be calculated fairly accurately.

The long term is not as clearly defined. Soft drinks, many of them with caffeine as part of their formula, have made an impact on usage. Many young adults prefer a soda in the morning, rather than a cup of coffee. This may change the demand figures in years to come and must be carefully considered.

The supply side of the equation is the one that often impacts pricing. The coffee tree is not a dependable producer. Its yields can radically increase (by as much as tenfold) for no apparent reason, producing bumper crops for a few years. This can be followed by several years of sparse production. Yet, no apparent pattern has been determine.

The trees are also very sensitive to wind and cold weather. Fear of frost at harvest can send prices soaring. The times to watch for are June and July for the

Brazilian crop, and October through March for Columbia, and November to April for the Ivory Coast (African crop).

Seasonality

Coffee is unique in that there is no clear cut seasonality to its pricing. The reason is twofold. First, coffee is harvested throughout the year, and almost all production is exported from the country of origin. Therefore, there is a steady supply coming on the market all year long.

Secondly, the green coffee beans can easily be stored for long periods of time without loss of quality. This also tends to level off the supply side of the equation.

Price Determinants

As discussed earlier, weather is the major determinant of price in the short term. However, there are other factors you must track.

Transportation—Coffee must move from its origin to where it will be processed and consumed. Anything that interferes with this movement (dock strikes, war, etc.) will impact price.

Inventories—The ability of coffee to retain its taste and aroma for long periods of time makes inventory levels an important factor.

Government Restrictions—The producing countries are considered to be somewhat unstable in some circles. Brazil at one time went as far as to burn much of its crop in an attempt to manipulate prices.

International Coffee Agreement of 1976—This agreement set an annual production quota for countries belonging to the International Coffee Organization. In turn, export and import quotas are set for both producing and consuming countries that belong to the ICO. The objective is to stabilize prices. Seventy-five nations, including the United States, are members. The status of this agreement can be a critical factor on pricing.

Understanding the impact of the supply/demand equation requires attention to a lot of data available from the USDA, the National Coffee Association, and the International Coffee Association.

Trader's Notes

Trading weather markets is a tricky business at best. Trading coffee is that much more complicated because it is a very thin futures market. This means that even a small amount of trading activity can result in very wide price swings. In other words, it can be very dangerous.

Since arabica contracts are traded on the New York Coffee, Sugar and Cocoa Exchange and robusta is on the London Exchange, some traders spread these two types of coffee depending on the price relationship. Intra-contract spreads are less interesting because there is basically no crop year.

Overview of the Cocoa Market

Cocoa

Cocoa is an ancient crop and drink of Central America. At times, it was important enough to be used as a medium of exchange. Cocoa appeared in Europe in the 16th century, but it wasn't until 1828 that a Dutch processor discovered that the fat of the cocoa bean, called cocoa butter, could be extracted. Combining sugar with the cocoa butter produced chocolate. Later in the 19th century, Swiss candy makers pioneered the use of adding milk to the cocoa butter and sugar—thus the world began to enjoy milk chocolate.

Supply Side

Cocoa beans grow on trees in tropical climates. They grow in an area that is between twenty degrees North and twenty degrees South of the equator and require at least fifty inches of rain per year. It takes five years for the trees to produce a bean crop. After that, the trees yield for another forty to fifty years with peak production coming around the fifteenth year.

The longevity of the trees makes cocoa very inelastic in the short run from a supply standpoint. High prices do not increase tree plantings, nor do low prices reduce new plantings or yields.

In the major producing countries (Ivory Coast, Brazil, Ghana, Cameroon, Nigeria, parts of Asia and Oceania), the main crop comes in from October through March. This accounts for three-quarters of the world's production. A "mid-crop" is harvested from May to August. The reason for these long harvesting periods is that the cocoa bean matures slowly and unevenly. With the production in the tropics and the majority of consumers in the temperate zones, the bulk of the crop must be shipped to the confection manufacturers. This makes transportation an important part of the price equation.

The bean cannot be stored in the tropics without being processed. Historically, all the processing (and therefore, inventory held) was done in the developed, user countries, especially the United States and Europe. Some of the producing countries, Brazil for example, are now doing some of the processing. This creates another level of inventory. There is also a third inventory level. Candy manufacturers and other users routinely carry a three to nine month supply, averaging about six months.

The processing of cocoa beans is a complex process. First, the ripe fruit or pods are cut from the trees, which grow to a height of twenty-five feet. The pods are split and twenty to forty seeds (beans) that look like almonds are removed. The beans are then fermented for two to nine days. This kills the bean's germ and activates enzymes, which produces the unique flavor.

After fermentation, the beans are dried, bagged, and shipped to the processor. The processor cleans, blends, and roasts the beans. After roasting, the thin shells, or hulls, of the beans are cracked and removed. The beans are now called "nibs." The nibs (meat of the bean) contain approximately 54 percent cocoa butter.

The nibs are crushed and ground to release the cocoa butter. The mixture of cocoa butter and finely ground nibs is called chocolate "liquor." It can be used at this stage, stored, or further processed into baking chocolate, cocoa, milk chocolate or sweet and semi-sweet chocolate. The cocoa we drink, by the way, contains 22 percent fat.

Demand Side

Cocoa is a very unique commodity in that its uses are very limited (candy, cocoa, flavoring foods), and there really isn't any substitute. On the other hand, it is a luxury item consumed mainly in high income countries, like the United States, West Germany, and the Netherlands. For this reason, it is insulated from price fluctuations (both up or down). If prices drop substantially, demand varies little. If prices skyrocket, sufficient demand is still there.

Price Determinant

While the retail buying is reasonably stable, on the wholesale and futures markets, there is plenty of price activity.

> Rumors—The cocoa market is very susceptible to the rumor mill. The reason for this is the commodity is produced in remote areas, where estimating supplies is difficult. Small, totalitarian governments may hold back information or disseminate misinformation.

> Weather—Cocoa trees require a lot of rain. If it doesn't come, production is reduced. Too much rain brings crop diseases. A severe "harmattan" (a dry, dusty wind from the Sahara Desert) can severely damage the Ivory Coast crop, for example.

> Income & Population—Increased wealth in a nation almost always leads to increased consumption. The only exception has been on the continent of Asia.

> Politics—Several of the producing countries have highly controlled economies. By maintaining a fixed price to farmers, they have held back production increases. The International Cocoa Agreement (ICA) has been as successful at price stabilization as the International Coffee Agreement was successful.

Sugar—Sugar is the other major ingredient in chocolate. One would expect the price of sugar to impact the price of cocoa. It doesn't because sugar candy is the major competitor of chocolate. When sugar candy prices go up, so does the price of chocolate candy and vice-versa.

Transportation—Moving unprocessed beans out of the tropics is critical. Any disruption or threat of disruption runs prices up.

Dollar—A strong U.S. dollar tends to decrease the world price of cocoa.

Inventory Levels—The three tiered inventory situation keeps a substantial supply of cocoa in the market. This is the major stabilizing factor in the market.

Seasonality

Because of the long growing season and complex inventory system, there is very little seasonality. Most often the lows occur in the first quarter. Highs come in July and August. This is reflective of the main crop harvest which takes place October through March.

Traders Notes

This is a tough market to figure out for both the fundamentalist and the technical trader. The fundamentalist must rely on notoriously unreliable data. The technician must deal with relatively wide bid-ask spreads, high margins and price movements that represent $10 per point. All in all, it is a fast moving market that can easily whipsaw even the most experienced trader. Whenever possible, trade with a broker who has a substantial amount of experience.

Overview of the Orange Juice Market

Orange Juice

Oranges are grown in a variety of countries throughout the world, other than the United States—Brazil, Spain, Japan and Italy to name a few. At the moment, the United States is still the dominant producing country.

Florida is the leading producer state, growing over 60 percent of the U.S. crop. It has had oranges under cultivation since the 1500s. California comes in second with about 30 percent of the crop. Its orange juice crop was first planted circa 1700. Texas and Arizona also produce a crop.

Orange juice became a popular breakfast drink all year long with the development of a process that freezes the juice without loss of flavor. This was achieved by Dr. L. G. MacDowell and two associates in 1947. His process called for over-concentrating the juice into a thick syrup, then adding more fresh orange juice and other flavorings prior to freezing. Thus we have Frozen Concentrated Orange Juice (FCOJ).

One of the key ingredients of FCOJ is sugar. Fruit buyers are concerned about "pounds solids" when they buy oranges for FCOJ. This refers to the amount of solids dissolved in the juice. Sugar being the primary one. The orange crop becomes sweeter the longer it grows. Valencias make the best juice because they have a high concentration of solids and are a late maturing variety.

Supply Side

As mentioned earlier, Florida is the major U.S. and world supplier. Most of the early and mid-season crop is harvested in late January. The harvest period for late oranges ranges from mid-April to June.

The early and mid-season crops are very vulnerable to frost. This can make for some very exciting roller coaster rides on the price charts. In the early 1980s—specifically the first four crop years of this decade—Florida was hit with four early frosts in a row. Frost can be very damaging to the orange trees, as well as the fruit. Therefore, serious frost damage can impact future years.

Remember, Florida is the major producer of oranges for both eating and freezing. It particularly dominates the FCOJ industry by providing as much as 75 percent of the fruit. However, because of the frost in the early 1980s, Florida's ability to be a reliable supplier, has been questioned.

At the same time, Brazil's crop is increasing significantly. Their government is providing its growers incentives and subsidies. In time, Brazil could mount a challenge to the Florida crop. By the way, it takes about five years from the time an orange tree is planted until it begins to bear fruit.

Demand Side

Most commodities are affected by supply and demand. This is not necessarily true with FCOJ. With orange juice, the supply side dominates the price equation.

Historically, oranges were shipped fresh and squeezed into juice in the home or peeled and eaten. They were a seasonal treat. When they were not available, we did without. Now FCOJ is always available in the freezer case. If it gets too expensive, we either do without or switch to a less expensive fruit, juice, or drink. If it is there, we partake. If not, we don't. It is somewhat similar to chocolate in this respect, but there are probably more chocolate "addicts" than "OJ junkies."

In other words, the demand is elastic. It will respond to changes in price. If the price moves up sharply, demand decreases. A plentiful supply and lower prices will spark demand.

Besides using oranges for juice and eating fruit, oranges have some other uses. The peel can be candied, dried or made into marmalade. An oil, pectin, can be squeezed from the peel. It is used as a flavoring or as a scent in perfumes. The pulp left over after commercial squeezings can be fed to livestock.

Seasonality

Like most crops, the price in the cash and futures markets tends to peak prior to harvest and decline afterward. For FCOJ, the highs traditionally come in November and the lows in June.

Price Determinants

Weather has a greater impact on the supply of oranges than on just about any other commodity. Winter freezes, from late November to mid-February, can wipe out the crop and the trees. Orange groves require warmth and moisture. A shortage of water during blooming can be devastating, and too much rain or irrigation can hurt as well. In addition, insects take their toll. Sudden heat waves can cause young fruit to prematurely drop. Even strong winds will hurt yields. This is a difficult crop to grow.

Since this is a supply driven market, worldwide competition, particularly Brazil, is a major factor. Analysts must track the total available crop and the number of newly producing trees coming into production.

FCOJ can be stored indefinitely. Therefore, inventory levels must be watched carefully. These inventories are held on several levels—the concentrate processors, brokers, warehousers, and major grocery chains.

The market for FCOJ has primarily been in the United States. It is slowly spreading to other developed countries. If this trend continues, it could impact price.

The ever-changing taste of consumers will also affect price. Recently, the amount of chilled, as opposed to frozen concentrate, juice has been steadily increasing. Again, this trend requires watching.

Trader's Notes

Trading frozen orange juice is a lot like trading pork bellies—it's for traders who like to skydive on weekends. Sudden and significant price changes occur unexpectedly. You should be firm of heart and deep of pocket when trading this market.

GLOSSARY OF TERMS

Actuals: The physical or cash commodity, as distinguished from commodity futures contracts.

Administrative Law Judge (ALJ): A CFTC official authorized to conduct a proceeding and render a decision in a formal complaint procedure.

Aggregation: The policy under which all futures positions owned or controlled by one trader or a group of traders are combined to determine reporting status and speculative limit compliance.

Arbitrage: The simultaneous purchase of one commodity against the sale of another in order to profit from distortions from usual price relationships. See also Spread, Straddle.

Arbitration: A forum for the fair and impartial settlement of disputes that the parties involved are unable to resolve between themselves. NFA's arbitration program provides a forum for resolving futures related disputes.

Associated Person (AP): An individual who solicits orders, customers, or customer funds on behalf of a Futures Commission Merchant, an Introducing Broker, a Commodity Trading Advisor, or a Commodity Pool Operator and who is registered with the Commodity Futures Trading Commission (CFTC) via the National Futures Association (NFA).

At the market: See Market Order.

At the money: An option whose strike price is equal, or approximately equal, to the current market price of the underlying futures contract.

Award: See Reparations Award.

Basis: The difference between the cash or spot price and the price of the nearby futures contract.

Bear market (bear/bearish): A market in which prices are declining. A market participant who believes prices will move lower is called a "bear." A news item is considered bearish if it is expected to produce lower prices.

Bid: An offer to buy a specific quantity of a commodity at a stated price.

Board of Trade: Any exchange or association of persons who are engaged in the business of buying or selling any commodity or receiving the same for sale on consignment. It usually means an exchange where commodity futures and/or options are traded. See also Contract Market or Exchange.

Break: A rapid and sharp price decline.

Broad Tape: The term commonly applied to newswires carrying price and background information on securities and commodities markets. This contrasts to the exchanges' own price transmission wires, which use a narrow ticker tape.

Broker: A person paid a fee or commission for acting as an agent in making contracts or sales; floor broker in commodities futures trading, a person who actually executes orders on the trading floor of an exchange; account executive (associated person) is the person who deals with customers and their orders in commission house offices. See Registered Commodity Representative.

Brokerage: A fee charged by a broker for execution of a transaction—an amount charged per transaction or a percentage of the total value of the transaction; it is usually referred to as a commission fee.

Bucket, Bucketing: Illegal practice of accepting orders to buy or sell without executing such orders; the illegal use of the customer's margin deposit without disclosing the fact of such use.

Bull Market (bull/bullish): A market in which prices are rising. A participant in futures who believes prices will move higher is called a "bull." A news item is considered bullish if it is expected to bring on higher prices.

Buy or Sell on Close or Opening: To buy or sell at the end or the beginning of the trading session.

Buying Hedge (or Long Hedge): Buying futures contracts to protect against possible increased cost of commodities slated for futures uses. See Hedging.

Call (option): The buyer of a call option acquires the right but not the obligation to purchase a particular futures contract at a stated price on or before a particular date. Buyers of call options generally hope to profit from an increase in the futures price of the underlying commodity.

Car(s): This is a colloquialism for futures contract(s). It came into common use when a railroad car or hopper of corn, wheat, etc. equaled the amount of a commodity in a futures contract. See Contract.

Carrying Broker: A member of a commodity exchange, usually a clearinghouse member, through whom another broker or customer, chooses to clear all or some trades.

Carrying Charges: Costs incurred in warehousing the physical commodity, generally including interest, insurance, and storage.

Carryover: That part of the current supply of a commodity consisting of stocks from previous production/marketing seasons.

Cash Commodity: Actual stocks of a commodity, as distinguished from futures contracts; goods available for immediate delivery or delivery within a specified period following sale; or a commodity bought or sold with an agreement for delivery at a specified future date. See Actuals and Forward Contracting.

Cash Forward Sale: See Forward Contracting.

Certificated Stock: Stocks of a commodity that have been inspected and found to be of a quality deliverable against futures contracts, stored at the delivery points designated as regular or acceptable for delivery by the commodity exchange.

Charting: The use of graphs and charts in the technical analysis of futures markets to plot trends of price movements, average movements of price volume, and open interest. See Technical Analysis.

Churning: Excessive trading of the customer's account by a broker, who has control over the trading decisions for that account, to make more commissions while disregarding the best interests of the customer.

Clearing: The procedure through which trades are checked for accuracy. Once the trades are validated, the clearinghouse or association becomes the buyer to each seller of a futures contract and the seller to each buyer.

Clearing Member: A member of a clearinghouse or an association. All trades of a non-clearing member must be registered and eventually settled through a clearing member.

Clearinghouse: An agency connected with commodity exchanges through which all futures contracts are made, offset, or fulfilled through delivery of the actual commodity and through which financial settlement is made; often, is a fully chartered separate corporation rather than a division of the exchange proper.

Clearing Price: See Settlement Price.

Close (the): The period at the end of the trading session, officially designated by the exchange, during which all transactions are considered made "at the close."

Closing Range: A range of closely related prices at which transactions took place at the closing of the market; buy and sell orders at the closing might have been filled at any point within such a range.

Commission: 1) A fee charged by a broker to a customer for performance of a specific duty, such as the buying or selling of futures contracts. 2) Sometimes used to refer to the Commodity Futures Trading Commission (CFTC).

Commission Merchant: One who makes a trade, either for another member of the exchange or for a non–member client, in his or her own name and becomes liable as principal to the other party to the transaction.

Commodity: An entity of trade or commerce, services, or rights in which contracts for future delivery may be traded. Some of the contracts currently traded are wheat, corn, cotton, livestock, copper, gold, silver, oil, propane, plywood, currencies, Treasury bills, bonds, and notes.

Commodity Exchange Act: The federal act that provides for federal regulation of futures trading.

Commodity Futures Trading Commission (CFTC): A commission set up by Congress to administer the Commodity Exchange Act which regulates trading on commodity exchanges.

Commodity Pool: An enterprise in which funds contributed by a number of persons are combined for the purpose of trading futures contracts and/or options on futures. Not the same as a joint account.

Commodity Pool Operator (CPO): An individual or organization which operates or solicits funds for a commodity pool. Generally required to be registered with the Commodity Futures Trading Commissions.

Commodity Trading Advisor (CTA): Individuals or firms that, for a fee, issue analysis or reports concerning commodities, advise others on the value or the advisability of trading in commodity futures, options, or leverage contracts.

Confirmation Statement: A statement sent by a commission house to a customer when a futures or options position has been initiated. The statement shows the number of contracts bought or sold and the prices at which the contracts were bought or sold. Sometimes combined with a Purchase and Sale Statement.

Complainant: The individual who files a complaint seeking a reparations award against another individual or firm.

Consolidation: A pause in trading activity in which price moves sideways, setting the stage for the next move. Traders evaluate their positions during periods of consolidation.

Contract: A term of reference describing a unit of trading for a commodity.

Contract Grades: Standards or grades of commodities listed in the rules of the exchanges which must be met when delivering cash commodities against futures contracts. Grades are often accompanied by a schedule of discounts and premiums allowable for delivery of commodities of lesser or greater quality than the contract grade.

Contract Market: A board of trade designated by the Commodity Futures trading Commission to trade futures or option contracts on a particular commodity. Commonly used to mean any exchange on which futures are traded. See also Board of Trade and Exchange.

Contract Month: The month in which delivery is to be made in accordance with a futures contract.

Controlled Account: See Discretionary Account.

Corner: To secure control of a commodity so that its price can be manipulated.

Correction: A price reaction against the prevailing trend of the market. Common corrections often amount to 33 percent, 50 percent or 66 percent of the most recent trend movement. Sometimes referred to as a retracement.

Cost of Recovery: Administrative costs or expenses incurred in obtaining money due the complainant. Included are costs such as, administrative fees, hearing room fees, charge for clerical services, travel expenses to attend the hearing, attorney's fees, and filing costs.

Cover: To offset a previous futures transaction with an equal and opposite transaction. Short covering is a purchase of futures contracts to cover an earlier sale of an equal number of contracts of the same delivery month; liquidation is the sale of futures contracts to offset the obligation to take delivery on an equal number of futures contracts of the same delivery month purchased earlier.

Current Delivery (Month): The futures contract which will come to maturity and become deliverable during the current month; also called "spot month."

Customer Segregated Funds: See Segregated Account.

Day Order: An order that if not executed expires automatically at the end of the trading session on the day it was entered.

Day Traders: Commodity traders, generally members of the exchange active on the trading floor, who take positions in commodities and then liquidate them prior to the close of the trading day.

Dealer Option: A put or call on a physical commodity, not originating on or subject to the rules of an exchange, written by a firm which deals in the underlying cash commodity.

Debit Balance: Accounting condition where the trading losses in a customer's account exceed the amount of equity in the customer's account.

Deck: All of the unexecuted orders in a floor broker's possession.

Default: 1) In the futures market, the failure to perform on a futures contract as required by exchange rules, such as a failure to meet a margin call or to make or take delivery. 2) In reference to the federal farm loan program, the decision on the part of a producer of commodities not to repay the government loan, but instead to surrender his or her crops. This usually floods the market driving prices lower.

Deferred Delivery: The distant delivery months in which futures trading is taking place, as distinguished from the nearby futures delivery month.

Delivery: The tender and receipt of an actual commodity or warehouse receipt or other negotiable instrument covering such commodity, in settlement of a futures contract.

Deliverable Grades: See Contract Grades.

Delivery Month: A calendar month during which a futures contract matures and becomes deliverable.

Delivery Notice: Notice from the clearinghouse of a seller's intention to deliver the physical commodity against a short futures position; it precedes and is distinct from the warehouse receipt or shipping certificate, which is the instrument of transfer of ownership.

Delivery Points: Those locations designated by commodity exchanges at which stocks of a commodity represented by a futures contract may be delivered in fulfillment of the contract.

Delivery Price: The official settlement price of the trading session during which the buyer of futures contracts receives through the clearinghouse a notice of the seller's intention to deliver and the price at which the buyer must pay for the commodities represented by the futures contract.

Discount: 1) A downward adjustment in price allowed for delivery of stocks of a commodity of lesser than deliverable grade against a futures contract. 2) Sometimes used to refer to the price difference between futures of different delivery months, as in the phrase "July at a discount to May," indicating that the price of the July future is lower than that of the May.

Discovery: The process which allows one party to obtain information and documents relating to the dispute from the other party(ies) in the dispute.

Discretionary Account: An arrangement by which the holder of the account gives written power of attorney to another, often a broker, to make buying and selling decisions without notification to the holder; often referred to as a managed account or controlled account.

Elasticity: A characteristic of commodities which describes the interaction of the supply, demand, and price of a commodity. A commodity is said to be elastic in demand when a price change creates an increase or decrease in consumption. The supply of a commodity is said to be elastic when a change in price creates change in the production of the commodity. Inelasticity of supply or demand exists when either supply or demand is relatively unresponsive to changes in price.

Equity: The dollar value of a futures trading account if all open positions were offset at the going market price.

Exchange: An association of persons engaged in the business of buying and selling commodity futures and/or options. See also Board of Trade and Contract Market.

Exercise: Exercising an option means you elect to accept the underlying futures contract at the option's strike price.

Exercise Price: The price at which the buyer of a call (put) option may choose to exercise his right to purchase (sell) the underlying futures contract. Also called strike price.

Expiration Date: Generally the last date on which an option may be exercised.

F.O.B. (Free on board): Indicates that all delivery, inspection, and elevation or loading costs involved in putting commodities on board a carrier have been paid.

Feed Ratios: The variable relationships of the cost of feeding animals to market weight sales prices, expressed in ratios, such as the hog/corn ratio. These serve as indicators of the profit return or lack of it in feeding animals to market weight.

Fibonacci Number or Sequence of Numbers: The sequence of numbers (0,1,2,3,5,8,13,21,34,55,89,144,233...), discovered by the Italian mathematician Leonardo de Pise in the 13th century. It is the mathematical basis of the Elliott Wave Theory, where the first two terms of the sequence are 0 and 1 and each successive number is the sum of the previous two numbers.

Fiduciary Duty: Responsibility imposed by operation of law (from congressional policies underlying the Commodity Exchange Act) which requires that the broker act with special care in the handling of a customer's account.

First Notice Day: First day on which notices of intention to deliver cash commodities against futures contracts can be presented by sellers and received by buyers through the exchange clearinghouse.

Floor Broker: An individual who executes orders on the trading floor of an exchange for any other person.

Floor Trader: Members of an exchange who are personally present, on the trading floors of exchanges, to make trades for themselves and their customers. Sometimes called scalpers or locals.

Forwarding Contracting: A cash transaction common in many industries, including commodities, in which the buyer and seller agree upon delivery of a specified quality and quantity of goods at a specified future date. Specific price may be agreed upon in advance or there may be agreements that the price will be determined at the time of delivery on the basis of either the prevailing local cash price or a futures price.

Free Supply: Stocks of a commodity which are available from commercial sale, as distinguished from government-owned or controlled stocks.

Fully Disclosed: An account carried by the Futures Commission Merchant in the name of the individual customer; it is the opposite of an omnibus account.

Fundamental Analysis: An approach to analysis of futures markets and commodity futures price trends which examine the underlying factors which will affect the supply and demand of the commodity being traded in futures. (See also Technical Analysis.)

Futures Commission Merchant (FCM): An individual or organization which solicits or accepts orders to buy or sell futures contracts or commodity options and accepts money or other assets from customers in connection with such orders. The individual or organization must be registered with the Commodity Futures Trading Commission.

Futures Contract: A standardized binding agreement to buy or sell a specified quantity or grade of a commodity at a later date, i.e., during a specified month. Futures contracts are freely transferable and can be traded only by public auction on designated exchanges.

Futures Industry Association (FIA): The national trade association for the futures industry.

Gap: A trading day during which the daily price range is completely above or below the previous day's range causing a gap between them to be formed. Some traders then look for a retracement to "fill the gap."

Grantor: A person who sells an option and assumes the obligation but not the right to sell (in the case of a call) or buy (in the case of a put) the underlying futures contract or commodity at the exercise price. See also Writer.

Gross Processing Margin (GPM): Refers to the difference between the cost of soybeans and the combined sales income of the soybean oil and meal which results from processing soybeans.

Guided Account: An account that is part of a program directed by a Commodity Trading Advisor (CTA) or Futures Commission Merchant (FCM). The CTA or FCM plans the trading strategies. The customer is advised to enter and/or liquidate specific trading positions. However, approval to enter the order must be given by the customer. These programs usually require a minimum initial investment and may include a trading strategy that will utilize only a part of the investment at any given time.

Hedging: The sale of futures contracts in anticipation of future sales of cash commodities as a protection against possible price declines or the purchase of futures contracts in anticipation of future purchases of cash commodities as a protection against increasing costs. See also Buying Hedge, Selling Hedge.

Inelasticity: A characteristic that describes the interdependence of the supply, demand, and price of a commodity. A commodity is inelastic when a price change does not create an increase or decrease in consumption; inelasticity exists when supply and demand are relatively unresponsive to changes in price. See also Elasticity.

Initial Margin: Customers' funds required at the time a futures position is established, or an option is sold, to assure performance of the customer's obligations. Margin in commodities is not a down payment, as it is in securities. See also Margin.

In the Money: An option having intrinsic value. A call is in the money if its strike price is below the current price of the underlying futures contract. A put is in the money if its strike price is above the current price of the underlying futures contract.

Intrinsic Value: The absolute value of the in the money amount; that is, the amount that would be realized if an in the money option were exercised.

Introducing Broker (IB): A firm or individual that solicits and accepts commodity futures orders from customers but does not accept money, securities, or property from the customer. An IB must be registered with the Commodity Futures Trading Commission and must carry all of its accounts through an FCM on a fully disclosed basis.

Inverted Market: Futures market in which the nearer months are selling at premiums over the more distant months; it is, characteristically, a market in which supplies are currently in shortage.

Invisible Supply: Uncounted stocks of a commodity in the hands of wholesalers, manufacturers, and producers which cannot be identified accurately; the stocks are outside commercial channels but theoretically available to the market.

Last Trading Day: Day on which trading ceases for the maturing (current) delivery month.

Leverage: Essentially, it allows an investor to establish a position in the marketplace by depositing funds that are less than the value of the contract.

Leverage Contract: A standardized agreement calling for the delivery of a commodity with payments against the total cost spread out over a period of time.

Its principal characteristics include standard units and quality of a commodity and of terms and conditions of the contract, payment and maintenance of margin close out by offset or delivery (after payment in full) and no right to or interest in a specific lot of the commodity. Leverage contracts are not traded on exchanges.

Leverage Transaction Merchant (LTM): The firm or individual through whom leverage contracts are entered. LTMs must be registered with the Commodity Futures Trading Commission.

Life of Contract: Period between the beginning of trading in a particular future and the expiration of trading in the delivery month.

Limit: See position limit, price limit, variable limit, and reporting limit.

Limit Move: A price that has advanced or declined the limit permitted during one trading session as fixed by the rules of a contract market.

Limit Order: An order in which the customer sets a limit on either price or time of execution, or both, as contrasted with a market order, which implies that the order should be filled at the most favorable price as soon as possible.

Liquidation: Usually the sale of futures contracts to offset the obligation to take delivery of an equal number of futures contracts of the same delivery month purchased earlier. Sometimes refers to the purchase of futures contracts to offset a previous sale.

Liquidity (or liquid market): A broadly traded market where buying and selling can be accomplished with small price changes and bid and offer price spreads are narrow.

Liquid Market: A market where selling and buying can be accomplished easily due to the presence of many interested buyers and sellers.

Loan Program: It is the primary means of government agricultural price support operations. The government lends money to farmers at announced rates, with using the crops as collateral. Default on these loans is the primary method by which the government acquires stocks of agricultural commodities.

Long: One who has bought a cash commodity or a commodity futures contract, in contrast to a short, who has sold a cash commodity or futures contract.

Long Hedge: Buying futures contracts to protect against possible increased prices of commodities. See also Hedging.

Maintenance Margin: The amount of money that must be maintained on deposit while a futures position is open. If the equity in a customer's account drops under the maintenance margin level, the broker must issue a call for money that will restore the customer's equity in the account to required initial levels. See also Margin.

Margin: In the futures industry, it is an amount of money deposited by both buyers and sellers of futures contracts to ensure performance against the contract. It is not a down payment.

Margin Call: A call from a brokerage firm to a customer to bring margin deposits back up to minimum levels required by exchange regulations; similarly, a request by the clearing–house to a clearing member firm to make additional deposits to bring clearing margins back to minimum levels required by clearinghouse rules.

Market Order: An order to buy or sell futures contracts which is to be filled at the best possible price and as soon as possible. A limit order, in contrast, may specify requirements for price or time of execution. See also Limit Order.

Maturity: Period within which a futures contract can be settled by delivery of the actual commodity; the period between the first notice day and the last trading day of a commodity futures contract.

Maximum Price Fluctuation: See Limit Move.

Minimum Price Fluctuation: See Point.

Misrepresentation: An untrue or misleading statement concerning a material fact relied upon by a customer when making his/her decision about an investment.

Momentum Indicator: A line that is plotted to represent the difference between today's price and the price of a fixed number of days ago. Momentum can be measured as the difference between today's price and the current value of a moving average. Often referred to as momentum oscillators.

Moving Average: A mathematical procedure to smooth or eliminate the fluctuations in data. Moving averages emphasize the direction of a trend, confirm trend reversals, and smooth out price and volume fluctuations or "noise" that can confuse interpretation of the market.

National Association of Futures Trading Advisors (NAFTA): The national trade association of Commodity Pool Operators (CPOs, Commodity Trading Advisors (CTAs), and related industry participants.

National Futures Association (NFA): The industry–wide self-regulatory organization of the futures industry.

Nearby Delivery (Month): The futures contract closest to maturity.

Nearbys: The nearest delivery months of a futures market.

New Asset Value: The value of each unit of a commodity pool. Basically, it is a calculation of assets minus liabilities plus or minus the value of open positions (marked-to-the-market) divided by the number of units.

Net Performance: An increase or decrease in net asset value exclusive of additions, withdrawals, and redemptions.

Net Position: The difference between the open long (buy) contracts and the open short (sell) contracts held by any one person in any one futures contract month or in all months combined.

Nominal Price: Declared price for a futures month sometimes used in place of a closing price when no recent trading has taken place in that particular delivery month; usually it is an average of the bid and asked prices.

Nondisclosure: Failure to disclose a material fact needed by the customer to make a decision regarding an investment.

Normalizing: An adjustment to data, such as a price series, to put it within normal or more standard range. A technique used to develop a trading system.

Notice Day-See First Notice day.

Notice of Delivery: See Delivery Notice.

Offer: An indication of willingness to sell at a given price—the opposite of bid.

Offset: The liquidation of a purchase of futures through the sale of an equal number of contracts of the same delivery months or the covering of a short sale of futures contracts through the purchase of an equal number of contracts of the same delivery month. Either action transfers the obligation to make or take delivery of the actual commodity to someone else.

Omnibus Account: An account carried by one futures commission merchant with another where the transactions of two or more persons are combined, rather than designated separately, and the identity of the individual accounts is not disclosed.

Open: The period at the beginning of the trading session officially designated by the exchange during which all transactions are considered made "at the open."

Open Interest: The total number of futures contracts of a given commodity which have not yet been offset by opposite futures transactions nor fulfilled by delivery of the actual commodity; the total number of open transactions where each transaction has a buyer and a seller.

Open Outcry: Method of public auction for making bids and offers in the trading pits or rings of commodity exchanges.

Opening Range: The range of closely related prices at which transactions took place at the opening of the market; buying and selling orders at the opening might be filled at any point within such a range.

Open Trade Equity: The unrealized gain or loss on open positions.

Option Contract: A unilateral contract which gives the buyer the right, but not the obligation, to buy or sell a specified quantity of a commodity or a futures contract at a specific price within a specified period of time, regardless of the market price of that commodity or futures contract. The seller of the option has the obligation to sell the commodity or futures contract or buy it from the option buyer at the exercise price if the option is exercised. See also Call (Option) and Put (Option).

Option Premium: The money, securities, or property the buyer pays to the writer(grantor) for granting an option contract.

Option Seller: See Grantor.

Order Execution: The handling of a customer order by a broker, including receiving the order verbally or in writing from the customer, transmitting it to the trading floor of the exchange where the transaction takes place, and returning confirmation (fill price) of the completed order to the customer.

Orders: See Market Order, Stop Order.

Original Margin: The term applied to the initial deposit of margin money required of clearing member firms by clearinghouse rules; it parallels the initial margin deposit required of customers.

Out of the Money: A call option with a strike price higher or a put option with a strike price lower than the current market value of the underlying asset.

Overbought: A technical opinion that the market price has risen too steeply and too fast in relation to underlying fundamental factors.

Oversold: A technical opinion that the market price has declined too steeply and too fast in relation to underlying fundamental factors.

P & S Statement: See Purchase and Sale Statement.

Par: A particular price, 100 percent of principal value.

Parity: A theoretically equal relationship between farm product prices and all other prices. In farm program legislation, parity is defined in such a manner that the purchasing power of a unit of an agricultural commodity is maintained at its level during an earlier historical base period.

Pit: A specially constructed arena on the trading floor of some exchanges where trading in a futures or options contract is conducted by open outcry. On other exchanges, the term "ring" designates the trading area for a futures or options contract.

Point: The minimum fluctuation in futures prices or options premiums.

Point Balance: A statement prepared by Futures Commission Merchants to show profit or loss on all open contracts by computing them to an official closing or settlement price.

Pool: See Commodity Pool.

Position: A market commitment. For example, a buyer of futures contracts is said to have a long position and, conversely, a seller of futures contracts is said to have a short position.

Position Limit: The maximum number of futures contracts that one can hold in certain regulated commodities, according to the provisions of the CFTC. Reference Reporting Limits.

Position Trader: A commodity trader who either buys or sells contracts and holds them for an extended period of time, as distinguished from the day trader, who will normally initiate and liquidate a futures position within a single trading session.

Premium: 1) The additional payment allowed by exchange regulations for delivery or higher-than-required standards or grades of a commodity against a futures contract. In speaking of price relationships between different delivery months of a given commodity, one is said to be trading at a premium over another when its price is greater than that of the other. 2) It can also mean the amount paid a grantor or writer of an option by a trader.

Price Limit: Maximum price advance or decline from the previous day settlement price permitted for a commodity in one trading session by the rules of the exchange.

Primary Markets: The principal market for the purchase and sale of a cash commodity.

Principal: Refers to a person that is a principal of a particular entity; 1) Any person including, but not limited to, a sole proprietor, general partner, officer or director, or person occupying a similar status or performing similar functions, having the power, directly or indirectly, through agreement or otherwise, to exercise a controlling influence over the activities of the entity; 2) Any holder or any beneficial owner of 10 percent or more of the outstanding shares of any class of stock of the entity; 3) Any person who has contributed 10 percent or more of the capital of the entity.

Private Wires: Wires leased by various firms and news agencies for the transmission of information to branch offices and subscriber clients.

Proceeding Clerk: The member of the commission's staff in the Office of Proceedings who maintains the Commission's reparations docket, assigns reparation cases to an appropriate CFTC official, and acts as custodian of the records of proceedings.

Producer: A person or entity that produces (grows, mines, etc.) a commodity.

Public Elevators: Grain storage facilities, licensed and regulated by state and federal agencies, in which space is rented out to whomever is willing to pay for it; some are also approved by the commodity exchanges for delivery of commodities against futures contracts.

Purchase Price: The total actual cost paid by a person for entering into a commodity option transaction, including premium, commission, or any other direct or indirect charges.

Purchase and Sale Statement (P&S): A statement sent by a commission house to a customer when a futures or options position has been liquidated or offset. The statement shows the number of contracts bought or sold, the gross profit or loss, the commission charges, and the net profit or loss on the transaction. Sometimes combined with a confirmation statement.

Put (option): An option that gives the option buyer the right, but not the obligation, to sell the underlying futures contract at a particular price on or before a particular date.

Pyramiding: The use of profits on existing futures positions as margins to increase the size of the position, normally in successively smaller increments—such as, the use of profits on the purchase of five futures contracts as margin to purchase an additional four contracts, whose profits will in turn be used to margin an additional three contracts.

Quotation: The actual price or the bid or ask price of either cash commodities or futures or options contracts at a particular time. Often called quote.

Rally: An upward movement of prices. See also Recovery.

Rally Top: The point where a rally stalls. A bull move will usually make several rally tops over its life.

Rang: The difference between the high and low price of a commodity during a given period, usually a single trading session.

Reaction: A short term countertrend movement of prices.

Recovery: An upward movement of prices following a decline.

Receivership: A situation in which a receiver has been appointed. A receiver is a person appointed by a court to take custody and to control, and to manage the property or funds of another, pending judicial action concerning them.

Registered Commodity Representative (RCR): See Broker or Associated Person (AP).

Regulations (CFTC): The regulations adopted and enforced by the federal overseer of futures markets, the Commodity Futures Trading Commission, in order to administer the Commodity Exchange Act.

Reparations: Compensation payable to a wronged party in a futures or options transaction. The term is used in conjunction with the Commodity Futures Trading Commission's customer claims procedure to recover civil damages.

Reparations Award: The amount of monetary damages a respondent may be ordered to pay to a complainant.

Reporting Limit: Sizes of positions set by the exchange and/or by the CFTC at or above which commodity traders must make daily reports to the exchange and/or the CFTC as to the size of the position by commodity, by delivery month, and according to the purpose of trading, i.e., speculative or hedging.

Resistance: The price level where a trend stalls. It is the opposite of a support level. Prices must build momentum to move through resistance.

Respondents: The individuals or firms against which the complaint is filed and a reparations award is sought.

Retender: The right of holders of futures contracts who have been tendered a delivery notice through the clearinghouse to offer the notice for sale on the open market, liquidating their obligation to take delivery under the contract; it is applicable only to certain commodities and only within a specified period of time.

Retracement: A price movement in the opposite direction of the prevailing trend. See Correction.

Ring: A circular area on the trading floor of an exchange where traders and brokers stand while executing futures or options trades. Some exchanges use pits rather than rings.

Round Lot: A quantity of a commodity equal in size to the corresponding futures contract for the commodity, as distinguished from a job lot, which may be larger or smaller than the contract.

Round Turn: The combination of an initiating purchase or sale of a futures contract and offsetting sale or purchase of an equal number of futures contracts to the same delivery month. Commission fees for commodity transactions cover the round turn.

Rules (NFA): The standards and requirements to which participants who are required to be Members of National Futures Association must subscribe and conform.

Sample Grade: In commodities, usually the lowest quality acceptable for delivery in satisfaction of futures contracts. See Contract Grades.

Scalper: A speculator on the trading floor of an exchange who buys and sells rapidly, with small profits or losses, holding positions for only a short time during a trading session. Typically, a scalper will stand ready to buy at a fraction below the last transaction price and to sell at a fraction above, thus creating market liquidity.

Security Deposit: See Margin.

Segregated Account: A special account used to hold and separate customer's assets from those of the broker or firm.

Selling Hedge: Selling futures contracts to protect against possible decreased prices of commodities which will be sold in the future. See Hedging and/or Short Hedge.

Settlement Price: The closing price, or a price within the range of closing prices, which is used as the official price in determining net gains or losses at the close of each trading session.

Short: One who has sold a cash commodity or a commodity futures contract; a long, in contrast, is one who has bought a cash commodity or futures contract.

Short Hedge: Selling futures to protect against possible decreasing prices of commodities. See also Hedging.

Speculator: One who attempts to anticipate commodity price changes and make profits through the sale and/or purchase of commodity futures contracts. A speculator with a forecast of advancing prices hopes to profit by buying futures contracts and then liquidating the obligation to take delivery with a later sale of an equal number of futures of the same delivery month at a higher price. A speculator with a forecast of declining prices hopes to profit by selling commodity futures contracts and then covering the obligation to deliver with a later purchase of futures at a lower price.

Spot: Market for the immediate delivery of the product and immediate payment. May also refer to the nearest delivery month of a futures contract.

Spot Commodity: See Cash Commodity.

Spread (or Straddle): The purchase of one futures delivery month against the sale of another futures delivery month of the same commodity; the purchase of one delivery month of one commodity against the sale of the same delivery month of a different commodity; or the purchase of one commodity in one market against the sale of that commodity in another market, to take advantage of and profit from the distortions from the normal price relationships that sometimes occur. The term is also used to refer to the difference between the price of one futures month and the price of another month of the same commodity. See also Arbitrage.

Stop Loss: A risk management technique used to close out a losing position at a given point. See Stop Order.

Stop Order: An order that becomes a market order when a particular price level is reached. A sell stop is placed below the market, a buy stop is placed above the market. Sometimes referred to as a stop loss order.

Strike Price: See Exercise Price.

Support: A price level at which a declining market has stopped falling. It is the opposite of a resistance price range. Once this level is reached, the market trades sideways for a period of time.

Switch: Liquidation of a position in one delivery month of a commodity and simultaneous initiation of a similar position in another delivery month of the same commodity. When used by hedgers, this tactic is referred to as "rolling forward" the hedge.

Technical Analysis: An approach to analysis of futures markets and anticipated future trends of commodity prices. It examines the technical factors of market activity. Technicians normally examine patterns of price range, rates of change, changes in volume of trading, and open interest. There data are often charted to show trends and formations which serve as indicators of likely future price movements.

Tender: The act on the part of the seller of futures contracts of giving notice to the clearinghouse, that he or she intends to deliver the physical commodity in satisfaction of the futures contract. The clearinghouse in turn, passes along the notice to oldest buyer of record in that delivery month of the commodity. See also Retender.

Tick: Refers to a change in price up or down. See also Point.

Ticker Tape: A continuous paper tape transmission of commodity or security prices, volume, and other trading and market information which operates on private or lease wires by the exchanges. It is available to their member firms and other interested parties on a subscription basis.

Time Value: Any amount by which an option premium exceeds the option's intrinsic value.

To-Arrive contract: A type of deferred shipment in which the price is based on delivery at the destination point. The seller pays the freight in shipping it to that point.

Traders: 1) People who trade for their own account. 2) Employees of dealers or institutions who trade for their employer's account.

Trading Range: An established set of price boundaries with a high and a low price within which a market will spend a marked period of time.

Transferable Notice: See Retender.

Trend line: A line drawn that connects either a series of highs or lows in a trend. The trend line can represent either support (as in an uptrend line) or resistance (as in a downtrend line). Consolidations are marked by horizontal trend lines.

Unauthorized Trading: Purchase or sale of commodity futures or options for a customer's account without the customer's permission.

Underlying Futures Contract: The specific futures contract that the option conveys the right to buy (in the case of a call) or sell (in the case of a put).

Variable Limit: A price system that allows price movements for larger than normally allowed price movements under certain conditions. In periods of extreme volatility, some exchanges permit trading and price levels to exceed regular daily limits. At such times, margins may be automatically increased.

Variation Margin Call: A mid-session call by the clearinghouse on a clearing member requiring the deposit of additional funds to bring clearing margin monies up to minimum levels in relation to changing prices and the clearing member's net position.

Volatility: A measure of a commodity's tendency to move up and down in price based on its daily price history over a period of time.

Volume of Trade: The number of contracts traded during a specified period of time.

Warehouse Receipt: Document guaranteeing the existence and availability of a given quantity and quality of a commodity in storage; it is commonly used as the instrument of transfer of ownership in both cash and futures transactions.

Wirehouse: See Futures Commission Merchant (FCM).

Write: See Grantor.

Note: This glossary is included to assist the reader. It is not a set of legal definitions, nor a guide to interpreting the Commodity Exchange Act or any other legal instrument. For all legal assistance, contract your personal attorney.

SOURCES FOR MORE INFORMATION

We'd first like to call your attention to two reference guides that will provide you with a broad overview of information you can access. Then we'll zero in on several books we believe are particularly valuable for future study.

For Publications—"The Individual Investor's Guide to Investment Publications" describes more than 150 newsletter, magazines and other publications plus software and financial databases. The futures section fills sixteen pages. Here's a sample of our listing to give you an idea of the information provided.

"Futures and Options Factors—The Futures Portfolio Advisor" (188)

Publisher—Wasendorf & Associates, Inc.; 802 Main Street., P.O. Box 849, Cedar Falls, IA 50613, 319/268-0441

Editor/Background: Russell R. Wasendorf

Sixteen years experience in the futures market, author of *Commodities Trading: The Essential Primer* (Dow Jones/Irwin 1984), founder of Center for Futures Education.

Philosophy—To provide long-term investment strategies in the futures and options markets using portfolio theory and index analysis.

Description—Publishes a unique series of index charts each week. These charts are the result of extensive research into Index Analysis, an adaptation of the Dow Theory. Called the Wasendorf Series of Commodity Indexes, these charts are analyzed in the newsletter and specific recommendations for trades in individual futures markets are advised. Covers all futures markets including grains, meats, metals, food/fiber, stock indexes, currencies, debt instruments, and petroleum markets. A daily telephone hotline is included.

Format—Newsletter; Frequency—Weekly; No. Pages—8; First Issue— 12/80; Circulation—2,000; Subscription Prices—1 yr., $228

Previously Known As—THE FUTURES PORTFOLIO ADVISOR

More information about this guide can be obtained from International Publishing Corporation, Inc., 625 N. Michigan Ave., Suite 1920, Chicago, IL 60611. Phone: 312/943-7354. If you'd like a sample of our newsletter, just give Wasendorf & Associates a call at 1-800-553-1711.

For Other Services—Brokerage firms, commodity trading advisors (CTAs), commodity pool operators (CPOs), computer/electronic price quotation and news services, publishers, professional services (education, legal), exchanges, futures and option industry organizations and more, you can browse through the "Futures Magazine's Annual Reference Guide" published each June. This annual reference guide covers a very wide range of products and services, but provides only the name, address, phone number and product-service category for most firms. It will give you a list of firms to contact. It is available from Oster Communication, 219 Parkade, Cedar Falls, IA 50613. Phone: 319/277-6341.

For Reference Book—Naturally, you should contact your local library. There are many very good ones. We'd like to single out the following as being particularly useful.

Baratz, Morton, *The Investor's Guide to Futures Money Management*, Revised Edition, (1989) LJR Communications, Inc., Columbia, MD.

Bernstein, Jake, *Facts on Futures: Insights and Strategies for Winning in the Futures Markets*, (1987) Probus Publishing Company, Chicago, IL.

Bernstein, Jake, *The Investor's Quotient*, (1981) John Wiley & Sons, New York, NY.

Chance, Don M., *An Introduction to Options and Futures*, (1989) The Dryden Press, Chicago, IL.

Chicago Board of Trade Commodity Trading Manual, (1989) Board of Trade of the City of Chicago, (Updated and revised approximately every other year. Check for latest edition.).

Dewey, Edward R., *Cycles, Selected Writings*, (1970) Foundation for the Study of Cycles, Pittsburgh, PA.

Dunn, D. and Hargitt, E., *Point and Figure Commodity Trading: A Computer Evaluation*, (1971) Dunn and Hargitt, West Lafayette, IN.

Elliott, R.N., *The Wave Principle*, (1938) Elliott, New York, NY.

Gann, William D., *How to Make Profits in Commodities*, (1951) Lambert-Gann, Pomeroy, WA.

Herbst, Anthony F., *Commodity Futures: Markets, Methods of Analysis, and Management of Risks*, (1986) John Wiley & Sons Inc., New York, NY.

Hieronymus, Thomas, *Economics of Futures Trading for Commercial and Personal Profit*, (1977) Commodity Research Bureau, New York, NY.

Jiler, William L., *How Charts Can Help You in the Stock Market*, (1962) Standard & Poor's Corporation, New York, NY.

Kaufman, Perry J., *Handbook of Futures Markets: Commodity, Financial, Stock Index, and Options*, (1984) John Wiley & Sons, Inc., New York, NY.

Kolb, Robert W., *Understanding Futures Markets*, 3rd Edition, (1991) Kolb Publishing Inc., Miami, FL.

Labuszewski, John and Singuefield, Jeanne Cavins, *Inside the Commodity Options Market*, (1985) John Wiley & Sons, New York, NY.

Luft, Carl F., *The Investor's Self-Teaching Seminar Series: Understanding and Trading Futures*, (1991) Probus Publishing Company, Chicago, IL.

Natenberg, Sheldon, *Option Volatility and Pricing Strategies*, (1988) Probus Publishing Company, Chicago, IL.

Petzel, Todd E., *Financial Futures and Options*, (1989) Quorum Books, New York, NY.

Schwager, Jack O., *A Complete Guide to the Futures Markets: Fundamental Analysis, Technical Analysis, Trading, Spreads, and Options*, (1984) John Wiley & Sons Inc., New York, NY.

Shaleen, Kenneth H., *Volume and Open Interest*, (1991) Probus Publishing Company, Chicago, IL.

Siegel, Daniel R. and Siegel, Diane F., *The Futures Markets*, (1990) Probus Publishing Company, Chicago, IL.

Sklarew, Arthur, *Techniques of a Professional Commodity Chart Analyst*, (1980) Commodity Research Bureau, Inc., New York, NY.

Teweles, Richard J., Harlow, Charles V. and Stone, Herbert L., *The Commodity Futures Game: Who Wins? Who Loses? Why?*, (1974) McGraw-Hill, New York, NY.

Wasendorf, Russell R., *Commodities Trading: The Essential Primer*, (1985) Dow Jones-Irwin, Homewood, IL.

For Compliance Assistance, the following organizations regulate the futures and securities industries or they have related enforcement powers.

Alliance Against Fraud Telemarketing
c/o National Consumers League
815 15th St. NW, Suite 516
Washington, DC 20005

American Association of Individual Investors
612 North Michigan Avenue
Chicago, IL 60611
312/280-0170

Commodity Futures Trading Commission
2033 K Street NW
Washington, DC 20581
202/254-6387

Council of Better Business Bureaus
1515 Wilson Boulevard
Arlington, VA 22209
703/276-0100

Federal Bureau of Investigation
Justice Department
9th St. & Pennsylvania Ave., NW
Washington, DC 20580
202/326-3650

Federal Trade Commission
6th St. & Pennsylvania Ave., NW
Washington, DC 20580
202/326-3650

National Association of Securities Dealers
1735 K Street, NW
Washington, DC 20006
202/728-8044

National Consumers League
815 15th St., NW
Suite 516
202/639-8140

National Futures Association
200 W. Madison, Suite 1600
Chicago, IL 60606
Toll-free: 800/621-3570
In IL: 800/621-3570

North American Securities Administration Association
2930 SW Wanamaker Drive
Suite 5
Topeka, KS 66614
913/273-2600

Securities and Exchange Commission
450 Fifth St., NW
Washington, DC 20006
202/728-8233

United States Postal Service
Chief Postal Inspector
Room 3021
Washington, DC 20260-2100
202/268-4267

Here's a list of the exchanges. Each has a public information department and will send information on request.

AMEX Commodities Corp.
86 Trinity Place
New York, New York 10006
212/306-8940

Board of Trade of Kansas City, Missouri, Inc.
4800 Main Street
Kansas City, Missouri 64112
816/753-7500

Chicago Board of Trade
141 West Jackson Boulevard
Chicago, Illinois 60604
312/435-3620

Chicago Mercantile Exchange
30 S. Wacker Drive
Chicago, Illinois 60606
312/930-1000

Chicago Rice & Cotton Exchange
444 West Jackson Boulevard
Chicago, Illinois 60606
312/341-3078

Coffee, Sugar & Cocoa Exchange
4 World Trade Center
New York, New York 10048
212/938-2800

Commodity Exchange Incorporated (COMEX)
4 World Trade Center
New York, New York 10048
212/938-2900

MidAmerica Commodity Exchange
141 West Jackson Boulevard
Chicago, Illinois 60604
312/341-3000

Minneapolis Grain Exchange
150 Grain Exchange Building
Minneapolis, Minnesota 55415
612/338-6212

New York Cotton Exchange
4 World Trade Center
New York, New York 10048
212/938-2702

New York Futures Exchange
20 Broad Street
New York, New York 10005
212/656-4949

New York Mercantile Exchange
4 World Trade Center
New York, New York 10048
212/938-2222

Philadelphia Board of Trade
Philadelphia Stock Exchange Building
1900 Market Street
Philadelphia, Pennsylvania 19105
215/496-5000

THE MOST COMMONLY ASKED QUESTIONS ABOUT INVESTING IN EXCHANGE TRADED OPTIONS

What is an option?

An option is the right, but not the obligation, to buy or sell an underlying futures contract at a specified price (strike price) during a specified period of time.

How much profit can I make?

There is no way of predicting exactly what your profits will be with any investment, including options. However, if you anticipate market trends correctly, with options your potential profits can be unlimited.

When you offset an option position, you can easily determine your profits or losses by subtracting the retail price (includes commission and fees) you paid from the amount you receive.

How much can I lose?

The buying of options on futures is a speculative investment. Option traders can expect to incur losses. If the market moves against you or doesn't move at all, you can lose your entire investment (premium, commissions, and fees). However, you can never lose more than your initial investment, as long as you do not exercise the option.

How are options traded?

Like futures contracts, all options on futures are bought and sold at competitive auctions in the option pits on the floor of the exchanges. The "open outcry" trading system provides fair and orderly price discovery for option premiums and permits close supervision by the Exchange Compliance and Surveillance Departments which monitor trading. At the end of each trading day, all options transactions are accepted and cleared by the clearing association, assuring performance on all contract obligations. This frees buyers and sellers of any further direct obligation to each other.

What is a "call option"?

A call option conveys the right, but not the obligation, to buy a futures contract at a specific price during a specified time period. You would buy a call option if you expected prices of the underlying futures contract to rise.

What is a "put option"?

A put option conveys the right, but not the obligation, to sell a futures contract at a specific price during a specified time period. You would buy a put option if you expected prices of the underlying futures contract to decline.

What is the "strike price"?

The strike price is the price at which you may buy (in the case of a call option) or sell (in the case of a put option) the underlying futures contract.

Who establishes the strike price?

The various exchanges—such as COMEX, IMM, and Chicago Board of Trade—establish strike prices for call and put options. Additional strike prices are added in accordance with futures price movements by applying a formula.

As futures prices rise or fall, options with higher or lower strike prices are introduced according to the preset formula. The result is to create "new" options on the same futures contract. This allows option strategies and opportunities to reflect current market conditions.

What is meant by "at the money"?

It is an option with the strike price that is nearest to the current underlying futures price.

What is meant by "in the money"?

It is a put option with the strike price that is higher than the current underlying futures price or a call option whose strike price is lower than the current underlying futures price.

What is meant by "out of the money"?

It is a put option whose strike price is lower than the current underlying futures price or a call option whose strike price is higher than the current underlying futures price.

How long does an option run?

Options run between one day and one year or more. Just as strike prices vary, so do option months. Bear in mind, and this is extremely important—that the option month refers to the futures contract delivery month rather than to the month in which the option actually expires. For instance, a July option is an option to buy (in the case of a call) or sell (in the case of a put) a July futures contract.

Options expiration dates vary from commodity to commodity and exchange to exchange. Options expire before the underlying futures contract does, often several weeks prior. Your account executive will provide full details.

Does the length of an option affect its cost?

Yes. All else being equal, an option with a longer period before expiration at the same strike price will cost more than one with less time to expiration, since it affords more time for a favorable price move to occur.

How much do options cost?

The retail purchase price is what you pay your broker for an option. The retail purchase price includes the premium, brokerage commissions, fees to the NFA, the exchange, and the clearing firm. The premium is the portion of the retail purchase price used to buy the option from the writer or issuer of the option.

Premiums vary according to the size of the option, commodity, strike price, length of the option, market conditions, and/or trends. Generally, very speculative options (out of the money, contrary to market trends or ones near to expiration) cost less than conservative options (those with more time to expiration, ones that are in the money or those moving with market trends). Premiums can range from just a few hundred dollars to several thousand dollars.

How is the premium determined?

It is determined by supply and demand—that is, by competition between buyers and sellers. Simply stated, option premiums must be high enough to induce sellers to write them and low enough to induce buyers to purchase them.

How do option premiums change?

If there is a change in the price of the underlying futures contract, is there a cent-for-cent relationship? Generally, no, except in the case of an option which is significantly in the money. At any other time, an increase or decrease in the futures price normally results in a smaller increase or decrease in the option premium. The less time an option has remaining until expiration and the deeper it is out-of-the-money, the smaller the premium response is likely to be in relation to a change in the underlying futures price.

What is meant by "leverage"?

Leverage is the "financial muscle" you create when you use a small amount of money to control an investment worth much more. Leverage can convert modest investments into large profits, sometimes doubling, tripling, or even quadrupling your money in just months.

How do you determine leverage with options?

Simply take the value of the underlying futures contract at the strike price and divide by the cost of the option.

How do I take profits?

Let's assume you own a call option. The price of the underlying futures contract has risen substantially with a consequent increase in the value of your option. The simplest way to take your profit is to sell your option. All you have to do is tell your account executive, and he or she will then place an order. The sell order will be executed on the trading floor of the exchange authorized to trade in that option. This is called offsetting your position.

Indeed, a major advantage of exchange traded options is that the market is designed to make available to buyers and sellers a continuous secondary market—a market in which an option, once purchased, can later be sold.

Are there any hidden charges in selling my option?

No. For example, you pay no insurance fees, no maintenance fees, and no interest payments. You do pay the premium, brokerage commission, exchange, NFA, and clearing firm fees.

Who guarantees my option?

The clearing house guarantees and is solely responsible for fulfillment of your option.

How much should I invest and what type of options should I buy?

The answers to both of these questions depends on many factors unique to you as an individual investor—for example, your goals, age, income, assets, financial responsibilities, marital status, and emotional make-up. In general, we recommend that your portfolio be well diversified and that you invest no more than you can comfortably afford to lose. While the profit potential of buying options can be enormous, there is always the possibility that the markets will not behave as you expect and you could lose 100 percent of your investment.

FUTURES MARKET
CONTRACT SPECIFICATIONS

U.S. Markets—Contract Specifications

COMMODITY	EXCH.	TRADING HRS. Central Time	DELIVERY MONTHS	CONTRACT SIZE	PRICE QUOTE	PT. VALUE FLUCTUATION	MIN. PRICE	DAILY LIMITS
Aluminum	COMMEC	7:30-1:10	F,H,K,N,U,Z	40,000 lbs	¢/lb	1pt = $4.00	5pts = $20.00	None
Australian Dollar	IMM	7:20-2:00	F,H,J,M,N,U,V,Z	100,000 AD	¢/AD	1pt = $10.00	1pt = $10.00	None
British Pound	IMM	7:20-2:00	H,M,U,Z	62,500 BP	¢/£	1pt = $6.25	2pts = $12.50	None
British Pound	MA	7:20-2:15	H,M,U,Z	12,500 BP	¢/£	1pt = $1.25	2pts = $2.50	None
CRB Index	NYSE	8:00-1:45	H,K,N,U,Z	500xCRB Index	100ths/pt	1pt = $5.00	5pts = $25.00	None
Can. Dollar	IMM	7:20-2:00	H,M,U,Z	100,000 CD	¢/CD	1pt = $10.00	1pt = $10.00	None
Can. Dollar	MA	7:20-2:15	H,M,U,Z	50,000 CD	¢/CD	1pt = $5.00	1pt = $5.00	None
Cattle, Fdr.	CME	9:05-1:00	F,H,J,K,Q,U,V,X	44,000 lbs	$/cwt	1pt = $4.40	2.5pts = $11.00	1.5¢ = $600 = 150pts
Cattle, Live	CME	9:05-1:00	G,J,M,Q,V,Z	40,000 lbs	$/cwt	1pt = $4.00	2.5pts = $10.00	1.5¢ = $600 = 150pts
Cattle, Live	MA	9:05-1:15	G,J,M,Q,V,Z	20,000 lbs	$/cwt	1pt = $2.00	2.5pts = $5.00	1.5¢ = $300 = 150pts
Cocoa (Metric)	NYCSCE	8:30-1:15	H,K,N,U,Z	10M ton (22,046)	$/M ton	1pt = $10.00	1pt = $10.00	$880 = 88pts
Coffee "C"	NYCSCE	8:15-12:58	H,K,N,U,Z	37,500 lbs	¢/lb	1pt = $3.75	5pts = $18.75	6¢/600pts(1)
Copper, High Grade	COMMEX	8:25-1:00	F,H,K,N,U,Z	25,000 lbs	¢/lb	1pt = $2.50	5pts = $12.50	None
Corn	CBOT	9:30-1:15	H,K,N,U,Z	5,000 bu	¢/bu	1¢ = $50.00	¢ = $12.50	10¢ = $500(5)
Corn	MA	9:30-1:45	H,K,N,U,Z	1,000 bu	¢bu	1¢ = $10.00	1/8¢ = 1.25	10¢ = $100
Cotton	NYCTE	9:30-1:40	H,K,N,U,Z	50,000 lbs	¢/lb	1pt = $5.00	1pt = $5.00	2¢/200pts(4)
Crude Oil	NYME	8:45-2:10	All Months	1,000 barrels	$/barrel	1pt = $10.00	1pt = $10.00	(12)
Deutschemark	IMM	7:20-2:00	H,M,U,Z	125,000 DM	¢/DM	1pt = $12.50	1pt = $12.50	None
Deutschemark	MA	7:20am-2:15pm 6:00pm-9:30pm	H,M,U,Z	62,500 DM	¢/DM	1pt = $6.25	1pt = $6.25	None
Eurodollar	IMM	7:20-2:00	H,M,U,Z	$1,000,000	basis pts	1pt = $25.00	1pt = $25.00	None
Euro. Currency Unit	IMM	7:10-1:30	H,M,U,Z	125,000 ECUs	¢/ECU	1pt = $12.50	1pt = $12.50	None
Gasoline, Unleaded	NYME	8:50-2:10	All Months	42,000 gal	¢/gal	1pt = $4.20	1pt = $4.20	
Gold	CBOT	7:20-1:40	G,J,M,Q,V,Z	32.15 troy oz	$/oz	10¢ = $3.215	10¢ = $3.215	$50/t.oz = $1,607.50
Gold	IMM	7:20-2:00		100 troy oz	$/oz	1pt = $1.00	10pts = $10.00	None
Gold	COMEX	7:20-1:30	G,J,M,Q,V,Z	100 troy oz	$/oz	1pt = $1.00	10pts = $10.00	None

(table continues)

Gold	MA	7:20-1:40	33.2 troy oz	$/oz	1pt = $.33	10pts = $3.32	None
Heating Oil	NYME	8:50-2:10	42,000 gal	¢/gal	1pt = $4.20	1pt = $4.20	(7)
Hogs	CME	9:10-1:00	40,000 lbs	$/cwt	1pt = $4.00	2.5pts = $10.00	1.5¢ = $600 = 150 pts
Hogs	MA	9:10-1:15	20,000 lbs	$/cwt	1pt = $2.00	2.5pts = $5.00	1.5¢ = $300 = 150pts
Japanese Yen	IMM	7:20-2:00	12,500,000 JY	¢/JY	1pt = $12.50	1pt = $12.50	None
Japanese Yen	MA	7:20am-2:15pm 6:00pm-9:30pm	6,250,000 JY	¢/JY	1pt = $6.25	1pt = $6.25	None
Lumber	CME	9:00-1:05	160,000 bd ft	$/m/bd ft	1pt = $1.60	10pts = $16.00	$5./500pts
M.M.I. Index	CBOT	8:15-3:15	250xMMI	1000ths/pt	1pt = $2.50	5pts = $12.50	(6)
Municipal Bonds	CBOT	7:20-2:00	$100,000	32nds/pt	1/32 - $41.25	1/32 = $31.25	96/32 = $3000(8)
Natural Gas	NYME	8:20-2:10	10,000 MMBtu	$/MMBtu	1pt = $10.00	1pt = $10.00	.10¢ = $1000=100pts
Nikkie Index	CME	8:00-3:15	500 x Index	100ths/pt	1pt = $5.00	5pts = $25.00	(11)
NYSE Index	NYFE	8:30-3:15	500 x Index	100ths/pt	1pt = $5.00	5pts = $25.00	(6)
Oats	CBOT	9:30-1:15	5,000 bu	¢/bu	1¢ = $50.00	1/4¢ = $12.50	10¢ = $500(5)
Oats	MA	9:30-145	1,000 bu	¢/bu	1¢ = $10.00	1/8¢ = $1.25	10¢ = $100
Orange Juice	NYCTE	9:15-1:15	15,000 lbs	¢/lb	1pt = $1.50	5pts = $7.50	5¢ = $750 = 500 pts
Palladium	NYME	7:10-1:20	100 troy oz.	$/oz	1pt = $1.00	5pts = $5.50	$6/600pts(3)
Platinum	NYME	7:20-1:30	50 troy oz.	$/oz	1pt = $.50	10pts = $5.00	$25/2500pts(3)
Pork Bellies	CME	9:10-1:00	40,000 lbs	¢/lb	1pt = $4.00	2.5pts = $10.00	2¢ = $800 = 200 pts
Propane	NYME	8:15-2:10	42,000 gal	$/gal	1pt = $4.20	1pts = $4.20	4¢ = $1680 = 400 pts
Rough Rice	MA	9:15-1:30	200,000 LBS	¢/cwt	1pt = $2.00	5pts = $10.00	30¢ = $600(5)
S&P 500 Index	IOM	8:30-3:15	500xS&P 500 Index	100ths/pt	1pt = $5.00	5pts = $25.00	(6)
Silver	COMEX	7:25-1:25	5,000 troy oz	¢/oz	1pt = $.50	50pts = $25.00	None
Silver, New	CBOT	7:25-1:25	1,000 troy oz	¢/oz	1pt = $.10	10pts = $1.00	$1.00 = $1000(3)
Silver	MA	7:25-1:40	1,000 oz	¢/oz	1pt = $.10	10pts = $1.00	None
Soybean Meal	CBOT	9:30-1:15	100 tons	$/ton	1pt = $1.00	10pts = $10.00	$10/1000pts(5)
Soybean Oi	CBOT	9:30-1:15	60,000 lbs	¢/lb	1pt = $6.00	1pt = $6.00	1¢ /100pts(5)
Soybeans	CBOT	9:30-1:15	5,000 bu	¢/bu	1¢ = $50.00	1/4¢ = $12.50	30¢ = $1500(5)
Soybeans	MA	9:30-1:15	1,000 bu	¢/bu	1pt = $10.00	1/8¢ = $1.25	30¢ = $300
Sugar	NYCSCE	9:00-12:43	112,000 lbs	¢/lb	1pt = $11.20	1pt = $11.20	1/2¢/50pts(1)
Swiss Franc	IMM	7:20-2:00	125,000 SF	¢/SF	1pt = $12.50	1pt = $12.50	None
Swiss Franc	MA	7:20-2:15	62,500 SF	¢/SF	1pt = $6.25	1pt = $6.25	None
T-Bills 90-Days	IMM	7:20-2:00	$1,000,000	basis pts	1pt = $25.00	1pt = $25.00	None

Contract	Exchange	Trading Hours	Months	Contract Size	Quote	Min. Fluctuation	Value	Daily Limit
Treasury Bills	MA	7:20-2:15	H,M,U,Z	$500,000	basis pts	1pt = $12.50	1pt = $12.50	None
T-Bonds 10 yr.	CBOT	7:20am-2:00pm 6:00pm-9:30pm	H,M,U,Z	$100,000	32nds/pt	1/32 = $31.25	1/32 = $15.62	96/32 = $3000(5)
Treasury Bonds	MA	7:20-3:15	H,M,U,Z	$50,000	32nds/pt	1/32 = $15.62	1/32 = $15.62	96/32 = $1500
Treasury Notes 10 year	CBOT	7:20am-2:00pm 6:00pm-9:30pm	H,M,U,Z	$100,000	32nds/pt	1/32 = $31.25	1/32 = $31.25	96/32 = $3000
T-Notes 5 yr.	CBOT	7:20-2:00	H,M,U,Z	$100,000	32nds/pt	1/32 = $15.63	1/64 = $15.63	96/32 = $3000(5)
U.S. Dollar Index	NYCTE	7:20-2:00	H,M,U,Z	500x Index	100ths/pt	1pt = $5.00	1pt = $5.00	200pts(10)
Value Line Index	KCBT	8:30-3:15	H,M,U,Z	500x Index	100ths/pt	1pt = $5.00	5pts = $25.00	(6)
Value Line, Mini	KCBT	8:30-3:15	H,M,U,Z	100x Index	100ths/pt	1pt = $1.00	5pts = $5.00	(6)
Wheat	CBOT	9:30-1:15	H,K,N,U,Z	5,000 bu	¢/bu	1¢ = $50.00	1/4¢ = $12.50	20¢ = $1000(5)
Wheat	KCBT	9:30-1:15	H,K,N,U,Z	5,000 bu	¢/bu	1¢ = $50.00	1/4¢ = $12.50	25¢ = $1250
Wheat	MPLS	9:30-1:45	H,K,N,U,Z	5,000 bu	¢/bu	1¢ = $10.00	1/4¢ = $12.50	20¢ = $200
Wheat	MA	9:30-1:45	H,K,N,U,Z	1,000 bu	¢/bu	1¢ = $10.00	1/8¢ = $1.25	20¢ = $200

Exchanges:

CBT	Chicago Board of Trade
CME	Chicago Merchantile Exchange
COMEX	Commodity Exchange, Inc. (NY)
IMM	International Monetary Market
IOM	Index and Option Market
KCBT	Kansas City Board of Trade
NYCSCE	New York Coffee, Sugar, and Cocoa Exchange
NYCTE	New York Cotton Exchange
NYFE	New York Futures Exchange
NYME	New York Mercantile Exchange

Abbreviations for Months

Month	1st yr.	2nd yr.
JAN	F	D
FEB	G	E
MAR	H	I
APR	J	L
MAY	K	O
JUN	M	P
JUL	N	T
AUG	Q	R
SEP	U	B
OCT	V	C
NOV	X	W
DEC	Z	Y

There are two sets of abbreviations for the months because the futures contracts roll from one year to the next. For example, June of 1992 would be "P" and June of 1993 would be "M." This would alternate for 1994 and 1995 and so on. You also need to double check with the quotation service you are using to make sure they use these conventions. If not, the theory will be the same, even if the letters vary.

Non-U.S. Markets—Contract Specifications

COMMODITY	EXCHANGE	TRADING HRS Central Time	DELIVERY MONTHS	CONTRACT SIZE	PRICE QUOTE	PT. VALUE FLUCTUATION	MIN PRICE	DAILY LIMITS
B-Pound	SIMEX	6:25pm-3:15am*	H,M,U,Z	£62,500			2 pt = $12.50	None
Brent Crude Oil	IPE	3:25am-2:13pm	All Months	1000 BBL			1pt = $10.00	None
D-Mark	SIMEX	6:20pm-3:10am*	H,M,U,Z	DM 125,000			1pt = $12.50	None
Eurodollar	LIFFE	2:15am-10:10am 10:26am-11:56am	H,M,U,Z	$1,000,000			1pt = $25.00	None
Eurodollar	SIMEX	5:45pm-3:20am*	H,M,U,Z	$1,000,000			1pt = $25.00	None
Euro-mark	LIFFE	2:05am-10:05am 10:29am-11:59am	H,M,U,Z	DM 1,000,000			1pt = DM25	None
FTSE 100 Index	LIFFE	2:35am-10:10am	All Months	£25xIndex			5pts = £12.50	None
German Bund	LIFFE	2:05am-10:00am 10:25am-11:55am	H,M,U,Z	DM250,000			1 pt = $12.50	None
Japanese Yen	SIMEX	6:15pm-3:05am*	H,M,U,Z	12,500,000 JY			1pt = $12.50	None
Long Gilt	LIFFE	2:30am-10:15am	H,M,U,Z	£50,000			1/32pt = £15.625	None
Nikkie Index	SIMEX	6:00pm-12:15am	H,M,U,Z	500xInd Fut Price			5pt = 2.500 JY	None
National Bond	MATIF	2:00am-9:00am	F,H,M,U,Z	FRF500,000			2pts = FRF100	250 pts
U.S. T-Bonds	SIMEX	5:30pm-3:00am 7:15am-9:00am*	H,M,U,Z	$100,000			1/32pt = $31.25	$3,000 = 96/32pt
U.S. T-Bonds	LIFFE	2:15am-10:10am 10:29am-11:59am	H,M,U,Z	$100,000	32nds pt		1/32pt = $31.25	None
3 Month Pibor	MATIF	1:30am-9:00am	H,M,U,Z	FRF5,000,000	Basis Pts		1pt = FRF125	60 pts
3 Month Sterling	LIFFE	2:20am-10:02	H,M,U,Z	£500,000	Basis Pts		1pt = £12.50	None

* During Daylight Savings, SIMEX times move back one hour (i.e., DMARK 7:20pm-4:10am)

Exchange for Physical (EFP)
EFP Gold   COMEX Gold (minimum contracts:1)
EFT Silver   COMEX Silver (minimum contracts:1)
EFP Currency   IMM Currency (minimum contracts:5)
EFP Bonds   CBOT Bonds (minimum contracts:varies)
EFP Platinum   NYME Platinum (minimum contracts:5)

For less active markets, consult your order desk before placing orders.

To trade these markets, we must have a foreign markets risk disclosure on file.

Footnotes:
(1) No limits front 2 months.
(2) Contact your broker for updated information.
(3) No limits front month.
(4) No limits after 1st Notice Day.
(5) No limits starting day before 1st Notice Day.
(6) Circuit breaker rule—ask your broker for details.
(7) Initial limit for front 2 months=2000 pts.; Total limit=4000 pts.; Back months initial limit=200 pts.; Total limit=2000 pts.
(8) No limits starting first or second day of/or prior to delivery month.
(9) The day prior to bank holidays and/or 3-day weekends, these markets may close at Noon. Contact your broker for details.
(10) No limits last one-half hour of trading daily and on last trading day. Also, adjustable intraday limits apply.
(11) Less than 2000.00-600.00 pts; 2000.00-3000.00-900.00 pts; 3000.00-4000.00-1200.00 pts; Over 4000.00-1500.00 pts.
(12) Initial limit front 2 months=750 pts. Total limit=1500 pts. Back months initial limit=100 pts. Total limit=750 pts.

The information contained in this table is from sources believed to be reliable, but we cannot be held responsible for either its accuracy or completeness. All contract specifications are subject to change by action of the respective commodity exchange. Therefore, the speficiations can be changed, sometime without notice. You need to be in touch with your broker before entering any trade. Limits are subject to change and to variable limit rules of the receptive exchange.

INDEX

ABOUT THE AUTHORS

Thomas A. McCafferty's involvement in the cash commodities and futures industries goes back to 1973. He has traded futures for his own account and supervised brokers who traded for others. Additionally, he has a strong background in sales and marketing and is the author of *In-House Telemarketing: A Master Plan for Starting and Managing a Profitable Telemarketing Program* (Probus, 1987). Currently, Mr. McCafferty oversees the branch office system for Wasendorf & Son Company, an introducing broker.

Russell R. Wasendorf has been totally involved in the futures market since he took over the reins, in the late 1970s, of the Commodity Education Institute, which trained hundreds of futures brokers and traders. By the early 1980s, Mr. Wasendorf had developed his proprietary indexes and began the development of his index analysis system. By the mid-1980s, he had written *Commodities Trading: The Essential Primer* (Dow Jones-Irwin, 1985), began a newsletter to track his trading system, "Futures and Options Factors," and launched a commodity price charting service "Pocket Charts." Currently, he manages his own introducing brokerage firm, Wasendorf & Son Company.

Dear Reader:

We hope you enjoyed this book. More importantly, we hope it answered your questions regarding investing in the futures market. As you've learned, not everyone is suited to it. The risks involved are considerable—matched only by the potential returns.

If you'd like to follow the futures markets for awhile, we'll be happy to send you four free issues of our commodity price chart service, "Pocket Charts." It contains forty-eight individual charts covering thirty-eight distinct futures markets. Here's a breakdown:

5 METALS: Palladium, Platinum, Gold, Copper and Silver

14 FINANCIALS: British Pound, Dollar Index, D-Mark, Canadian Dollar, Japanese Yen, Swiss Franc, S & P 500, NYSE Comp. Index, Muni Bond, Value Line, T-Notes, T-Bonds, T-Bills, Eurodollars.

6 GRAINS (12 Charts): Corn (2 delivery months), Oats, Soybeans (2 delivery months), Soybean Oil, Soybean Meal, Chicago CBT Wheat (2 delivery months), Kansas City Wheat, Minneapolis Wheat.

4 MEATS: Live Cattle, Feeder Cattle, Live Hogs, and Pork Bellies.

6 FOOD & FIBERS: Cocoa, World Sugar, Orange Juice, Coffee, Lumber, Cotton.

3 PETROLEUMS: Heating Oil, Crude Oil, Unleaded Gas.

5 WASENDORF INDEXES: Composite, Grain, Meat, Metal, Food/Fiber.

To receive your free issues, simply mail the coupon below or give us a call at 1-800-553-1711.

Last of all, we'd like to thank you for the time, effort and money you've invested in the book. We sincerely wish you the best of luck with all your investments.

Sincerely,
Thomas McCafferty and Russell R. Wasendorf
Authors of *All About Futures*

Yes . . . I'd like to follow the markets for awhile. Please send me 4 weeks of your commodity price charting service, "Pocket Charts."

Call 1-800-553-1711. Or mail coupon to:
Wasendorf & Associates, Inc.
802 Main Street, P.O. Box 849
Cedar Falls, IA 50613

Name _____
Address _____
City _____
State _____ Zip _____
Phone ( ) _____

About the Publisher

PROBUS PUBLISHING COMPANY

Probus Publishing Company fills the informational needs of today's business professional by publishing authoritative, quality books on timely and relevant topics, including:

- Investing
- Futures/Options Trading
- Banking
- Finance
- Marketing and Sales
- Manufacturing and Project Management
- Personal Finance, Real Estate, Insurance and Estate Planning
- Entrepreneurship
- Management

Probus books are available at quantity discounts when purchased for business, educational or sales promotional use. For more information, please call the Director, Corporate/Institutional Sales at 1-800-PROBUS-1, or write:

Director, Corporate/Institutional Sales
Probus Publishing Company
1925 N. Clybourn Avenue
Chicago, Illinois 60614
FAX (312) 868-6250